FSOT
SECRETS

Study Guide
Your Key to Exam Success

FSOT Exam Review for the
Foreign Service Officer Test

Published by
Mometrix Test Preparation
FSOT Exam Secrets Test Prep Team

Written and edited by the FSOT Exam Secrets Test Prep Staff

Printed in the United States of America

This paper meets the requirements of ANSI/NISO Z39.48-1992 (Permanence of Paper).

Mometrix offers volume discount pricing to institutions. For more information or a price quote, please contact our sales department at sales@mometrix.com or 888-248-1219.

Mometrix Media LLC is not affiliated with or endorsed by any official testing organization. All organizational and test names are trademarks of their respective owners.

ISBN 13: 978-1-60971-698-1
ISBN 10: 1-60971-698-1

Dear Future Exam Success Story:

Congratulations on your purchase of our study guide. Our goal in writing our study guide was to cover the content on the test, as well as provide insight into typical test taking mistakes and how to overcome them.

Standardized tests are a key component of being successful, which only increases the importance of doing well in the high-pressure high-stakes environment of test day. How well you do on this test will have a significant impact on your future, and we have the research and practical advice to help you execute on test day.

The product you're reading now is designed to exploit weaknesses in the test itself, and help you avoid the most common errors test takers frequently make.

How to use this study guide

We don't want to waste your time. Our study guide is fast-paced and fluff-free. We suggest going through it a number of times, as repetition is an important part of learning new information and concepts.

First, read through the study guide completely to get a feel for the content and organization. Read the general success strategies first, and then proceed to the content sections. Each tip has been carefully selected for its effectiveness.

Second, read through the study guide again, and take notes in the margins and highlight those sections where you may have a particular weakness.

Finally, bring the manual with you on test day and study it before the exam begins.

Your success is our success

We would be delighted to hear about your success. Send us an email and tell us your story. Thanks for your business and we wish you continued success.

Sincerely,

Mometrix Test Preparation Team

Need more help? Check out our flashcards at: http://MometrixFlashcards.com/FSOT

TABLE OF CONTENTS

Top 20 Test Taking Tips.. 1
Communication.. 2
Correct Grammar, Organization, and Sentence Structure Required for Writing Reports..................... 28
Economics... 63
Management 75
Mathematics and Statistics 90
United States Government...105
United States Society and Culture..117
World History and Geography...158
Practice Test...187
    Answers and Explanations 209
Secret Key #1 - Time is Your Greatest Enemy 218
    Pace Yourself...218
Secret Key #2 - Guessing is not Guesswork..219
    Monkeys Take the Test..219
    $5 Challenge..220
Secret Key #3 - Practice Smarter, Not Harder 221
    Success Strategy 221
Secret Key #4 - Prepare, Don't Procrastinate 222
Secret Key #5 - Test Yourself...223
General Strategies...224
Special Report: How to Overcome Test Anxiety 229
    Lack of Preparation...229
    Physical Signals 230
    Nervousness 230
    Study Steps..232
    Helpful Techniques 233
Additional Bonus Material 237

Top 20 Test Taking Tips

1. Carefully follow all the test registration procedures
2. Know the test directions, duration, topics, question types, how many questions
3. Setup a flexible study schedule at least 3-4 weeks before test day
4. Study during the time of day you are most alert, relaxed, and stress free
5. Maximize your learning style; visual learner use visual study aids, auditory learner use auditory study aids
6. Focus on your weakest knowledge base
7. Find a study partner to review with and help clarify questions
8. Practice, practice, practice
9. Get a good night's sleep; don't try to cram the night before the test
10. Eat a well balanced meal
11. Know the exact physical location of the testing site; drive the route to the site prior to test day
12. Bring a set of ear plugs; the testing center could be noisy
13. Wear comfortable, loose fitting, layered clothing to the testing center; prepare for it to be either cold or hot during the test
14. Bring at least 2 current forms of ID to the testing center
15. Arrive to the test early; be prepared to wait and be patient
16. Eliminate the obviously wrong answer choices, then guess the first remaining choice
17. Pace yourself; don't rush, but keep working and move on if you get stuck
18. Maintain a positive attitude even if the test is going poorly
19. Keep your first answer unless you are positive it is wrong
20. Check your work, don't make a careless mistake

Communication

Errors of articulation

As a child learns a new language, he or she has a tendency to omit sounds from words. Over time, the child will include all of the sounds, but may not be able to effectively articulate some of the more difficult consonants. For instance, the "t" sound is one that is often omitted from words, as for instance in the contraction "don't," which is often pronounced as "don'." As an individual begins to speak more quickly, he or she is even more likely to omit these common consonant sounds. To a certain extent, these errors of articulation are not a problem. When they become chronic and extreme, however, they can make speech extremely difficult to understand.

Articulation of consonants

Consonant sounds are created by stopping or redirecting a sound. For instance, an "s" sound is formed by pressing the tongue to the palette to slow down an escaping sound. Because consonants often depend on a percussive motion, it is possible to draw them out for a long time. Similarly, because of their short duration, consonants do not have as much effect as vowels on the quality of an individual's voice. Because consonants are articulated quickly, they are often more difficult to hear. For this reason, speakers need to be especially sure to clearly articulate them. When a conversation is heard at a great distance, often all that can be discerned is a long string of vowels sounds. Similarly, individuals who mumble are doing a poor job of articulating consonants. Many individuals focus on pronunciation, but clear articulation of consonants is a prerequisite for this skill.

Pauses in vocal delivery

Human speech is not just a constant stream of syllables. The placement and use of pauses during speech also plays an important role in forming meaning. The study of pauses in human speech is a subcategory of paralinguistics. A short pause is often used to denote the end of a sentence or clause. In many ways, short pauses are used like commas. Long pauses, on the other hand, are more similar to periods or the ends of paragraphs. When a speaker takes a long pause, he or she may be allowing what has been said to sink into the minds of the audience. Individuals often pause as they search for the right word. Other times, individuals will insert a slight pause into a sentence to create a level of suspense before the thought is finished.

Nonverbal communication

Nonverbal communication is the ability to enhance or elaborate on the words of the speaker. In particular, hand gestures and changes in vocal rhythm and volume have the ability to add expressiveness to what is being said. Many times, the gestures and vocal mechanisms of the speaker simply emphasize his or her message; at other times, however, the speaker may detract from or undermine his or her message with contradictory gestures. Hand gestures and gesticulations have the ability to dramatize a communication event.

By giving the audience things other than words to concentrate on, the speaker engages and entertains them. Although nonverbal communication is typically thought of as supplementary to the words being spoken during a communication event, it can also serve a vital purpose as feedback. The gestures, eye movements, facial expressions, and posture of the audience often indicates their level of engagement more accurately and honestly than verbal criticism. It is very difficult to hide extreme boredom or rapt attention. The nonverbal communication of the audience will indicate their level of interest and acceptance of the message of the speaker. The speaker can then adjust his or her message accordingly.

At times, the nonverbal communication produced by a speaker will give a slightly different message than that of the speaker's words. This is often the case when a speaker is attempting to introduce an element of irony into his or her message. For instance, if at the conclusion of a bad movie one friend says to another, "Well, that was a good use of my time," but smiles while saying the words, the other friend might assume that the message is being delivered with sarcasm. In other words, the speaker does not literally mean that the movie was a good use of time, but rather wishes to indicate that it was a waste of time. A message is being delivered, but the nonverbal communication accompanying the words creates a complex message different than the mere words being spoken.

Sometimes, a speaker's nonverbal communication is contradictory to the words he or she is speaking. This can often create confusion and conflict. For instance, imagine a person is in distress. In some cultures, it is not considered dignified to ask another person for help, even in emergency situations. So a person in dire need of assistance might be saying he or she does not need help, even though observation of nonverbal signs says otherwise. Obviously, this will create conflict in the mind of the audience, who will want to obey the wishes of the person but will also want to lend assistance to a person in need. When an individual directly contradicts his or her words with his or her nonverbal communication, it becomes much more difficult for the communication message to be interpreted.

Listening

People often listen to one another as a demonstration of empathy. Empathy is the ability to understand and appreciate what another person is going through despite not having the same experience oneself. One of the ways a person can express understanding and compassion for others is simply by listening to them. Listening to someone indicates that his or her problems are worth your time. Most people find that not only is listening a good way to demonstrate empathy, but it is also a good way to develop empathy. It seems that when we listen to one another, we gradually develop a sense of each other's internal worlds, and we come to treat each other with more compassion.

Simply listening to another person can have profound psychological implications. Indeed, the entire field of psychoanalysis is largely based on the idea that having a sympathetic audience for one's problems is profoundly therapeutic. Many people pay a great deal of money simply to have a sympathetic listener who can offer some professional advice. Psychoanalysts are especially skilled at creative listening. That is, they are able to "unpack" the message of the speaker and discern new, possibly hidden meanings. Numerous studies have indicated that the process of verbally elaborating and describing personal issues eases the burden of stress on the mind, regardless of whether the interpretation of these issues is accurate or constructive.

Defensiveness can be extremely limiting to an individual's ability to listen properly. When a person is defensive, he or she is overly concerned with protecting his or her own interests. Defensiveness is especially prevalent in interpersonal communications in which the two parties do not trust one another. However, some paranoid individuals may be naturally more inclined to defensiveness than others. The problem with defensiveness is that it indicates that the attention of the listener is on his or her own concerns, rather than on the content of the message being delivered. To the degree that a listener is not focusing on the message being delivered, his or her ability to understand and respond to the message will be impaired.

Active listening

Active listening is a technique of communication reception in which the listener tries to develop an empathic relationship with the speaker. Proponents of this form of listening declare that a great deal of listening contains an unhelpful evaluative aspect, to the extent that the speaker continually feels in danger of being criticized by the listener. In active listening, on the other hand, the listener makes an effort to fully experience the thought process of the speaker before even beginning to judge. Perhaps most importantly, active listening is a skill that is developed over time. To fully engage with what someone is saying, the listener must practice subverting his or her own ego and focus instead on the perceived interests of the speaker.

Defensiveness

Speech communication theorists identify a number of ways in which defensiveness can impair effective and accurate communication. These ways are basically defined by the attitude of the listener. For instance, some defensive listeners adopt an overly evaluative posture, in which they indicate that it is up to them to decide whether the speaker is competent or not. Other defensive listeners adopt a self-consciously apathetic attitude, as if to indicate that they are above being interested in the message of the speaker. Another common listening attitude for a defensive individual is certainty, or the assumption that he or she already knows the content of the message. This attitude draws the speaker up short and makes it difficult for him or her to continue communicating.

Public speaking

Speech communication instructors often refer to public speaking as a "transaction," or a way of indicating the important active roles of both the speaker and audience. Too often, people consider speech-giving as a process in which one person actively provides information while another group of people passively receives information. Instead, the ideal public speaking relationship is one in which the speaker presents a message and the audience presents feedback. Even when the audience is not given an opportunity to speak, they provide feedback in the form of attention or inattention. By referring to public speaking as a transaction, instructors emphasize the roles and responsibilities of both speaker and audience. In general, speech communication instructors would define a transaction as any communication in which information passes from speaker to listener and vice versa.

For most people, the obvious goals of public speaking are political victories and support for social movements. Both are common motives of public speech, but they are not the only recognized intention of public communication. Public speech is often used to define an individual or a community. For instance, people may use speeches to describe particular attributes of themselves or of the group to which they belong. People also use speeches simply to disseminate information. Speeches can be used to inspire other people to action. Famous addresses like the "I Have a Dream" speech of Martin Luther King, Jr. exemplify this kind of speech. Finally, public speaking can be used to introduce arguments and to debate controversial questions in a community. The presidential debates before the general election are a good example of this.

- 4 -

There are a number of reasons for studying public speaking, but the most commonly cited are social, intellectual, and consumer motives. People need to learn to speak in public in order to function in society and to manage relationships, administrate social events, and minimize conflict. Intellectually, a study of public speaking gives insight into human thought, ethics, and persuasion. Public speeches can generate emotions and ideas in listeners as well as influence their existing thoughts and feelings. It is also important to study public speaking not only to improve one's own speaking skills, but to improve one's ability to analyze and interpret the speeches of others.

Informative speech

When one is delivering an informative speech, his or her primary goal is to instruct the audience on a particular subject. If the speech is effective, the audience members will leave with more knowledge and understanding. College lectures are a great example of an informative speech. Although informative speeches may be entertaining, the humor or "color" of the speech should not distract from the overall intention, which is to disseminate information. Informative speeches often contain specific statistical data and an organized set of arguments and supporting evidence. Many informative speeches contain mention of counter-arguments, including rebuttals.

Impromptu speech

An impromptu speech is one delivered "off-the-cuff"; that is, one delivered with a minimum amount of preparation and in an informal style. Not everyone is capable of delivering an effective impromptu speech. Most people can give a successful impromptu speech only if the topic is one on which they have discoursed before or if they are extremely familiar with their topic. Of course, we all make impromptu speeches as a matter of course in our daily lives. Every time you are asked to give your opinion on a subject or to explain an idea, you are in effect making an impromptu speech. By studying speech communication, however, people can learn the elements of effective impromptu speeches and improve their ability to deliver them.

Extemporaneous speech

An extemporaneous speech combines elements of preparation and improvisation. When one is delivering an extemporaneous speech, he or she is drawing on prepared research but not reading directly from a sheet of paper nor reciting the speech from memory. An extemporaneous speech is more conversational and informal than a written speech and is therefore more appropriate for casual gatherings. The colloquial and informal nature of an extemporaneous speech can be extremely helpful in cultivating a good rapport between speaker and audience. To deliver an effective extemporaneous speech, however, the speaker must be extremely familiar with his or her source material.

Persuasive speech

Persuasive speeches are designed to change the minds of the audience or motivate the audience to action. The precise goals of a persuasive speech are dependent on the particular cause promoted by the speaker. Moreover, the methods employed in a persuasive speech will depend on the subject matter and the speaker's rhetorical style. Some speakers employ a dry, data-driven style when making a persuasive speech.They hope to overwhelm their audience with the strength and breadth of information. Other speakers seek to beguile their audience by amusing and entertaining them.

This kind of speech is appropriate for general audiences and non-technical subjects. When a persuasive speech is being delivered to an audience of experts, or is centered on a complex issue, it must include cogent reasoning and supportive data.

Entertaining speech

The only goal of some speeches is to entertain and amuse the audience. Standup comedy is a type of entertaining speech. Many speeches that also contain information or persuasive content are primarily entertaining. The keynote speakers at conferences and conventions often cloak their arguments in witty anecdotes and jokes. Obviously, serious subjects are not appropriate content for entertaining speeches. However, many speakers will introduce some elements of an entertaining speech to first capture the attention of the audience and then persuade them to engage seriously with the more weighty elements of the speech.

Introductory speech

It is common for a speech of introduction to precede a keynote speech, a presentation, or a public performance of some kind. For instance, a symphony director will often give a brief speech of introduction before a concert. The best introductory speeches do not simply list the achievements or characteristics of the person or event that is to follow. Rather, they engage the interest of the audience and whet their appetite for what is to come. A good speech of introduction should not include any criticism of what is to follow. It is always a good rule of thumb for the introductory speaker to confer with those who are to follow so that his or her message can be as appropriate as possible.

Welcoming speech

A welcoming speech is often given at the beginning of a convention, meeting, or special event of some kind. Typically, the welcome will be delivered by a representative of the group or organization putting on the event. For instance, the chairman of a professional organization administering a business convention might deliver a speech of welcome to convention attendees. Welcoming speeches are typically light on substance and primarily provide an overview of the events to follow. Also, a welcoming speech typically includes a message of thanks to the organizers and administrators of the event. The speaker often indicates his or her personal goals for the event and may tell the audience how to make their questions and comments known to the event administrators.

Memorizing and reading a speech

When delivering a speech, the speaker may need to decide whether to memorize or read the text. There are advantages to each approach. When a speech is memorized, the speaker can make eye contact with the audience and use his or her hands to make illustrative gestures. Memorized speeches run the risk of sounding overly rehearsed, however, and the speaker may falter if he or she loses track of the speech. Some speakers prefer to read their speeches, often because they prefer to have a copy of the speech for reference. If the speaker plans to read his or her speech, he or she should become extremely familiar with the speech so it is not necessary to read every word from the paper. Regardless of whether a speech is memorized or read, the speaker should practice delivery to increase fluency.

Specific purposes for a speech

The first step in preparing a speech is knowing the specific purpose of that speech. This enables the speaker to focus on what is important and to research efficiently for relevant material. Knowing the specific purpose of the speech allows the speaker to emphazise the most important points within the speech. The specific purpose of a speech might be informing the audience on a particular point, changing a few minds on a particular subject, raising some money, or simply entertaining the audience. It is a good idea to make the specific purpose of the speech explicit in the speech. Although you do not want to beat your audience over the head with your intentions, there should be no question as to what the speech is meant to accomplish. In general, the specific purpose of a speech is defined in terms of the desired reaction from the audience.

Persuasion

Persuasion is the art of changing the attitudes, beliefs, or actions of other people. It can be used for any number of purposes: to sell a product, to make a friend, to advance a cause, or simply to win an argument. To a certain degree, even primarily informative speeches contain an element of persuasion. The speaker is encouraging his or her audience to understand a given subject in the same way he or she does. To be persuasive, the speaker must have a clear idea of what he or she is trying to accomplish. Also, it is important to understand the best persuasive strategy for achieving the desired effect. Persuasion can be styled as direct argument or as more indirect, even subversive, suggestion.

Students of rhetoric have long noticed the correlation between a charismatic personality and persuasion. Basically, if a speaker is able to establish strong personal relationships with his or her audience, he or she is much more likely to be an effective persuasive communicator. The most important thing a persuasive speaker can do is to establish trust from the outset. If a speaker can convince the audience that he or she has their best interests at heart and is a competent source of information, the work of persuasion is largely done. Establishing trust and respect with the audience is as much a matter of one's credentials as one's appearance and presentation. Speakers who can demonstrate expertise and empathy are likely to find success with the audience.

To be persuasive, an individual must be perceived as competent by the audience. Competence manifests itself in a number of characteristics, such as preparedness, poise, thoughtfulness, and clarity. A competent speaker should be able to answer questions from the audience on a specific subject, or should at least be able to explain where the answers could be found. A competent speaker must have supporting evidence for his or her arguments and must make this evidence clear to the audience. A competent speaker will also be able to organize his or her message effectively, giving the audience the best opportunity to educate themselves. Finally, a competent speaker will appear unhurried and calm.

Audiences seem to have a sixth sense for insincerity. They can tell when a speaker does not really believe his or her message. For this reason, effective persuasion is greatly benefited by the speaker's deep conviction in what he or she is saying. It is often said that before a speaker can persuade anyone else, he or she needs to be persuaded.

When the strength of a speaker's convictions is evident in his or her delivery, the natural empathy of the audience will assist in persuasion. Historically, a survey of the great persuasive orators (Martin Luther King Jr., Abraham Lincoln, Pericles, etc.) confirms that strong belief is a boon to persuasive rhetoric.

Another factor that can greatly influence a speaker's power of persuasion is reputation. When a speaker has a reputation for upright behavior and responsibility to the truth, an audience is much more likely to believe his or her message. The credibility of the speaker is imperative, regardless of the topic. If the content of the speech is highly specialized, the audience will want to know that the speaker has some advanced training in the subject. When an audience arrives for a speech already knowing the positive reputation of the speaker, the work of persuasion is almost complete. For many politicians and orators, building a reputation that encourages persuasion is the work of a lifetime.

Having direct knowledge of sources can be extremely beneficial to a speaker's power of persuasion. For instance, imagine a motivational speaker on the subject of weight loss. If that speaker has had the experience of being overweight and then successfully losing weight and becoming more healthy, the audience will be much more likely to take his or her words to heart. When a speaker can claim direct experience of the topic on which he or she speaks, the audience is unlikely to attribute the speaker's motives to personal gain or manipulation. The most effective speakers are able to present their personal experience as a model for the examination and consideration of the audience.

Unconscious mimicry or imitation can be one of the most powerful forces for persuasion. Human beings have a natural tendency to imitate the behavior of those they perceive to be leaders or role models. People often adopt beliefs or act in ways uncharacteristic of whom they really are in order to mirror the behavior of a leader. This phenomenon is due in part to the tendency of human beings to minimize differences between one another as a means of preventing conflict. Of course, to inspire imitation on the part of the audience, a speaker must appear competent and have a good reputation. The members of an audience should be particularly skeptical of speakers who encourage them to adopt a point of view simply because others are doing so.

Human beings have a natural tendency to believe what designated authority figures tell them. In part, this is an inherited characteristic. Early humans, in order to survive in the wild, often had to rely on the advice and guidance of their peers. In many cases, people will follow directions from an authority figure without considering the ramifications of their actions. This phenomenon was evidenced during the Nuremberg trials after World War II, as numerous Nazi officials defended their actions as "just following orders." The educational system also encourages people to trust authority figures and follow directions. Audience members should be aware of this tendency and should guard against blindly accepting the recommendations of a speaker.

A persuasive speaker may sometimes use a suggestion rather than a direct command to achieve his or her goal. A suggestion is simply a less forceful recommendation; it implies that the audience has the ability to decide for themselves whether or not to accept the guidance of the speaker. Suggestion is a good strategy for dealing with naturally skeptical audience members, who will resist any overt attempts to change their minds.

Because it is an indirect form of persuasion, however, suggestion requires a bit more subtlety on the part of the speaker. But because it gives the listener the impression that he or she has arrived independently at a conclusion, suggestion can be more effective than direction.

When an audience is considering the elements of a persuasive speech, they will likely give some thought to the motivations of the speaker. For instance, when approached by a salesperson, a customer is likely to assume that the salesperson has a vested personal interest in making a sale and does not necessarily have the best interests of the consumer at heart. In other contexts, however, the motivation of the speaker may be harder to discern. In an academic speech, forinstance, the audience will be aware that the speaker is attempting to promote a certain viewpoint, but they may not be able to determine exactly why the speaker supports that point of view. To the extent that the audience can discern the motivation of the speaker, they will be able to intellectually consider the merits of the speech, and not be swayed by emotion.

Audiences will naturally be resistant to persuasive arguments that attempt to take them out of their normal routine. People of all ages have a tendency to fall into habitual behaviors that can be difficult and even painful to interrupt. A persuasive speaker, however, is by nature one who attempts to convert an audience to a new way of living or thinking. He or she will therefore encounter the listeners' resistance, based on their entrenched habits. Habitual behavior can be attacked in a number of ways. One is to persuade the audience that these habits are detrimental. Another is to suggest the advantages that can be gained from a new way of living or thinking. In all cases, however, the speaker should remember that most behavioral change is incremental and not the result of sudden conversion.

One of the most common kinds of persuasive speech is one in which the speaker attempts to persuade the audience to change something. The speaker may be asking the listeners to change their behavior, their opinion on some subject, or the way in which some issue is handled in their community. These kinds of speeches usually follow a similar arc: first, the speaker describes the disastrous state of affairs at present. Second, the speaker introduces his or her proposal for remedying the situation. Third, the speaker indicates the rewards that the audience will obtain by accepting the proposal of the speaker. If the speech is effective, by its conclusion the audience should be practically intoxicated with the expansive vision of a positive future the speaker has outlined.

Another kind of persuasive speech is one in which the speaker attempts to persuade the audience to *not* change something. Like the speech in support of change, the speech against change has three classic components. First, the speaker argues that things are fine as they are. Second, the speaker argues against any proposals for change that have been made. Third, the speaker describes the negative consequences for the audience if changes are made. As with the speech in support of change, the speech against change begins by setting the general scene and only gradually works its way around to addressing the individual concerns of the audience members. In this way, the last impression the audience receives is that of the effects of change or stasis on their own lives.

Presentation

Over the last few years, the presentation has emerged as the most common speech form in the United States. Members of the business community frequently give presentations, but this form is also common to academic lectures, community discussions, and religious gatherings. One of the defining characteristics of a presentation is that it contains other media besides simply a speaker. It is common for a speaker to include PowerPoint slides, photographs, brochures and handouts, short videos, audio samples, in a presentation. Because presentations are often designed to be given over and over again to different audiences, they may be complex, detailed, and highly coordinated.

One of the defining characteristics of a presentation is the use of presentation aids. Speakers often include supplementary audio or visual materials that elaborate or reinforce their presentation points. Currently, the most popular presentation aid is PowerPoint, a software program that allows speakers to assemble a collection of slides to accompany their speech. Speakers also frequently include video samples in their presentations. In business, tables and charts are frequently used to illustrate the points of a presentation.

Eulogy

A eulogy is a speech that praises a particular individual and highlights his or her best qualities. Eulogies are often given at funerals as the speaker remembers the deceased in a positive light. Eulogies are not the appropriate form for criticism or objective analysis of a person's life.

On the other hand, a eulogy may fail if the audience finds it so excessively laudatory that it is not believable. In some cases, a eulogy of sorts may be given in praise of a particular event, community, or culture. Typically, a eulogy is delivered to an audience that is already disposed to think favorably of the subject. The speaker is typically someone who has extensive personal experience with the subject of the eulogy.

Audience analysis

In the study of speech communication, audience analysis is simply the practice of examining the characteristics and background of the audience in order to tailor a speech appropriately. For instance, one would want to know the general age, socioeconomic status, culture, and gender of an audience while preparing a speech. The type of speech appropriate to a group of elementary schoolgirls will be quite different from that appropriate to a group of older men, even if both speeches are on the same subject. The prejudices and pre-existing opinions of these two groups will be extremely different and thus, to be effective, a speaker must tailor and deliver his or her message to each group in very different ways.

When a seasoned public speaker conducts an audience analysis, he or she focuses on a few specific characteristics of the audience. For one thing, the speaker wants to know the audience's background as it relates to him or her and his or her subject matter.

Although much of audience analysis consists of determining the approximate ages and socioeconomic backgrounds of the audience, this is primarily because such information enables the speaker to estimate the audience's opinions and degree of familiarity with the subject matter and speaker. A speaker who is well-liked by the audience can employ a different rhetorical strategy than one with whom most of the audience disagrees.

Remembering the audience's capacity to act

When developing a speech, one should always remember the characteristics and capabilities of the audience. This is especially important when producing a persuasive speech. It does not make sense to encourage the audience to take an action they are not capable of taking. For instance, a politician would be foolish to make an impassioned plea for votes to a bunch of elementary school students, all of whom are years away from voter eligibility. When developing a persuasive speech, then, it is essential to remember the capacity of the audience to act.

Audience attitude

It is important for a speaker to gauge the attitude of the audience before delivering his or her speech. Attitude, because it is more subtle than age, ethnicity, or belief system, can only be determined through direct observation. Thus, if a speaker is able to observe the audience before delivering the speech, he or she can benefit greatly. Observing the audience beforehand can provide clues to what kind of general mood the audience is in, whether good or bad. If the audience is in a hostile mood, the speaker may want to avoid trying to joke with them. An audience that seems jovial and engaged, on the other hand, should not be alienated with strident rhetoric or harsh words. The job of the speaker is to establish and maintain a good rapport with the audience.

Beliefs

To accurately assess what an audience might be thinking, one must understand that audience's core beliefs. Strictly defined, beliefs are the facts, ideas, and opinions that the audience holds to be true. Objectively, some of these beliefs may actually be untrue. However, to deliver an effective message, a speaker must take into account the sum total of the audience's beliefs. If the purpose of the speech is to adjust the beliefs of the audience, the speaker must appeal to either the reasoning skills or the emotions of his or her listeners.

When describing the beliefs of an audience, speech communication instructors often distinguish between fixed and variable beliefs. The primary difference between the two is that fixed beliefs are harder to change. Typically, fixed beliefs have been held throughout an individual's life and most likely reinforced by his or her experience. Variable beliefs, on the other hand, may have been recently acquired and therefore may be less established in the individual's mind. A speaker is more likely to change variable beliefs and should therefore focus his or her attention on these. Variable beliefs are especially vulnerable to change when they are based on opinion rather than fact.

Facts and opinions

When considering the convictions of an audience, it is good to distinguish between facts and opinions. Facts are those convictions that can be proven in an objective sense. Scientific assertions, for instance, are considered facts. Opinions, on the other hand, cannot necessarily be supported by hard data. People often hold opinions for rather arbitrary individual reasons, such as those based on personal experience.

The fact that communities hold collective opinions must also be considered when making a speech. In general, it is easier for a speaker to adjust beliefs or convictions based on opinion than those based on fact.

> **Review Video: <u>Fact or Opinion</u>**
> *Visit **mometrix.com/academy** and enter **Code: 870899***

Basic elements of speechmaking

To master the speechmaking process one should clearly understand a few basic elements.. The central figure is the speaker; that is, the one delivering the speech. The speaker brings a self-conception as well as a conception, or impression, of the audience's general identity. In the study of speechmaking, the audience is sometimes referred to as the "receiver." Like the speaker, the audience members will have a self-image as well as an impression of the speaker. The setting in which the speech is delivered is known as the "situation." The speaker uses various channels of communication, including words and gestures, to communicate his or her message. The audience members will deliver their responses to the speech both verbally and through body language. This response to the speech is called feedback.

Preparing a speech

To successfully prepare a speech it is best to follow a basic set of established steps. By following these steps, the speaker (or speechwriter) can more efficiently develop an organized and effective presentation. The first step in preparing a speech is to select a subject, if the topic has not been predetermined. Next, the speaker should articulate to himself or herself the key ideas and arguments to be included in the speech. As he or she begin to formulate these ideas and arguments, it is important to take into account the characteristics of the intended audience. At this point, the speaker should begin gathering materials for the speech, whether through research or brainstorming. The next step is to outline the speech, and finally, write a draft of the speech. It is always a good idea to practice delivering the speech and to make revisions or adjustments where necessary.

During the preparation phase of speech composition, a speaker will begin to organize his or her research material. Once the speaker has decided upon the basic angle and structure of the speech, he or she may need to acquire more research materials for elaboration and support. Of course, it may take the speaker a while to find the appropriate thrust of the speech. Speakers should not be discouraged by numerous blind alleys or false starts during the preparation phase. Even when it seems that progress is not being made, the speaker should remember that each false start eliminates a possible point of entry bringing the ultimate goal closer.

Selecting a subject

Perhaps the most important component of an effective speech is an appropriate and interesting subject. When selecting a subject for a speech, one should look for a topic that is engaging to a general audience. While it is important for the speaker to have some familiarity with the subject, it is not necessarily a good idea to speak about a subject on which he or she is an expert. Too often, an expert delivering a speech to a general audience dwells too much in details and specificities, which has a tendency to bore the audience. It is a good idea for the speaker to have a passing familiarity with the subject, so that he or she will be able to find good research materials and judge what will be interesting to a general audience. However, the speaker should also make sure to emphasize the aspects of the subject that are relevant to the lives of the audience members.

Creativity

Sometimes it can be difficult to come up with a topic for a speech. All the "good topics" may seem to have already been covered, or there may be no one single subject on which a potentiall speaker has enough information to be effective. Effective speakers develop creative ways to come up with new speech topics. Being creative, however, does not mean sitting back and waiting for the muse of speech topics to visit. Creative speakers work proactively to develop new topics. They list their areas of interest and are constantly considering everything they see and read in terms of how it could be developed into a speech. Most creative speakers discard more ideas for speeches than they ever use.

After a speaker has decided upon a topic for a speech, the next move is to conduct a creative analysis of that topic—simply a detailed exploration of the topic. To begin with, the speaker assembles as much information as he or she can within the amount of time available. This may include interviews, books, and old periodicals. Experienced speakers will have a good working knowledge of the public or school library and will be able to acquire diverse basic materials in a short period of time. After all this information has been assembled, the speaker will sort through it, looking perhaps for an entry point for his exploration. An interesting narrative, a point of local interest, or a previously overlooked angle on the subject may all be ways for the speaker to engage the interest of the audience on a given subject.

Creative speech analysis

During the incubation phase of creative speech analysis, the speaker actually does not engage in any direct work on the speech. Instead, the speaker allows his or her subconscious to mull over the content of the speech. Even though it seems like no work is being done during this period, the incubation phase is actually very important, as it is during this period that the most creative thinking on the subject occurs. Also, the incubation phase gives the speaker a chance to freely imagine the speech, associate various ideas, and try unique combinations. Many speakers say their most unique and powerful ideas often occur to them when they are doing something totally different than speech preparation.

After the incubation phase, the speaker should have a solid structure as well as a number of creative ideas for the speech. In the succeeding illumination phase, he or she will apply the ideas gained during the incubation phase to the basic outline constructed during the preparation phase. It is very common for a speaker to feel a burst of enthusiasm during the illumination phase, as he or she discovers the unique ways in which his or heroriginal ideas will elaborate and improve upon the original structure. The illumination phase is still basically a brainstorming phase. Speakers are still experimenting with new ideas and combinations of materials.

The fourth and final part of the creative analysis of a speech topic is the verification phase. During this phase, the speaker looks over his or her notes carefully. Occasionally, some of the ideas that seemed so brilliant during the incubation and illumination phases turn out to be inappropriate or implausible. Other times, a careful examination of the speech will uncover holes in the reasoning of the argument or reveal the necessity of adding or removing a particular part of the speech. The verification phase of creative speech analysis can be seen as a final polishing of the materials gathered and organized during the first three phases.

Managing creativity during the development of a speech

For the process of creative speech analysis to be effective, a certain amount of discipline needs to be brought to bear on the creative instinct. This is one reason why the process of creative speech analysis includes four distinct phases. By adhering to a set procedural pattern, the speaker will limit the amount of time spent in any one area and will move along toward completion at a predictable pace. Also, by following an organized analysis process, it is easier to avoid the procrastination that commonly occurs during the creative process. As much as possible, a speaker should try to work at specific times without interruption to allow the creative subconscious to do its work.

Basic message units

In every speech, the content is divided into what are called basic message units. A basic message unit has two parts: the point the speaker is trying to make and the evidence or supporting material he or she has assembled. In order to be complete, a message unit needs to have both components. Otherwise, the speaker will be making points without offering any reasoning or evidence, or he will be giving factual information and argumentation without connecting the dots to make a larger point. The point stated by the speaker needs to be a complete and discrete thought. The supporting material must be pertinent to the point and sufficient to convince a reasonable person.

- 13 -

Logical analysis of a speech topic

A speaker should always perform what is known as a logical analysis before presenting his or her speech.This is simply an analysis of the message units that make up the speech, as well as the connections between these message units. To be effective, the logic of any speech must progress in a systematic and discernible manner and should include ample evidence and supporting materials. Speakers often create a brief outline for their speech, in which they sketch the basic structure of the speech's logic, leaving out the supplementary material. In any case, it is essential to make sure the logical skeleton of a speech is sturdy before focusing on other aspects.

As the speaker reviews his prepared speech and performs a logical analysis, he needs to be constantly asking himself whether each point and piece of supporting material is essential. Everything included in the speech should be there for a clear and explicit reason or else it must be considered superfluous. The speaker must also determine whether all of the evidence clearly and directly supports the points it is intended to support. Finally, the speaker must make sure every point in the speech follows a proper order, progressing logically to the speech's climax and ultimate conclusion.

Faulty attribution of causation

One of the most common errors of logic one can make in a speech is the faulty attributionof causation. This occurs when the speaker erroneously assumes that just because one thing followed another, the second thing was caused by the first. For instance, I may grab my umbrella on the way out the door before it starts raining, but if I later use my umbrella I cannot claim that bringing my umbrella caused the rain. When a speaker describes a major historical or social event and suggests such an event had only one cause, this is almost always a case of faulty attribution of causation. Major social and historical movements are simply too complex to be attributed to a single cause. At the very least, a speaker must provide detailed substantiation for any assertions of causation.

Circular reasoning

A common logical error in speeches is circular reasoning. A chain of logic is described as circular when the assumptions made at the beginning of the argument depend on the conclusion of the argument being true. For instance, imagine a speaker declaring that the Tigers baseball team will certainly lose their playoff series. As evidence for this claim, the speaker declares that the Tigers always lose their playoff series. This reasoning clearly does not hold up: In order to believe the Tigers will lose their playoff series, we have to assume they always lose their playoff series, which we do not really know yet, and which depends on their performance in the upcoming playoffs series. In other words, the claims made by the speaker depend for their support on the speaker's assumptions.

> ➤ **Review Video: Circular Reasoning**
> *Visit* **mometrix.com/academy** *and enter* **Code: 398925**

Contradictory argument

Occasionally, a speaker will fall victim to the logical error known as the contradictory argument. A contradictory argument is one in which the speaker introduces information that directly contradicts his main argument. For the most part, this error should be easy to avoid. After all, a speaker will be careful not to include information that undermines his main point. Speakers do, however, sometimes include inconsistent arguments in a speech and this can be highly detrimental to their purpose. Contradictory argument is especially problematic in a persuasive speech, in which the speaker is attempting to persuade the audience from their pre-existing opinions and hoping to sell them on the merits of an alternative view.

Expository supporting material

Most speeches include expository supporting material. The word "expository" comes from the same root as "expose" and refers to information that sheds light on areas about which the audience may know little. Some of the common forms of expository information are examples, analogies, and narratives. Expository supporting material is distinguished from argumentative supporting material in that it strives to remain as objective as possible When a speaker claims to be providing objective and impartial information, he or she will be held to that standard by the audience. For this reason, it is especially important for speakers who use expository supporting material to verify their sources.

Examples

A good speaker knows that examples can be effective because they provide concrete case studies through which the audience can assess the arguments of the speech. Examples are also good for humanizing an abstract speech. For instance, an audience may have a hard time listening to a speech about water conservation, but if the speaker introduces examples of how drought can affect individual people, they will be more likely to stay engaged. A good speaker includes examples that are appropriate and interesting, but which do not distract from his or her main points. Also, examples should not dominate a speech; they should simply add interest to the body of the speaker's message.

Successful speakers are likely to use both real and hypothetical examples in the course of a speech. Real examples are appropriate in speeches describing a particular historical or social topic that is grounded in reality. For instance, it would not be appropriate to use a hypothetical example in an argument about the Revolutionary War since there are plenty of real examples to illustrate points regarding that conflict. In more general speeches, however, it may be necessary to use a hypothetical situation as an example. When describing the possible results of some decision, for instance, a speaker might invoke the case of some hypothetical person as a means of dramatizing his or her argument. In general, real examples are treated with more respect by an audience and should be used whenever possible.

Analogies

An effective speaker will often elaborate and clarify his or her ideas with analogies. An analogy is simply an extended comparison between two things. For instance, a speech on economics might describe a current downturn in the economy as it relates to the Great Depression. In other words, the speaker is drawing an analogy between a current problem and a known historical event. The important thing to remember about an analogy is that the two things being compared will probably not be identical in all respects. The speaker should take care to indicate this and should not make claims that suggest the analogy is perfect. On the other hand, an effective analogy can be a useful predictive tool and can give the audience a way of engaging with the subject.

Narratives

Speakers often incorporate narratives into their speeches as a way of engaging interest and indirectly making a point. A narrative is simply a story. Narratives can be either fiction or nonfiction. As with examples, narratives tend to have more impact on an audience when they are true. However, an artfully told fictitious narrative can also captivate an audience.

 Recent scientific research suggests that audience members are mentally programmed to pay attention to information when it is presented as a story. That is, the human mind is naturally receptive to a narrative. Good speakers take advantage of this tendency by delivering information in the context of a narrative.

> ➢ **Review Video:** <u>Narratives</u>
> *Visit **mometrix.com/academy** and enter **Code: 280100***

Statistics

Speakers often use statistics to provide numerical evidence for their assertions. Basically, a loose definition of statistics is any information that contains numbers.To be effective, statistics must be clear and accurate. Statistics can have a great deal of sway over an audience, since they carry with them the impression of objectivity and mathematical truth. That being said, audience members should keep in mind that statistics are often highly subjective. For instance, by manipulating sample size, information taken into consideration, and scope of a statistical survey, a speaker can present information to support his point no matter how incorrect it is. Audience members should always be wary of statistics and should press the speaker to provide more information on the origin and methodology behind any statistics he or she uses.

Numbers

There are a few different ways to use numbers in a speech. One way is to use numbers as markers of evaluation. When we say a person weighs 120 pounds, for instance, we are using numbers to evaluate their weight. In a similar way, numbers can be used as a basis for comparison. By comparing the prices of two dishwashers, for instance, we obtain an important piece of information we can use in making a consumer decision. Numbers can also be used to make illustrative points. For instance, speakers often cite various statistics in support of an argument. It is important to emphasize that, although numbers suggest impartiality, they are calculated by human beings, who are highly subjective and whose intentions should be rigorously questioned.

Eyewitness testimony

Many speakers incorporate eyewitness testimony into their speeches to great effect. Of course, this kind of supporting material is only appropriate for certain kinds of speeches. For instance, when delivering a speech about the Battle of the Bulge, it might be very useful to quote some soldiers who fought in the battle. On the other hand, eyewitness testimony seems less appropriate to a speech about climate change , which is so widespread that no one person could view its entire effect globally. When using eyewitness testimony, it is important to establish the credentials of the person being quoted. Also, a speaker should take care to indicate the particular vantage point of the eyewitness, so the audience can consider his or her testimony in light of that point of view.

Expert testimony

Whenever possible, speakers attempt to incorporate expert testimony into their speeches. Any time a speaker can quote a well-known authority who agrees with his or her point of view, he or she will be eager to do so. Most members of an audience will probably feel relatively uninformed compared to the speaker and will be ready to listen to anyone who may be considered an expert. Of course, testimony is only expert and appropriate when it comes from an expert in that particular field. For example, most people would be less inclined to take seriously the political views of an expert in basketball than they would if those views came from a respected public servant. Nevertheless, an audience should remain skeptical about persuasive arguments, even when they are made by experts. The standards of logic required of experts apply to everyone else as well.

Ethics

To be effective as a public speaker, one needs to maintain a high degree of ethical rectitude. This is true not only because of the inherent virtues of ethical behavior, but also because an audience will not trust a speaker whom they believe to be unethical. To promote good ethics as a public speaker, one should always be as honest as possible. One should also try to promote the interests of the audience whenever appropriate. It is important to give members of the audience responsibility for making up their own minds, rather than attempting to browbeat them into submission with one's argument.

Title

It is very important to settle on a clear and appropriate title for a speech early on in the preparation process. The title should make explicit the central idea or concept to be discussed in the speech. The title should also indicate the intention of the speech. For instance, if the intent of the speech is to inform the audience about a particular subject, the title should clearly state the name of the subject. If the intention of the speech is to persuade the audience, the title should indicate the main arguments to be made by the speech. To be effective, a title should be succinct, clear, and, if possible, engaging.

Immediate aim and ultimate aim

On occasion, a speaker will have a slightly different intention in making a speech than is apparent from the speech itself. In the field of speech communication, this is known as the distinction between immediate aim and ultimate aim. An example would be a particular speech intended to be a small part of achieving a long-term goal. A prominent businessman, for example, might make a speech about ethics in public policy. Whereas on its face the speech might seem to be a simple address about local community issues, it might be also be part of the businessman's plan to develop his reputation in advance of a political campaign. The immediate aim of the speech, then, is to inform, while the ultimate aim is to advance the political ambitions of the speaker.

Location

When preparing a speech, one should always keep in mind the occasion for which the speech is intended as this will help determine what kind of speech is appropriate. Individuals who have gathered together for a summer picnic, for instance, will not be interested in hearing a long and complicated speech. A short, humorous address would be more appropriate for this setting.

A convention of professors, on the other hand, will be receptive to a more substantive speech that might also include relevant technical information. On rare occasions, a speaker may decide it is necessary to deliver a speech not entirely appropriate for the setting; this should only be done, however, when it is absolutely necessary.

Time limits

When preparing a speech, one must be aware of exactly how much time is available for presenting the material. The time limit will greatly influence the content of the speech. It is rarely possible, for instance, to effectively discuss a complicated subject in a short period of time. Nor will it be possible to hold an audience's interest over a long period of time without having a wealth of information and ideas. Giving an effective persuasive speech in particular requires sufficient time. This is especially true when one is trying to convert an audience's opinion on a subject with which they are unfamiliar or on which they already have firm opinions. Generally, it takes a strong argument, elaborated through a number of points, to alter an opinion already agreed upon by most members of the audience.

Many speakers handicap themselves from the start by selecting a subject that is either too expansive or too narrow for their needs. To be effective, a speech subject must be appropriate for the amount of time available for giving the speech. Obviously, a half-hour speech can go into much more detail and tackle a wider range of issues than can a five-minute speech. A very short speech should have only one main idea, whereas in a longer speech the speaker may have time to deliver several important points and give supporting information for each. Although the best way to determine the appropriate subject for the time limit is to gain experience as a public speaker, beginning speakers can nevertheless help themselves by considering the parameters of a speech as they begin to consider possible subjects.

Setting

When preparing a speech, a speaker should take into account any idiosyncrasies of the speech format or setting. For instance, in some situations a speaker will have specific guidelines and rules for his or her speech. When giving an address to the members of a particular religious or cultural group, for instance, one might need to abide by specific rules. Another thing to consider is the placement of the speech in the overall event. For instance, if other speeches are to follow, one might want to make sure there will be no overlap in speech content. Also, if the speech is to be given directly after a dinner, one should be aware that audience members will be less likely to pay close attention to the details of the speech. Finally, a good speaker will be aware in advance what the physical setting for the speech will be. That is, he or she will know beforehand such details as whether or not the speech is to be given standing or sitting and whether a podium will be available.

Research

To adequately prepare for delivering a speech, one needs to assemble all pertinent information and create a complete outline. One of the reasons why it is a good idea to select a familiar topic for one's speech is that less research will be required. At the very least, one should know where to look to find the information necessary to deliver an informative and comprehensive speech. Speakers may need to consult with experts in the given subject or peruse newspapers, magazines, and books for extra information. Many local and school libraries have extensive databases for performing research, and a thorough Internet search can often provide vast amounts of helpful material.

Composing a speech outline

Creating a detailed, comprehensive outline is the first step before actually writing the first draft of a speech. After assembling all the necessary material and information for the speech, the speaker can then begin organizing the main points of the speech and the arguments and evidence supporting his or her ideas and claims. It is important that all secondary ideas and claims also support the speech's main idea or claim. One should always introduce the most important claim, or thesis, at the beginning of the speech. The speaker can then spend the rest of the speech building a case for this thesis and elaborating other related points. When composing an outline, remember that the finished speech should ideally be much more colorful and engaging. An outline is not meant to entertain, but rather to clearly and succinctly indicate the organization of the speech.

Practicing speech delivery

Excellent speech delivery does not just happen. It is the result of extensive practice. After the speaker has outlined and drafted the speech, he or she needs to practice delivering it. Practicing a speech serves a number of purposes. For one thing, the speaker might not detect weak points in the speech until he or she actually speaks the words aloud. In addition, it is helpful to record oneself practicing the speech and then play back the tape to identify weaknesses in the delivery. It is often a good idea to practice delivering a speech in front of friends or family and then have them critique the performance. Perhaps the most important point is that practice delivering the speech allows the speaker to further familiarize himself or herself with the material, thus increasing the level of comfort and fluency in delivery.

Cultivating self-confidence

Most people struggle with some degree of anxiety when they are required to speak in public. One of the best things a person can do to reduce speech anxiety is to present a confident image. Naturally, one should always practice delivering a speech several times beforehand. Through repetition, the speaker becomes familiar with the appropriate gestures and rhythms of the speech, which gives rise to increasing confidence in his or her ability to deliver. Another good way to build confidence is to make eye contact with the audience during speech delivery. A forthright, steady gaze from the speaker connotes a feeling of confidence. Finally, confidence can be communicated through posture and body language. Standing up straight and emphasizing key points with hand gestures is a great way to communicate self-confidence.

Evaluation

There are a number of things to look for when evaluating the quality of a speech. All effective speeches share a few essential characteristics, such as a good introduction—one that engages the audience and introduces the main idea or argument of the speech. The introduction also establishes the tone of the rest of the speech. The body of the speech should include clear exposition of ideas and appropriate supporting material. The conclusion of the speech should reinforce the main idea or claim and solidify audience understanding. The presentation of the speech should be appropriate to the audience and setting and should be fluent in its delivery.

Message

The message of a speech is communicated not only with the words being spoken but also through the speaker's self-presentation. In other words, the quality of the speaker's voice and his or her body language contribute to the message as well. The message of the speech is generally considered to have three basic components: structure, content, and presentation. The structure of the speech is the order in which information is delivered. To be effective, a speech must have a logical and coherent structure. The content of the speech is the information it contains; even an entertaining or persuasive speech must have good content. Finally, the presentation of a speech is the style in which it is delivered to the audience. Different kinds of speeches require different presentation styles. The most important thing is to match the presentation to the intention of the speech.

Important attributes of a speaker

To be an effective speaker, one must have a clear intention, a good attitude, and extensive knowledge of the subject of the speech, as well as a degree of credibility with the audience. The speaker should fully understand the intention of the speech, even if that intention is not directly expressed in the speech. Sometimes a speaker will have a hidden motive or a long-term goal that cannot be expressed in the speech. To establish credibility, the speaker should possess a solid working knowledge of the subject of the speech. When the speaker is fluent in the subject he or she is discussing, the speech will flow more naturally and the speaker will be able to tailor his or her message to the audience's level of understanding. Referring to a speaker's "attitude" simply means his or her self-conception; that is, the image the speaker has of himself or herself. If a speaker has a positive self-image, he or she is more likely to deliver an effective speech.

Characteristics of the speech listener

The individual or group of individuals who listen to a speech bring their own characteristics to bear on the quality of the speech. For one thing, listeners will always have their own intentions. That is, they will always be seeking to obtain something from the speech, whether it is information or entertainment. Listeners will also have varying degrees of skill, meaning that some groups will be better at understanding a complex message. Listeners will also bring their pre-existing attitudes toward the speaker and the speaker's subject. To deliver an effective message, a speaker needs to perform an audience analysis to determine the characteristics of his or her listeners.

Feedback

Feedback is the response of the audience to the message delivered by a speaker. Although feedback is typically thought of as verbal responses to the message, it also includes body language, attention or inattention, and participation in dialogue after the speech. To be effective, a speaker must be attuned to all these kinds of feedback. In other words, he or she must monitor the audience throughout the speech to identify signs of boredom or engagement. The feedback a speaker receives while delivering his speech is called immediate feedback. The feedback the speaker receives after delivering the speech is called delayed feedback. Delayed feedback usually takes the form of critical comments, praise, or questions. A practiced speaker will use feedback to improve subsequent speeches.

Tailoring the subject of a speech for the appropriate audience

When deciding on the subject of the speech, the speaker must take into account the characteristics and ability level of the audience. The speaker should be aware of the audience's expectations. That is, whether they expect to be informed, entertained, or persuaded. Audience members may be annoyed if a speech has a drastically different tone from the one they were expecting. For instance, an audience expecting a serious speech will be impatient with a speaker who spends a great deal of

- 20 -

time trying to make them laugh. In some cases, it may be necessary to thwart the expectations of the audience, as for instance when a serious moral point must be made instead of providing sheer entertainment.

When deciding upon the subject matter of a speech, the speaker should take into account the audience's general intelligence level and subject-related knowledge. A speech will be ineffective if it is either too elementary or too advanced for the audience. If the speaker is unfamiliar with the knowledge base of the proposed audience, he or she should take steps to determine this knowledge before preparing the speech. For an unschooled audience, it is a good idea to focus on the most basic and important principles of a given subject. For an audience of experts in a given field, however, it is important to provide information that will be stimulating and informative.

Defining the purpose of the speech

In preparation for making a speech, it is important to strictly define the purpose of the speech. Without a firm idea of the intention of the speech, it will be too easy for the content to miss the mark. To begin with, the speaker should consider his or her own intentions as well as the intentions of the audience. As much as possible, the intentions of the speaker and those of the audience should be made to overlap. One should define the central argument or idea to be expressed in the speech and take care that this argument or idea is consistent with the intention of the speech. It is also important that the title of the speech indicates the intention as well as the central theme of the speech.

Idea and a claim

The goal of a speech is to disseminate information or persuade the audience. In other words, a speaker will either deliver ideas or make claims. A speaker who is delivering ideas is expressing information and opinions for their own sake, and not necessarily trying to change the minds of the audience. Informative speeches are usually on subjects about which the audience is not expected to know very much. The purpose of such a speech is to increase the knowledge of the audience rather than to convert them to any particular viewpoint. When a speaker makes claims, on the other hand, he or she is introducing opinions that may or may not be held by the members of the audience. The intention of this type of speech will be to provide arguments and evidence to support the speaker's claims.

Main idea

It is important when giving an informative speech to lay out the main idea in a manner comprehensible to the audience. The main idea of an informative speech should be presented near the beginning of the address and therefore should not require an audience to understand any concepts that will be explained later in the speech. The audience should be able to understand the gist of the main idea before the speaker goes on to elaborate. In the preparation of a speech, the speaker should define the main idea early on, so that he or she can procure evidence and supporting arguments appropriate to that main idea. Too often, speakers introduce evidence and arguments not directly supportive of the main idea of the speech. This causes confusion among the audience and waters down the effect of the speech.

When a speech is designed to present or advance a particular viewpoint, the speaker will need to pay special attention to the phrasing of the speech's main claim. The main claim should be phrased in such a way that it will be comprehensible to a general audience and will not offend casual listeners with a harsh or controversial tone. The degree of intensity appropriate to the claim will depend on the audience. A more strident tone can be used with an audience of like-minded individuals, whereas a diverse group of uncommitted listeners requires a more evenhanded tone. When constructing the main claim of a speech, the speaker should be sure to present only ideas that can be supported by available evidence and reasonable argument. If the main claim of a speech is far-fetched or unsupportable, even the more rational elements of the speech may be dismissed by a skeptical audience.

Well-organized speech

All well-organized speeches have certain qualities in common. For instance, a well-organized speech is comprehensible, meaning it can be understood by all members of the audience. A well-organized speech also has a formal unity, which means all of its parts contribute to the main idea. A unified speech has no extraneous parts. A well-organized speech is also comprehensive—it covers all the issues an audience member would expect to be addressed by a speech on the given subject. Finally, a well-organized speech does not have any repetition. Every major point should be covered in its entirety, but no points need to be repeated once they have been clearly delivered.

Proof speech

Speech communication instructors often refer to a "proof speech." This is a common type of speech, in which the speaker introduces his or her argument and then attempts to prove it. Proof speeches follow a consistent pattern. In brief, a proof speech has four components: introduction, argument, development, and conclusion. A speech that follows this pattern allows the audience to become acquainted with the thrust of the speaker's arguments before substantiation is offered. The lengths of the various components of a proof speech will vary, depending on the speaker's interests and the knowledge level of the audience. For instance, an audience already familiar with the subject matter may not require as much supporting material to be convinced.

Impromptu speech pattern

Any relatively informal speech on a light subject can be referred to as an impromptu speech. An impromptu speech may be given on very short notice and will therefore give evidence of much less preparation. Even so, impromptu speeches tend to follow a similar pattern. There are four basic steps in a typical impromptu speech: an engaging introduction, a brief overview, elaboration, and summary. Notice that the four components of an impromptu speech directly parallel the components of a proof speech. The only real difference is that the delivery will be looser and the style of delivery will endeavor to be more entertaining. An impromptu speech often begins with a humorous or intriguing anecdote and often ends with a light touch as well.

Problem-solving pattern of speech-making

In a problem-solving speech, the speaker outlines a particular problem, attempts to diagnose the cause, and then suggests a potential solution. Problem-solving speeches are at their heart persuasive speeches, since they attempt to convince the audience of the merits of adopting a particular strategy to solve a given problem. To be effective, however, a problem-solving speech needs to follow a logical pattern. These speeches typically begin with an introduction and a definition of the problem in question. The speaker will then summarize the possible causes of the problem and discuss some of the possible solutions. Following this, the speaker will make a case for one of the solutions and provide supporting evidence and argumentation. Finally, the speaker will attempt to rebut some of the possible counterarguments to the proposed solution.

Call-to-action speech

When speech communication instructors describe a call-to-action speech, they are referring to a speech that intends to inspire the audience to follow some recommended course of action. A call-to-action speech has five typical components: engaging the audience, describing why the audience should want to change something, explaining the best way to change, describing the positive consequences of making the change, and directly indicating how change can be made. It is not really possible to rearrange the steps in a call-to-action speech. Unless the argument is delivered in this order, the speech will likely be ineffective. It is important to end by outlining the positive consequences of change and making an emotional plea, as this leaves the audience on a high note, which is most likely to translate into direct action.

Denotative meaning

Denotative meaning is the way in which a word indicates something else. The word "table," for instance, denotes a flat surface with three or more legs. A speaker must always be conscious of the denotative meaning of the words he or she uses. The denotative meaning is not decided on an individual basis. Rather, it is the product of unconscious agreements on meaning made by the members of a community. In other words, to ensure that he or she communicates effectively with the audience, the speaker must have a familiarity with the denotative meanings that will be known to the members of that audience. Effective speakers continually refer to a dictionary during speech composition in order to solidify their understanding of denotative meanings.

Connotative meaning

Connotative meaning is any implication or a suggestion connected to a word that extends beyond the denotative meaning of the word. The connotative meaning of the word, then, is not strictly the definition of the word. Connotative meanings are often quite emotional in character. For instance, the denotative meaning of the word "whale" is a large mammal that lives in the ocean. When the same word is used in a certain way, however, its connotative meaning may refer to someone who is overweight.

Speakers need to be aware of both the connotative and the denotative meanings of the words they use. Otherwise, they run the risk of confusing or even offending the audience members. A detailed dictionary will often have explanations of the various connotative meanings of common words.

> **Review Video:** <u>**Denotative and Connotative Meanings**</u>
> *Visit **mometrix.com/academy** and enter **Code: 736707***

Avoiding distractions

As much as possible, an effective speaker will minimize distractions during a speech. Distractions can include things done by the audience as well as by the speaker him- or herself. Of course, it is not possible for a speaker to control the behavior of an audience, but he or she can exercise self-control. Too many speakers challenge the patience of the audience by hemming and hawing over their words, making distracting gestures, or engaging in frequent vocal tics. For many speakers, making noises like "uh" and "er" while searching for the right word is natural and unconscious. It can be very distracting to an audience, however, so a speaker would do well to practice delivering his or her message without incorporating these filler sounds.

Speaking in a manner appropriate to the topic and setting of the speech

Ideally, with experience a speaker develops the ability to deliver his or her message in a manner appropriate to the topic, the audience, and the setting. For instance, when speaking to a group of five or six people, it is inappropriate to use a booming voice and wild, dramatic gestures. Likewise, it takes a very sophisticated speaker to deliver an intimate, informal lecture to a group of two or three hundred. One of the best ways to develop a sense of what is appropriate for a given setting is to study effective speakers in various settings. Notice how they vary their vocal quality and nonverbal communication repertoire in different environments. To gain the attention and respect of the audience, the speaker needs to deliver his or her message in a manner that will meet their expectations.

Importance of nonverbal communication in delivering speech

Many speakers underestimate the positive effects that nonverbal communication can have on their success in delivering a message. By making assertive and forceful gestures, a speaker can create an image of credibility and confidence. Similarly, by making easy gestures, a speaker can promote an image of relaxation and expansiveness. The trick is to know which gestures are appropriate in which situations. Furthermore, an effective speaker will be able to modulate the volume and pitch of his or her voice in accordance with the requirements of the speech.

A bombastic tone is not appropriate to an academic discourse, nor is a dry delivery appropriate for a political rally. A speaker needs to be aware of the expectations of the audience, and only challenge them when such a challenge is necessary.

Procedure for improving one's own public speech

The process of improving public speech technique will vary depending on the individual's particular challenges. A few common remedies can be generally helpful however. For one thing, a person can record themselves and listen to the way they speak. Speakers are frequently unaware of their articulation problems while giving a speech, but these problems become clear upon review. With practice, speakers can train themselves to diagnose particular problems and can subsequently learn to self-correct them. Practice in producing the correct sound every day should result in almost immediate progress. After a while, the corrections will become habitual and will no longer need review or practice.

Posture

Many speakers fail to recognize the significance of proper posture in the delivery of a speech. As much as words or gestures, a speaker's posture transmits information about his or her attitude, credibility, and confidence. To present a message effectively, a speaker should stand up as straight and tall as possible. Slouching forward or bending over one's notes indicates a lack of interest and preparation. This kind of advice may seem trivial, but an audience will subconsciously pay closer attention to anyone whose posture indicates command and authority. Effective speakers pay close attention to their own posture and make sure that poor posture does not disrupt the transmission of their message.

Facial expression

The facial expressions made by a speaker can have a significant impact on the effectiveness of message delivery. The facial expressions of the speaker can either reinforce or contradict his or her words. If the words being spoken are amusing or colorful, it is appropriate for the speaker to be smiling and have a relaxed facial expression. If the speaker is addressing a serious subject while grinning, however, the audience will most likely discount what he or she is saying. A speaker needs to match his or her facial expressions to the subject matter and to the expectations of the audience. A large audience can expect the facial expressions of the speaker to be slightly exaggerated, while a small audience may be put off by what seems like a leering or grimacing speaker.

Eye contact

Speakers should never underestimate the importance of eye contact during message delivery. For one thing, it is very difficult for an audience member who is making eye contact with the speaker to lose interest. An effective speaker will often shift his or her gaze around the room, making eye contact with as many people as possible. Under no circumstances should a speaker look up in the air, stare at his or her notes, or fix his or her eyes on some point in the distance. At the same time, the speaker should not constantly move his or her eyes around the room, as this may be perceived as anxious behavior. Eye movements should be calm, regular, and smooth.

Gestures

A public speaker should make sure that his or her gestures are in harmony with the subject matter of the speech and the expectations of the audience. Many people are in the habit of either moving their hands frequently during speech or keeping their hands stationary. Both of these approaches are only appropriate in certain circumstances. When delivering a speech to a large audience, or delivering a speech with a high emotional content, a speaker may be advised to incorporate wide, energetic gestures. However, these kinds of motions are not appropriate for a more somber subject. And although gestures can amplify the meaning of the speaker's words, they should never become a distraction from the message of the speech.

Proper way to use notes

Many speakers will require notes, but they should rely on these notes as little as possible during delivery of the speech. For one thing, notes tend to prevent a speaker from making effective eye contact and using his or her hands expressively while speaking. Also, speakers who become reliant on notes may not be able to orient themselves in a speech if something goes wrong with the notes. Notes should only be used as a reference point of last resort. They should be kept down in front of the speaker, preferably out of view of the audience. They should not be held and should be on as few pieces of paper as possible, to prevent excessive shuffling during a speech. Finally, a speaker who requires notes should carefully look them over before a speech to make sure they are understandable and arranged properly.

Speech anxiety

Speech anxiety is a common malady but not one that should cause a person to lose heart. Even the most successful speakers have a bit of anxiety when delivering a message. In a way, this anxiety is a positive thing, because it focuses the attention and encourages concentration. Speech anxiety is a natural response to confronting an uncertain and unfamiliar situation. Research suggests that those who suffer from severe speech anxiety are often the most effective public speakers. Also, most speakers report that the anxiety they feel before delivering a speech is much greater than the anxiety they feel when actually in the process of speaking.

The abundance of nervous energy felt before delivering a speech can be used to the speaker's advantage. For one thing, many people find that speech anxiety sharpens their senses and focuses their concentration on the task at hand. Human beings are naturally inclined to focus their attention when they perceive a threat. The good thing about speech anxiety is that the attention is sharpened even though the threat is not significant. Many accomplished speakers use speech anxiety to increase their level of excitement and dynamism while delivering a speech. Indeed, many speakers say that without speech anxiety, they would not be able to achieve the rhetorical effects that have made them successful speakers.

State apprehension

To some extent, everyone grapples with speech anxiety. The fear of embarrassment or public disclosure can be overcome only with significant practice at public speaking. There are a couple of different kinds of speech anxiety. "State apprehension" is defined as speech anxiety that is only felt in specific situations. For instance, an individual who is comfortable talking in class but becomes anxious when required to speak informally with peers is experiencing state apprehension. Many people experience state apprehension in relation to delivering formal speeches in front of a group. State apprehension has both physical and mental symptoms, including vocal tics, sweaty palms, and a trembling voice.

Trait apprehension

Some people experience speech anxiety to a greater degree than others. Those aspects of speech anxiety that are unique to an individual are known as trait apprehensions. For instance, someone might have an aversion to public speaking because of a past experience. People who have an unnaturally high level of trait apprehension tend to avoid situations in which they will be required to speak to a large group. The good news for these individuals is that trait apprehension can be overcome with experience. Unfortunately, however, this means practicing public speaking until it becomes natural.

Channels of public communication

Normally, speech delivery is considered a simple transmission of words by one person to a group. However, this is only one of the channels through which information is delivered during a speech. In the technical language of speech communication, the speaker's words are said to pass through the verbal channel. At the same time, the speaker's tone of voice indicates his or her attitude through the aural channel. Some speakers use visual aids, which transmit information through the pictorial channel. Finally, a speaker transmits information about his or her attitude and self-image through gestures and facial expressions. This transmission is said to pass through the visual channel.

Physical setting

The physical setting in which a speech is delivered exerts significant influence over the expectations of the audience and should therefore be taken into account by the speaker beforehand. For instance, an audience that is required to stand during a speech will have less patience for a long-winded and complex oration. On the other hand, if the audience is seated in soft, plush chairs, they may be too relaxed to pay attention to a serious lecture. When the subject of a speech requires a fair amount of technical detail, it is a good idea for the audience to be seated in upright chairs and for the room to have sufficient light. In any case, the speaker should consider how physical setting will influence the mood of the audience and should adjust his or her speech accordingly.

Social context

When speakers consider the characteristics of the environment in which they will deliver their speech, they sometimes neglect to consider the social context. The social context is the set of relationships between the members of the audience and the speaker and between the members of the audience themselves. The speaker should know beforehand how he or she stands in relation to the audience. For instance, a speaker may be recognized as an expert, an entertainer, or an intriguing fraud. Also, the speaker should understand how the members of the audience st and in relation to one another; whether they are friends, colleagues, or strangers, for instance. The information gained by this consideration of social context should inform the construction and delivery of the speech.

Communication rules

Sometimes a speech will be delivered in a particular environment or to a particular group that is governed by specific communication rules. For instance, a speech delivered in church is unlikely to be followed by a question-and-answer period. As another example, some debating societies have strict rules for the presentation and critique of a speech. In more informal situations, some groups will have different expectations for speaker behavior. For instance, a gathering of senior citizens is unlikely to respond well to coarse humor. In other words, communication rules may be explicit or implicit. While preparing a speech, the speaker needs to address the formal considerations that will influence his or her message.

Correct Grammar, Organization, and Sentence Structure Required for Writing Reports

Writing preparation

Effective writing requires preparation. The planning process includes everything done prior to drafting. Depending on the project, this could take a few minutes or several months. Elements in planning include considering the purpose of the writing, exploring a topic, developing a working thesis, gathering necessary materials, and devising a plan for organizing the writing. The organizational plan may vary in length and components, from a detailed outline to a stack of research cards. The organizational plan is a guide to help draft a writing project. The plan may change as writing progresses, but having such a guide is essential to keeping a project on track. Planning is usually an ongoing process throughout the writing, but it is essential to begin with a structure.

Grammar

Grammar may be practically defined as the study of how words are put together or the study of sentences. There are multiple approaches to grammar in modern linguistics. Any systematic account of the structure of a language and the patterns it describes is grammar. Modern definitions state that grammar is the knowledge of a language developed in the minds of the speakers.

A grammar, in the broadest sense, is a set of rules internalized by members of a speech community, and an account, by a linguist, of such a grammar. This internalized grammar is what is commonly called a language. Grammar is often restricted to units that have meaning. The expanded scope of grammar includes morphology and syntax and a lexicon. Grammatical meaning is described as part of the syntax and morphology of a language, as distinct from its lexicon.

Nouns and pronouns

Nouns are names persons, places, things, animals, objects, time, feelings, concepts, and actions, and are usually signaled by an article (*a, an, the*). Nouns sometimes function as adjectives modifying other nouns. Nouns used in this manner are called noun/adjectives. Nouns are classified for a number of purposes: capitalization, word choice, count/no count nouns, and collective nouns are examples.

A pronoun is a word used in place of a noun. Usually the pronoun substitutes for the specific noun, called the antecedent. Although most pronouns function as substitutes for nouns, some can function as adjectives modifying nouns.

Pronouns may be classed as personal, possessive, intensive, relative, interrogative, demonstrative, indefinite, and reciprocal. Pronouns can cause a number of problems for writers, including pronoun-antecedent agreement, distinguishing between *who* and *whom*, and differentiating pronouns, such as *I* and *me*.

> ➢ **Review Video: Nouns and Pronouns**
> *Visit* **mometrix.com/academy** *and enter* **Code: 312073**

- 28 -

FREE Study Skills DVD Offer

Dear Customer,

Thank you for your purchase from Mometrix! We consider it an honor and privilege that you have purchased our product and want to ensure your satisfaction.

As a way of showing our appreciation and to help us better serve you, we have developed a Study Skills DVD that we would like to give you for <u>FREE</u>. **This DVD covers our "best practices" for studying for your exam, from using our study materials to preparing for the day of the test.**

All that we ask is that you email us your feedback that would describe your experience so far with our product. Good, bad or indifferent, we want to know what you think!

To get your **FREE Study Skills DVD**, email <u>freedvd@mometrix.com</u> with "FREE STUDY SKILLS DVD" in the subject line and the following information in the body of the email:

a. The name of the product you purchased.

b. Your product rating on a scale of 1-5, with 5 being the highest rating.

c. Your feedback. It can be long, short, or anything in-between, just your impressions and experience so far with our product. Good feedback might include how our study material met your needs and will highlight features of the product that you found helpful.

d. Your full name and shipping address where you would like us to send your free DVD.

If you have any questions or concerns, please don't hesitate to contact me directly.

Thanks again!

Sincerely,

Jay Willis
Vice President
<u>jay.willis@mometrix.com</u>
1-800-673-8175

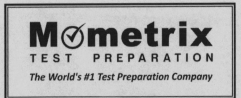

Verbs

The verb of a sentence usually expresses action or being. It is composed of a main verb and sometimes supporting verbs. These helping verbs are forms of *have, do,* and *be,* and nine modals. The modals are *can, could, may, might, shall, should, will, would,* and *ought.* Some verbs are followed by words that look like prepositions but are so closely associated with the verb as to be part of its meaning. These words are known as particles, and examples include *call off, look up,* and *drop off.*

The main verb of a sentence is always one that would change form from base form to past tense, past participle, present participle, and *–s* forms. When both the past-tense and past-participle forms of a verb end in *–ed,* the verb is regular. In all other cases, the verb is irregular. The verb *to be* is highly irregular, having eight forms instead of the usual five.

> ➤ **Review Video:** <u>**Action Verbs and Linking Verbs**</u>
> *Visit **mometrix.com/academy** and enter **Code: 743142***

Adjectives, articles, and adverbs

An adjective is a word used to modify or describe a noun or pronoun. An adjective usually answers one of these questions: Which one? What kind? How many? Adjectives usually precede the words they modify although they sometimes follow linking verbs, in which case they describe the subject.

Articles, sometimes classed as adjectives, are used to mark nouns. There are only three: the definite article *the* and the indefinite articles *a* and *an.*

An adverb is a word used to modify or qualify a verb, adjective, or another adverb. It usually answers one of these questions: When? Where? How? Why? Adverbs modifying adjectives or other adverbs usually intensify or limit the intensity of words they modify. The negators *not* and *never* are classified as adverbs.

Writers sometimes misuse adverbs, and multilingual speakers have trouble placing them correctly.

> ➤ **Review Video:** <u>**Adjectives and Adverbs**</u>
> *Visit **mometrix.com/academy** and enter **Code: 520888***

Prepositions and conjunctions

A preposition is a word placed before a noun or pronoun to form a phrase modifying another word in the sentence. The prepositional phrase usually functions as an adjective or adverb. There are a limited number of prepositions in English, perhaps around 80. Some prepositions are more than one word long. *Along with, listen to,* and *next to* are some examples.

> ➤ **Review Video:** <u>**Prepositions**</u>
> *Visit **mometrix.com/academy** and enter **Code: 946763***

Conjunctions join words, phrases, or clauses, and they indicate the relationship between the elements that are joined. There are coordinating conjunctions that connect grammatically equal elements, correlative conjunctions that connect pairs, subordinating conjunctions that introduce a subordinate clause, and conjunctive adverbs, which may be used with a semicolon to connect independent clauses. The most common conjunctive adverbs include *then, thus,* and *however.* Using conjunctions correctly helps avoid sentence fragments and run-on sentences.

> ➤ **Review Video:** <u>**Coordinating and Correlative Conjunctions**</u>
> *Visit **mometrix.com/academy** and enter **Code:** **390329***

Linking verbs, transitive verbs, and intransitive verbs

Linking verbs link the subject to a subject complement, a word, or word group that completes the meaning of the subject by renaming or describing it.

A transitive verb takes a direct object, a word, or word group that names a receiver of the action. The direct object of a transitive verb is sometimes preceded by an indirect object. Transitive verbs usually appear in the active voice, with a subject doing the action and a direct object receiving the action. The direct object of a transitive verb is sometimes followed by an object complement, a word or word group that completes the direct object's meaning by renaming or describing it.

Intransitive verbs take no objects or complements. Their pattern is subject + verb.

A dictionary will disclose whether a verb is transitive or intransitive. Some verbs have both transitive and intransitive functions.

Subject of a sentence

The subject of a sentence names who or what the sentence is about. The complete subject is composed of the simple subject and all of its modifiers.

To find the complete subject, ask, who? Or, what? Insert the verb to complete the question. The answer is the complete subject. To find the simple subject, strip away all the modifiers in the complete subject.

In imperative sentences, the verb's subject is understood, but not actually present in the sentence. Although the subject ordinarily comes before the verb, in sentences that begin with *There are* or *There was*, the subject follows the verb.

The ability to recognize the subject of a sentence helps in editing a variety of problems, such as sentence fragments and subject-verb agreement, as well as the choice of pronouns.

> ➤ **Review Video:** <u>**Subjects and Verbs**</u>
> *Visit **mometrix.com/academy** and enter **Code:** **987207***

Sentence patterns

Sentence patterns fall into five common modes with some exceptions. They are:
1. Subject + linking verb + subject complement
2. Subject + transitive verb + direct object
3. Subject + transitive verb + indirect object + direct object

4. Subject + transitive verb + direct object + object complement
5. Subject + intransitive verb

Common exceptions to these patterns are questions and commands, sentences with delayed subjects, and passive transformations. Writers sometimes use the passive voice when the active voice would be more appropriate.

Subordinate word groups

Subordinate word groups cannot stand alone. They function only within sentences, as adjectives, adverbs, or nouns.

Prepositional phrases begin with a preposition and end with a noun or noun equivalent, called its object. Prepositional phrases function as adjectives or adverbs.

Subordinate clauses are patterned like sentences, having subjects, verbs, and objects or complements. They function within sentences as adverbs, adjectives, or nouns.

Adjective clauses modify nouns or pronouns and begin with a relative pronoun or relative adverb.

Adverb clauses modify verbs, adjectives, and other adverbs.

Noun clauses function as subjects, objects, or complements. In both adjective and noun clauses words may appear out of their normal order. The parts of a noun clause may also appear in their normal order.

Verbal phrases

A verbal phrase is a verb form that does not function as the verb of a clause. There are three major types of verbal phrases:
1. Participial phrases: These always function as adjectives. Their verbals are always present participles, always ending in *–ing*, or past participles frequently ending in *–d,–ed,–n,–en*, or *–t*. Participial phrases frequently appear immediately following the noun or pronoun they modify.
2. Gerund phrases: Gerund phrases are built around present participles, and they always function as nouns, usually as subjects, subject complements, direct objects, or objects of a preposition.
3. Infinitive phrases are usually structured around *to* plus the base form of the verb. They can function as nouns, as adjectives, or as adverbs. When functioning as a noun, an infinitive phrase may appear in almost any noun slot in a sentence, usually as a subject, subject complement, or direct object. Infinitive phrases functioning as adjectives usually appear immediately following the noun or pronoun they modify. Adverbial phrases usually qualify the meaning of the verb.

Appositive and absolute phrases

Strictly speaking, appositive phrases are not subordinate word groups. Appositive phrases function somewhat as adjectives do, to describe nouns or pronouns. Instead of modifying nouns or pronouns, however, appositive phrases rename them. In form, they are nouns or noun equivalents. Appositives are said to be in apposition to the nouns or pronouns they rename. For example, in the

- 31 -

sentence "Terriers, hunters at heart, have been dandied up to look like lap dogs," *hunters at heart* is in apposition to the noun *terriers*.

An absolute phrase modifies a whole clause or sentence, not just one word, and it may appear nearly anywhere in the sentence. It consists of a noun or noun equivalent usually followed by a participial phrase. Both appositive and absolute phrases can cause confusion in their usage in grammatical structures. They are particularly difficult for a person whose first language is not English.

Sentence classification

Sentences are classified in two ways: according to their structure or to their purpose.

Writers use declarative sentences to make statements, imperative sentences to issue requests or commands, interrogative sentences to ask questions, and exclamatory sentences to make exclamations.

Depending on the number and types of clauses they contain, sentences may be classified as simple, compound, complex, or compound-complex.

Clauses come in two varieties: independent and subordinate. An independent clause is a full sentence pattern that does not function within another sentence pattern; it contains a subject and modifiers plus a verb and any objects, complements, and modifiers of that verb, and it either stands alone or could stand alone. A subordinate clause is a full sentence pattern that functions within a sentence as an adjective, an adverb, or a noun but cannot stand alone as a complete sentence.

Sentence structure

The four major types of sentence structure are:
1. Simple sentences: Simple sentences have one independent clause with no subordinate clauses. A simple sentence may contain compound elements—a compound subject, verb, or object, for example—but does not contain more than one full sentence pattern.
2. Compound sentences: Compound sentences are composed of two or more independent clauses with no subordinate clauses. The independent clauses are usually joined with a comma and a coordinating conjunction or with a semicolon.
3. Complex sentences: A complex sentence is composed of one independent clause with one or more dependent clauses.
4. Compound-complex sentences: A compound-complex sentence contains at least two independent clauses and at least one subordinate clause. Sometimes they contain two full sentence patterns that can stand alone. When each independent clause contains a subordinate clause, this makes the sentence both compound and complex.

> ➤ **Review Video:** <u>Sentence Structure</u>
> Visit ***mometrix.com/academy*** *and enter* ***Code:*** **700478**

Subject and verbs agreement

In the present tense, verbs agree with their subjects in number, (singular or plural) and in person (first, second, or third). The present tense ending *–s* is used with a verb if its subject is third person

- 32 -

singular; otherwise, the verb takes no ending. The verb *to be* varies from this pattern, and, alone among verbs, it has special forms in both the present and past tense.

Problems with subject-verb agreement tend to arise in certain contexts:
1. Words between subject and verbs
2. Subjects joined by *and*
3. Subjects joined by *or* or *nor*
4. Indefinite pronouns, such as *someone*
5. Collective nouns
6. Subject after the verb
7. Pronouns *who, which*, and *that*
8. Plural form, singular meaning
9. Titles, company names, and words mentioned as words

Problems that can be encountered when using verbs

The verb is the heart of the sentence. Verbs have several potential problems, including the following:
1. Irregular verbs: These are verbs that do not follow usual grammatical rules.
2. Tense: Tenses indicate the time of an action in relation to the time of speaking or writing about the action.
3. Mood: There are three moods in English: the indicative, used for facts, opinions, and questions; the imperative, used for orders or advice; and the subjunctive, used for wishes. The subjunctive mood is the most likely to cause problems. The subjunctive mood is used for wishes and in *if* clauses expressing conditions contrary to facts. The subjunctive, in such cases, is the past tense form of the verb; in the case of *be*, it is always *were*, even if the subject is singular. The subjunctive mood is also used in *that* clauses following verbs such as *ask, insist, recommend*, and *request*. The subjunctive, in such cases, is the base, or dictionary, form of the verb.

Pronouns and problems encountered with pronouns

Pronouns are words that substitute for nouns: *he, it, them, her, me,* and so on. Four frequently encountered problems with pronouns include the following:
1. Pronoun-antecedent agreement: The antecedent of a pronoun is the word the pronoun refers to. A pronoun and its antecedent agree when they are both singular or plural, or of the same gender.
2. Pronoun reference: A pronoun should refer clearly to its antecedent. A pronoun's reference will be unclear if it is ambiguous, implied, vague, or indefinite.
3. Personal pronouns: Some pronouns change their case form according to their grammatical structure in a sentence. Pronouns functioning as subjects appear in the subjective case, those functioning as objects appear in the objective case, and those functioning as possessives appear in the possessive case.
4. Who or whom: *Who*, a subjective-case pronoun, can be used only as subjects and subject complements. *Whom*, an objective-case pronoun, can be used only for objects. The words *who* and *whom* appear primarily in subordinate clauses or in questions.

Adjective and adverb

Adjectives modify nouns or pronouns; adverbs modify verbs, adjectives, or other adverbs. Adjectives are often misused in place of adverbs to modify verbs in casual or nonstandard speech. Adverbs usually answer one of these questions: When?, Where?, How?, Why?, How often?, To what degree?. Many adverbs are formed by adding *–ly* to adjectives. However, not all words ending in *–ly* are adverbs. Some adjectives end in *–ly*, and some adverbs do not.

Adjectives ordinarily precede nouns, but they can also function as subject complements following linking verbs. When an adjective functions as a subject complement, it describes the subject.

Most adjectives and adverbs have three forms: the positive, the comparative, and the superlative. The comparative should be used to compare two things, the superlative to compare three or more things.

Repairing a sentence fragment

As a rule, a part of a sentence should not be treated as a complete sentence. A sentence must be composed of at least one full independent clause. An independent clause has a subject and a verb and can stand alone as a sentence. Some fragments are clauses that contain a subject and a verb but begin with a subordinating word. Other fragments lack a subject, verb, or both.

A sentence fragment can be repaired by combining the fragment with a nearby sentence, punctuating the new sentence correctly, or turning the fragment into a sentence by adding the missing elements. Some sentence fragments are used by writers for emphasis. Although sentence fragments are sometimes acceptable, readers and writers do not always agree on when they are appropriate. A conservative approach is to write in complete sentences only unless a special circumstance dictates otherwise.

Run-on sentence

Run-on sentences are independent clauses that have not been joined correctly. An independent clause is a word group that does or could stand alone in a sentence. When two or more independent clauses appear in one sentence, they must be joined in one of these ways:
1. Revision with a comma and a coordinating conjunction
2. Revision with a semicolon, a colon, or a dash, used when independent clauses are closely related and their relationship is clear without a coordinating conjunction
3. Revision by separating sentences, used when both independent clauses are long or if one is a question and one is not: Separate sentences may be the best option in this case.
4. Revision by restructuring the sentence: For sentence variety, consider restructuring the sentence, perhaps by turning one of the independent clauses into a subordinate phrase or clause.

Usually one of these choices will be an obvious solution to the run-on sentence. The fourth technique above is often the most effective solution but requires the most revision.

Avoiding a double negative or a double superlative

Standard English allows two negatives only if a positive meaning is intended. "The team was not displeased with its performance" is an example. Double negatives used to emphasize negation are nonstandard.

Negative modifiers—such as *never, no*, and *not*—should not be paired with other negative modifiers or negative words, such as *none, nobody, nothing*, and *neither*. The modifiers *hardly, barely,* and *scarcely* are also considered negatives in Standard English, so they should not be used with other negatives, such as *not, no one,* or *never*.

Do not use double superlatives or comparatives. When –*er* or –*est* has been added to an adjective or adverb, avoid using *more* or *most*. Avoid expressions such as *more perfect* and *very round*. Either something is or is not. It is not logical to suggest that absolute concepts come in degrees. Use the comparative to compare two things and the superlative to compare three or more things.

Comma

The comma was invented to help readers. Without it, sentence parts can run together, making meanings unclear. Various rules for comma use include the following:
1. Use a comma between a coordinating conjunction joining independent clauses.
2. Use a comma after an introductory clause or phrase.
3. Use a comma between items in a series.
4. Use a comma between coordinate adjectives not joined with *and*. Do not use a comma between cumulative adjectives.
5. Use commas to set off nonrestrictive elements. Do not use commas to set off restrictive elements.
6. Use commas to set off transitional and parenthetical expressions, absolute phrases, and elements expressing contrast.
7. Use commas to set off nouns of direct address, the words *yes* and *no*, interrogative tags, and interjections.
8. Use commas with dates, addresses, titles, and numbers.
9. Use commas to prevent confusion.
10. Use commas to set off direct quotations.

Situations in which commas are unnecessary

1. Do not use a comma between compound elements that are not independent clauses.
2. Do not use a comma after a phrase that begins with an inverted sentence.
3. Do not use a comma between the first or after the last item in a series or before the word *although*.
4. Do not use a comma between cumulative adjectives, between an adjective and a noun, or between an adverb and an adjective.
5. Do not use commas to set off restrictive or mildly parenthetical elements or to set off an indirect quotation.
6. Do not use a comma to set off a concluding adverb clause that is essential to the meaning of the sentence or after the word *although*.

7. Do not use a comma to separate a verb from its subject or object. 8. Do not use a comma after a coordinating conjunction or before a parenthesis.
8. Do not use a comma with a question mark or an exclamation point.

> ➢ **Review Video: Commas**
> *Visit **mometrix.com/academy** and enter **Code: 644254***

Semicolon

The semicolon is used to connect major sentence elements of equal grammatical rank. Some rules regarding semicolons include the following:
1. Use a semicolon between closely related independent clauses not joined with a coordinating conjunction.
2. Use a semicolon between independent clauses linked with a transitional expression.
3. Use a semicolon between items in a series containing internal punctuation.
4. Avoid using a semicolon between a subordinate clause and the rest of the sentence.
5. Avoid using a semicolon between an appositive word and the word it refers to.
6. Avoid using a semicolon to introduce a list.
7. Avoid using a semicolon between independent clauses joined by *and, but, or, nor, for, so,* or *yet.*

> ➢ **Review Video: Semicolon Usage**
> *Visit **mometrix.com/academy** and enter **Code: 370605***

Colon

The colon is used primarily to call attention to the words that follow it. In addition, the colon has some other conventional uses:
1. Use a colon after an independent clause to direct attention to a list, an appositive, or a quotation.
2. Use a colon between independent clauses if the second summarizes or explains the first.
3. Use a colon after the salutation in a formal letter, to indicate hours and minutes, to show proportions, between a title and subtitle, and between city and publisher in bibliographic entries.

A colon must be preceded by a full independent clause. Avoid using colons in the following situations:
1. Between a verb and its object or complement
2. Between a preposition and its object
3. After *such as, including,* or *for example*

Apostrophe

An apostrophe is used to indicate that a noun is possessive. Possessive nouns usually indicate ownership, as in *Bill's coat* or *the dog's biscuit.* Sometimes ownership is only loosely implied, as in *the dog's coat* or *the forest's trees.* If it is unclear whether a noun is possessive, turning it into a phrase may clarify it.

If the noun is plural and ends in *–s,* add only an apostrophe. To show joint possession, use *–'s* with the last noun only. To show individual possession, make all nouns possessive.

- 36 -

An apostrophe is often optional in plural numbers, letters, abbreviations, and words mentioned as words. Common errors in using apostrophes include the following:
1. Using an apostrophe with nouns that are not possessive
2. Using an apostrophe in the possessive pronouns *its, whose, his, hers, ours, yours,* and *theirs*

> ➤ **Review Video: Apostrophes**
> *Visit **mometrix.com/academy** and enter **Code: 213068***

Quotation marks

Use quotation marks to enclose direct quotations of a person's words, spoken or written. Do not use quotation marks around indirect quotations. An indirect quotation reports someone's ideas without using that person's exact words.

Set off long quotations of prose or poetry by indenting. Use single quotation marks to enclose a quotation within a quotation. Quotation marks should be used around the titles of short works: newspaper and magazine articles, poems, short stories, songs, episodes of television and radio programs, and subdivisions of books or web sites.

Punctuation is used with quotation marks according to convention. Periods and commas are placed inside quotation marks, whereas colons and semicolons are placed outside quotation marks. Question marks and exclamation points are placed either inside or outside quotation marks, depending on the rest of the material in the sentence.

Note: Do not use quotation marks around the title of your own essay.

> ➤ **Review Video: Quotation Marks**
> *Visit **mometrix.com/academy** and enter **Code: 884918***

Essays

Essays are generally defined to describe a prose composition, are relatively brief (rarely exceeding 25 pages), and deal with a specific topic. Originally, essays tended to be informal in tone and exploratory and tentative in approach and conclusions. In more modern writing, essays have been divided into the formal and informal. The formal essays have dominated the professional and scientific fields, whereas the informal style is written primarily to entertain or give opinions. Writers should be mindful of the style of essay their subject lends itself to and conform to the conventions of that style.

Some types of essays, particularly scientific and academic writing, have style manuals to guide the format and conventions of the writing. The Modern Language Association and the American Psychological Association have two of the most widely followed style manuals. They are widely available for writers' reference.

Dash, parentheses, and brackets

Dashes are used for the following purposes:
1. To set off parenthetical material that deserves emphasis
2. To set off appositives that contain commas
3. To prepare for a list, a restatement, an amplification, or a dramatic shift in tone or thought

Unless there is a specific reason for using the dash, omit it. It can give text a choppy effect.

Parentheses are used to enclose supplemental material, minor digressions, and afterthoughts. They are also used to enclose letters or numbers, labeling them items in a series. Parentheses should be used sparingly, as they break up text in a distracting manner when overused.

Brackets are used to enclose any words or phrases that have been inserted into an otherwise word-for-word quotation.

End punctuations

Use a period to end all sentences except direct questions or genuine exclamations. Periods should be used in abbreviations according to convention. Problems can arise when there is a choice between a period and a question mark or exclamation point. If a sentence reports a question rather than asking it directly, it should end with a period, not a question mark.

Question marks should be used following a direct question. If a polite request is written in the form of a question, it may be followed by a period. Questions in a series may be followed by question marks even when they are not in complete sentences.

Exclamation marks are used after a word group or sentence that expresses exceptional feeling or deserves special emphasis. Exclamation marks should not be overused, being reserved for appropriate exclamatory interjections.

Ellipsis mark and the slash

The ellipsis mark consists of three spaced periods (...) and is used to indicate when certain words have been deleted from an otherwise word-for-word quotation. If a full sentence or more is deleted in the middle of a quoted passage, a period should be inserted before the ellipsis dots. The ellipsis mark should not be used at the beginning of a quotation. It should also not be used at the end of a quotation unless some words have been deleted from the end of the final sentence.

> ➤ **Review Video:** Ellipsis
> *Visit **mometrix.com/academy** and enter **Code: 402626***

The slash (/) may be used to separate two or three lines of poetry that have been run into a text. If there are more than three lines of poetry they should be handled as an indented quotation. The slash may occasionally be used to separate paired terms such as passed/failed or either/or.

In this case, a space is not placed before or after the slash. The slash should be used sparingly, only when it is clearly appropriate.

> **Review Video: <u>Slash</u>**
*Visit **mometrix.com/academy** and enter **Code:** **881954***

Choosing topics

Very often the choice of a subject may be assigned or determined by someone besides the writer. When the choice is left to the writer, it is sometimes wise to allow the topic itself to select the writer. That is to say, those topics that interest, engage, puzzle, or stimulate someone may be good choices. Engaging the writer is the most important factor in choosing a topic. Engagement notes a strong interest and spirit of inquiry about the subject. It is a signal that the subject and author are interacting in some creative sense, which usually encourages good writing.

Even with an assigned topic, a particular aspect of the subject may interest the writer more than others do. The key to any writer's choice of topic is the likelihood of a subject to inspire the author to question, speculate, inquire, and interact. From this natural interest and attraction, some of the most creative writing develops.

Understanding a writing assignment

Many writing assignments address specific audiences (physicians, attorneys, and teachers) and have specific goals. These writers know for whom and why they are writing. This can clarify the writing significantly. Other assignments, particularly in academic settings, may appear with no specific subject, audience, or apparent purpose. Assignments may come with some variables—such as a specified audience, subject, or approach—and leave the rest up to the writer. Because of these variables, it is useful to consider the following questions:
1. What specifically is the assignment asking the writer to do?
2. What information or knowledge is necessary to fulfill the assignment?
3. Can the topic be broadened or limited to more effectively complete the project?
4. Are there specific parameters or other requirements for the project?
5. What is the purpose of the assignment?
6. Who is the intended audience for the work?

These questions can clarify the writing task and open avenues for exploration.

Purpose in writing

What is the main purpose of the proposed piece? This may be very clear and focused, or it may be ambiguous. A writer should be clear about the purpose of his or her writing, as this will determine the direction and elements of the work. Generally, purposes may be divided into three groups:
1. To entertain
2. To persuade or convince
3. To educate or inform

Considering an audience

The careful consideration of the anticipated audience is a requisite for any project. Although much of this work is intuitive, some guidelines are helpful in the analysis of an audience.
1. Specifically identify your audience. Are they eclectic, or do they share common characteristics?
2. Determine qualities of the audience, such as age, education, sex, culture, and special interests.
3. Understand what the audience values; brevity, humor, originality, honesty are examples.
4. What is the audience's attitude toward the topic: Skeptical? Knowledgeable? Pro or con?
5. Understand the writer's relationship to the audience: Peer, authority, advocate, or antagonist?

Understanding the qualities of an audience allows the writer to form an organizational plan tailored to achieve the objectives of the writing with the audience in mind. It is essential to effective writing.

Understanding the topic

Easily overlooked is the basic question of ascertaining how knowledgeable the writer is about the subject. A careful evaluation should be made to determine what is known about the topic and what information must be acquired to undertake the writing assignment. Most people have a good sense of how to go about researching a subject, using the obvious available resources: libraries, the Internet, journals, research papers, and other sources. There are, however, some specific strategies that can help a writer learn more about a subject and, just as important, what is not known and must be learned. These strategies or techniques are useful not only in researching a subject but also when problems come up during the actual writing phase of the assignment. These strategies include brainstorming, free writing, looping, and questioning.

Brainstorming

Brainstorming is a technique used frequently in business, industry, science, and engineering. It is accomplished by tossing out ideas, usually with several other people, to find a fresh approach or a creative way to approach a subject. This can be accomplished by an individual by simply free associating about a topic. Sitting with paper and pen, every thought about the subject is written down in a word or phrase. This is done without analytical thinking, just recording what arises in the mind about the topic. The list is then read over carefully several times.

The writer looks for patterns, repetitions, clusters of ideas, or a recurring theme. Although brainstorming can be done individually, it works best when several people are involved. Three to five people are ideal. This allows an exchange of ideas and points of view and often results in fresh ideas or approaches.

Looping

Looping is a variation of free writing that focuses a topic in short five-minute stages, or loops. Looping is done as follows:
1. With a subject in mind, spend five minutes free writing without stopping. The results are the first loop.
2. Evaluate what has been written in the first loop. Locate the strongest or most recurring thought, which should be summarized in a single sentence. This is the center of gravity and the starting point of the next loop.
3. Using the summary sentence as a starting point, do another five-minute cycle of free writing. Evaluate the writing and locate the center of gravity for the second loop, and summarize it in a single sentence. This will be the start of the third loop.
4. Continue this process until a clear, new direction to the subject emerges. Usually this will yield a starting point for a whole new approach to a topic.

Looping can be very helpful when a writer is blocked or unable to generate new ideas on a subject.

Questioning and investigating a subject

Asking and answering questions provides a more structured approach to investigating a subject. Several types of questions may be used to illuminate an issue.
1. Questions to describe a topic: Questions—such as what is it? What caused it? What is it like or unlike? What is it a part of? What do people say about it?—help explore a topic systematically.
2. Questions to explain a topic: Examples include who, how, and what is it? Where does it end and begin? What is at issue? How is it done?
3. Questions to persuade involve the claims that can be made about it. What evidence supports the claims? Can the claims be refuted? What assumptions support the claims?

Questioning can be a very effective device, as it leads the writer through a systematic process to gain more information about a subject.

Thesis

A thesis states the main idea of the essay. A working or tentative thesis should be established early on in the writing process. This working thesis is subject to change and modification as writing progresses. It will serve to keep the writer focused as ideas develop.

The working thesis has two parts: a topic and a comment. The comment makes an important point about the topic. A working thesis should be interesting to an anticipated audience; it should be specific and limit the topic to a manageable scope.

Three criteria are useful tools to measure the effectiveness of any working thesis. The writer applies these tools to ascertain the following:
1. Is the topic of sufficient interest to hold an audience?
2. Is the topic specific enough to generate interest?
3. Is the topic manageable? Too broad? Too narrow? Can it be adequately researched?

Research

Many writing assignments require research. Research is the process of gathering information for the writer's use. There are two broad categories of research:

1. Library research should be started after a research plan is outlined. Topics that require research should be listed and catalogues, bibliographies, periodical indexes checked for references. Librarians are usually an excellent source of ideas and information on researching a topic.
2. Field research is based on observations, interviews, and questionnaires. This can be done by an individual or a team, depending on the scope of the field research.

The specific type and amount of research will vary widely with the topic and the writing assignment. A simple essay or story may require only a few hours of research, whereas a major project can consume weeks or months.

Organizing information

Organizing information effectively is an important part of research. The data must be organized in a useful manner so that it can be effectively used. Here are three basic ways to organize information.

1. Spatial organization is useful, as it lets the user see the information, to fix it in space. This has benefits for those individuals who are visually adept at processing information.
2. Chronological organization is the most common presentation of information. This method places information in the sequence in which it occurs. Chronological organization is very useful in explaining a process that occurs in a step-by-step pattern.
3. Logical organization includes presenting material in a logical pattern that makes intuitive sense. Some patterns that are frequently used are illustrated, definition, compare/contrast, cause/effect, problem/solution, and division/classification. Each of these methods is discussed next.

There are six major types of logical organization that are frequently used:

1. Illustrations may be used to support the thesis. Examples are the most common form of this organization.
2. A series of definitions identifying what something is or is not is another way of organization. What are the characteristics of the topic?
3. Dividing or classifying information into separate items according to their similarities is a common and effective organizing method.
4. Comparing, focusing on the similarities of things, and contrasting, highlighting the differences between things, together form an excellent tool to use with certain kinds of information.
5. Cause and effect is a simple tool to logically understand relationships between things. A phenomenon may be traced to its causes for organizing a subject logically.
6. Problem and solution is a simple and effective manner of logically organizing material. It is very commonly used and lucidly presents information.

Initial or rough plan

After information gathering has been completed and the fruits of the research organized effectively, the writer now has a rough or initial plan for the work. A rough plan may be informal, consisting of a few elements such as introduction, body, and conclusions, or a more formal outline. The rough plan may include multiple organizational strategies within the overall piece, or it may isolate one or two that can be used exclusively. At this stage, the plan is just that, a rough plan subject to change as new ideas appear, and the organization takes a new approach. In these cases, the need for more research sometimes becomes apparent, or existing information should be considered in a new way. A more formal outline leads to an easier transition to a draft, but it can also limit the new possibilities that may arise as the plan unfolds. Until the parameters of the piece become clear, it is usually best to remain open to possible shifts in approaching the subject.

First draft

Drafting is a mysterious art and does not easily lend itself to rules. Generally, the more detailed the formal or informal outline is, the easier is the transition to a first draft. Drafting is a learning process, and planning, organizing, and researching may be ongoing. Drafting is an evaluative process as well, and the whole project will be under scrutiny as the draft develops. The scope may be narrowed or widened, the approach may change, and different conclusions may emerge.

The process itself is shaped by the writer's preferences for atmosphere during the writing process. Time of day or night, physical location, ambient conditions, and any useful rituals can all play into the writer's comfort and productivity. The creation of an atmosphere conducive to the writer's best work is a subtle but important aspect of writing that is often overlooked. Although excellent writing has often been done in difficult situations, it is not the best prescription for success.

Evaluating a draft

Once a draft is finished, an evaluation is in order. This can often mean reviewing the entire process with a critical eye. There is no formal checklist that ensures a complete and effective evaluation, but there are some elements that can be considered:
1. It should be determined whether sufficient research was done to properly develop the assignment. Are there areas that call for additional information? If so, what type?
2. What are the major strengths of the draft? Are there any obvious weaknesses? How can these be fixed?
3. Who is the audience for this work and how well does the material appeal to them?
4. Does the material actually accomplish the goals of the assignment? If not, what needs to be done?

This is a stage for stepping back from the project and giving it an objective evaluation. Changes made now can improve the material significantly. Take time here to formulate a final approach to the subject.

Effective questions to ask in obtaining a critical response to the draft

Now is the time to obtain objective criticisms of the draft. It is helpful to provide readers with a list of questions to be answered about the draft. Some examples of effective questions are:
1. Does the introduction catch the reader's attention? How can it be improved?
2. Is the thesis clearly stated and supported by additional points?
3. What type of organizational plan is used? Is it appropriate for the subject?
4. Are paragraphs well developed, and is there a smooth transition between them?
5. Are the sentences well written, and do they convey the appropriate meaning?
6. Are words used effectively and colorfully in the text?

7. What is the tone of the writing? Is it appropriate to the audience and subject?
8. Is the conclusion satisfactory? Is there a sense of completion that the work is finished?
9. What are main strengths and weaknesses of the writing? Are there specific suggestions for improvement?

Supporting the thesis of the work

It is most important that the thesis of the paper be clearly expounded and adequately supported by additional points. The thesis sentence should contain a clear statement of the major theme and a comment about the thesis. The writer has an opportunity here to state what is significant or noteworthy of this particular treatment of the subject. Each sentence and paragraph in turn should build on the thesis and support it.

Particular attention should be paid to ensuring the organization properly uses the thesis and supporting points. It can be useful to outline the draft after writing, to ensure that each paragraph leads smoothly to the next, and that the thesis is continually supported. The outline may highlight a weakness in flow or ideation that can be repaired. It will also spatially illustrate the flow of the argument and provide a visual representation of the thesis and its supporting points. Often things become clearer when outlined than they do with a block of writing.

Title, introduction, and conclusion

A good title can identify the subject, describe it in a colorful manner, and give clues to the approach and sometimes the conclusion of the writing. It usually defines the work in the mind of the reader.

A strong introduction follows the lead of the title; it draws the readers into the work and clearly states the topic with a clarifying comment. A common style is to state the topic, and then provide additional details, finally leading to a statement of the thesis at the end. An introduction can also begin with an arresting quote, question, or strong opinion, which grabs the reader's attention.

A good conclusion should leave readers satisfied and provide a sense of closure. Many conclusions restate the thesis and formulate general statements that grow out of it. Writers often find ways to conclude in a dramatic fashion through a vivid image, quotation, or a warning. This is done in an effort to give the ending punch and to tie up any existing points.

Examining paragraphs and sentences

Paragraphs are a key structural unit of prose used to break up long stretches of words into more manageable subsets and to indicate a shift in topics or focus. Each paragraph may be examined by identifying the main point of the section and ensuring that every sentence supports or relates to the main theme. Paragraphs may be checked to make sure the organization used in each is appropriate and that the number of sentences is adequate to develop the topic.

Sentences are the building blocks of the written word, and they can be varied by paying attention to sentence length, sentence structure, and sentence openings. These elements should be varied so that writing does not seem boring, repetitive, or choppy. A careful analysis of a piece of writing will expose these stylistic problems, and they can be corrected before the final draft is written. Varying sentence structure and length can make writing more inviting and appealing to a reader.

Words and tone

A writer's choice of words is a signature of his or her style. A careful analysis of the use of words can improve a piece of writing. Attention to the use of specific nouns rather than general ones can enliven language. Verbs should be active whenever possible to keep the writing stronger and energetic, and there should be an appropriate balance between numbers of nouns and verbs. Too many nouns can result in heavy, boring sentences.

Tone may be defined as the writer's attitude toward the topic and to the audience. This attitude is reflected in the language used in the writing. The tone of a work should be appropriate to the topic and to the intended audience. Some writing should avoid slang and jargon although it may be fine in a different piece. Tone can range from humorous to serious and all levels in between. It may be more or less formal, depending on the purpose of the writing and its intended audience. All these nuances in tone can flavor the entire writing and should be kept in mind as the work evolves.

Editing process

Time must always be allowed for thorough and careful editing to ensure clean and error-free work. It is helpful to create a checklist of editing to use as the manuscript is proofed. Patterns of editing problems often become apparent, and understanding these patterns can eliminate them. Examples of patterns of errors include misuse of commas, difficulty in shifting tenses, and spelling problems. Once these patterns are seen, it is much easier to avoid them in the original writing. A checklist should be prepared based on every piece of writing, and it should be cumulative. In this manner, progress may be checked regularly, and the quantity and type of errors should be reduced over time. It is often helpful to have a peer proof a manuscript, to get a fresh set of eyes on the material. Editing should be treated as an opportunity to polish and perfect a written work rather than a chore that must be done. A good editor usually turns into a better writer over time.

Proofreader

As a proofreader, one's goal is always to eliminate all errors. This includes typographical errors as well as any inconsistencies in spelling and punctuation. Begin by reading the prose aloud, calling out all punctuation marks and ensuring that all sentences are complete and no words are left out. It is helpful to read the material again, backwards, so the focus is on each individual word and the tendency to skip ahead is avoided.

A computer is a blessing to writers who have trouble proofreading their work. Spelling and grammar check programs may be used to reduce errors significantly. However, it is still important for a writer to do the manual proofing necessary to ensure errors of pattern are not repeated. Computers are a wonderful tool for writers, but they must be employed by the writer rather than as the writer. Skillful use of computers should result in a finely polished manuscript free of errors.

Primary and secondary sources of research material

Primary sources are the raw material of research. This can include results of experiments, notes, and surveys or interviews done by the researcher. Other primary sources are books, letters, diaries, eyewitness accounts, and performances attended by the researcher.

Secondary sources consist of oral and written accounts prepared by others. This includes reports, summaries, critical reviews, and other sources not developed by the researcher.

Most research writing uses both primary and secondary sources: primary sources from first-hand accounts and secondary sources for background and supporting documentation. The research process calls for active reading and writing throughout. As research yields information, it often calls for more reading and research, and the cycle continues.

Formulating a research question and developing a hypothesis

The result of a focusing process is a research question, which is a question or problem that can be solved through research data. A hypothesis is a tentative answer to the research question that must be supported by the research. A research question must be manageable, specific, and interesting. Additionally, it must be argumentative, capable of being proved or disproved by research.

It is helpful to explore a topic with background reading and notes before formulating a research question and a hypothesis. Create a database containing the knowledge to be used in approaching the task of identifying the research question. This background work will allow the writer to formulate a specific question and a tentative answer, the hypothesis. The process of exploring a topic can include brainstorming, free-writing, and scanning your memory and experience for information.

Observing and recording data

Collecting data in the field begins with direct observation, noting phenomena totally objectively and recording it. This requires a systematic approach to observation and recording information. Before beginning the observation process, certain steps must be accomplished:
1. Determine the purpose of the observation and review the research question and hypothesis to see that they relate to each other.
2. Set a limited time for the observations.
3. Develop a system for recording information in a useful manner.
4. Obtain proper materials for taking notes.
5. Consider the use of cameras, video recorders, or audiotape recorders.
6. Use the journalistic technique of asking who, what, where, when, and why to garner information.

Planning and conducting research interviews

After determining the exact purpose of the interview, check it against the research question and hypothesis.

Set up the interview in advance, specifying the amount of time needed. Prepare a written list of questions for the interview, and try out questions on peers before the interview. Prepare a copy of your questions, leaving room for notes. Ensure that all the necessary equipment is on hand, and record the date, time, and subject of the interview.

The interview should be businesslike and take only the allotted time. A flexible attitude will allow for questions or comments that have not been planned for but may prove helpful to the process. Follow-up questions should be asked whenever appropriate. A follow-up thank-you note is always appreciated and may pave the way for further interviews. Be mindful at all times of the research question and hypothesis under consideration.

- 46 -

Drafting the research essay

Before beginning the research essay, revisit the purpose, audience, and scope of the essay. An explicit thesis statement should summarize major arguments and approaches to the subject. After determining the special format of the essay, a survey of the literature on the subject is helpful. If original or first-hand research is involved, prepare a summary of the methods and conclusions.

A clustering strategy assembles all pertinent information on a topic in one physical place. The preparation of an outline may be based on the clusters, or a first draft may be developed without an outline. Formal outlines use a format of thesis statement, main topic, and supporting ideas to shape the information.

Drafting the essay can vary considerably among researchers, but it is useful to use an outline or information clusters to get started. Drafts are usually done on a point-to-point basis.

The introduction to a research essay is particularly important, as it sets the context for the essay. It needs to draw the reader into the subject and provide necessary background to understand the subject. It is sometimes helpful to open with the research question and explain how the question will be answered. The major points of the essay may be forecast or previewed to prepare readers for the coming arguments.

In a research essay, it is a good idea to establish the writer's credibility by reviewing credentials and experience with the subject. Another useful opening involves quoting several sources that support the points of the essay, again to establish credibility. The tone should be appropriate to the audience and subject, maintaining a sense of careful authority while building the arguments. Jargon should be kept to a minimum, and language should be carefully chosen to reflect the appropriate tone.

The conclusion to a research essay helps readers summarize what they have learned. Conclusions are not meant to convince, as this has been done in the body of the essay. It can be useful to leave the reader with a memorable phrase or example that supports the argument. Conclusions should be both memorable and logical restatements of the arguments in the body of the essay.

A specific-to-general pattern can be helpful, opening with the thesis statement and expanding to more general observations. A good idea is to restate the main points in the body of the essay, leading to the conclusion. An ending that evokes a vivid image or asks a provocative question makes the essay memorable. The same effect can be achieved by a call for action, or a warning. Conclusions may be tailored to the audience's background, in terms of language, tone, and style.

Checklist for Reviewing a Draft of a Research Essay
1. Introduction: Is the reader's attention gained and held by the introduction?
2. Thesis: Does the essay fulfill the promise of the thesis? Is it strong enough?
3. Main points: Are the main points listed and ranked in order of importance?
4. Organization: What is the organizing principle of the essay? Does it work?
5. Supporting information: Is the thesis adequately supported? Is the thesis convincing?
6. Source material: Are there adequate sources and are they smoothly integrated into the essay?
7. Conclusion: Does the conclusion have sufficient power? Does it summarize the essay well?
8. Paragraphs, sentences, words: Are these elements effective in promoting the thesis?
9. Overall review: Evaluate the essay's strengths and weaknesses. What revisions are needed?

Modern Language Association style

The Modern Language Association style is widely used in literature and languages as well as other fields. The MLA style calls for noting brief references to sources in parentheses in the text of an essay and adding an alphabetical list of sources, called "Works Cited," at the end. Specific recommendations of the MLA include the following:
1. "Works Cited": Include in this section only works actually cited. List on a separate page the author's name, title, and publication information, which must include the location of the publisher, the publisher's name, and the date of publication.
2. Parenthetical citations: MLA style uses parenthetical citations following each quotation, reference, paraphrase, or summary to a source. Each citation is made up of the author's last name and page reference, keyed to a reference in Works Cited.
3. Explanatory notes: Explanatory notes are numbered consecutively and identified by superscript numbers in the text. The full notes may appear as endnotes or as footnotes at the bottom of the page.

American Psychological Association style

The American Psychological Association style is widely followed in the social sciences. The APA parenthetical citations within the text direct readers to a list of sources. In APA style, this list is called "References." References are listed on a separate page, and each line includes the author's name, publication date, title, and publication information. Publication information includes the city where the publisher is located and the publisher's name. Set in italics (or underline) the titles of books and periodicals, but not articles.

APA parenthetical expressions citations include the author's last name, the date of publication, and the page number. APA style allows content footnotes for information needed to be expanded or supplemented, marked in the text by superscript numbers in consecutive order. Footnotes are listed under a separate page, headed "Footnotes" after the last page of text. All entries should be double-spaced.

Early assessment of a writing assignment

An early assessment of the writing assignment is very helpful. Understanding the subject, and your relationship to it, is important. Determine if this subject is broad enough for the assignment, or perhaps it must be narrowed to be effectively addressed. If a choice of topics is offered, it is wise to select one of which you have significant prior knowledge or one that can be reasonably investigated in the time given for the work. An important part of assessing the topic will be to decide how much detail to use in writing.

Where will the information for the project come from? Will field research be necessary or will secondary sources suffice? Is there a need to use personal interviews, questionnaires, or surveys to accumulate information? How much reading will need to be done? What kind of documentation will be used? Answering these questions will help estimate the time needed for research.

Controlling length and document design

Writers seldom have control over length and document design. Usually an academic assignment has a specified length; journalists work within tight word-count parameters. Document design often follows the purpose of a writing project. Specific formats are required for lab reports, research papers, and abstracts. The business world operates within fairly narrow format styles: the business letter, memo, and report, allowing only a small departure from the standard format.

Some assignments allow the writer to choose the specific format for the work. The increased flourishes provided by computers allow a great deal of creativity in designing a visually stimulating and functional document. Improving readability is always a worthwhile goal for any project, and this is becoming much easier with available software.

Determining tentative focus and plan

As the topic of the writing assignment is explored, various possibilities will emerge as to focusing the material. This is an ideal time to settle on a tentative central idea. This tentative idea may change during the course of the assignment. Often a central idea may be stated in one sentence, which is called a thesis sentence. The thesis prepares the reader for the supporting points in the work. The thesis will usually appear in the opening paragraph of the text. The thesis contains a key word or phrase that provides the focus of the writing. This is usually a limiting or narrowing of the main subject.

After determining a thesis, the writer may proceed to an informal outline. This can be as simple as writing the thesis followed by a list of major supporting ideas. Clustering diagrams may also be used to formulate informal outlines.

Preparing formal outlines

A formal outline may be useful if the subject is complex and includes many elements. Following is a guide to preparing formal outlines:
1. Always put the thesis at the top so it may be referred to as often as necessary during the outlining.
2. Make subjects similar in generality as parallel as possible in the formal outline.
3. Use complete sentences rather than phrases or sentence fragments in the outline.
4. Use the conventional system of letters and numbers to designate levels of generality.
5. Assign at least two subdivisions for each category in the formal outline.
6. Limit the number of major sections in the outline. If there are too many major sections, combine some of them and supplement with additional subcategories.
7. Remember the formal outline is still subject to change; remain flexible throughout the process.

Introduction

An introduction announces the main point of the work. It will usually be a paragraph of 50 to 150 words, opening with a few sentences to engage the reader, and concluding with the essay's main point. The sentence stating the main point is called the thesis sentence. If possible, the sentences leading to the thesis should attract the reader's attention with a provocative question, vivid image, description, paradoxical statement, quotation, or anecdote. The thesis sentence could also appear at the beginning of the introduction. Some types of writing do not lend themselves to stating a thesis in one sentence. Personal narratives and some types of business writing may be better served by conveying an overriding purpose of the text, which may or may not be stated directly. The important point is to impress the audience with the rationale for the writing.

Creating an effective thesis

Creating an effective thesis is an art. The thesis should be a generalization rather than a fact and should be neither too broad nor too narrow in scope. A thesis prepares readers for facts and details, so it may not be a fact itself. It is a generalization that requires further proof or supporting points. Any thesis too broad may be an unwieldy topic and must be narrowed. The thesis should have a sharp focus and avoid vague, ambivalent language. The process of bringing the thesis into sharp focus may help in outlining major sections of the work. This process is known as blueprinting, and it helps the writer control the shape and sequence of the paper. Blueprinting outlines major points and supporting arguments that are used in elaborating on the thesis. A completed blueprint often leads to a development of an accurate first draft of a work. Once the thesis and opening are complete, it is time to address the body of the work.

Filling out the body and writing a conclusion

The body of the essay should fulfill the promise of the introduction and thesis. If an informal outline has not been done, now is the time for a more formal one. Constructing the formal outline will create a skeleton of the paper. Using this skeleton, the writer finds it much easier to fill out the body of an essay. It is useful to block out paragraphs based on the outline to ensure they contain all the supporting points and are in the appropriate sequence.

The conclusion of the essay should remind readers of the main point, without belaboring it. It may be relatively short, as the body of the text has already made the case for the thesis. A conclusion can summarize the main points and offer advice or ask a question. Never introduce new ideas in a conclusion. Avoid vague and desultory endings, instead close with a crisp, often positive, note. A dramatic or rhetorical flourish can end a piece colorfully.

Global revisions

Global revisions address the larger elements of writing. They usually affect paragraphs or sections, and may involve condensing or merging sections of text to improve meaning and flow. Sometimes material may be rearranged to better present the arguments of the essay. It is usually better for the writer to get some distance from the work before starting a global revision. Reviewers and editors can be usefully employed to make suggestions for revision. If reviewers are used, it is helpful to emphasize the focus on the larger themes of the work rather than the finer points. When undertaking a global review, the writer might wish to position himself or herself as the audience rather than the writer. This provides some additional objectivity and can result in a more honest appraisal of the writing and revisions that should be made. Global revisions are the last major changes a writer will make in the text.

Answering the following questions as objectively as possible will allow for a useful global revision:
1. Purpose: Does the draft accomplish its purpose? Are the material and tone appropriate for the intended audience? Does it account for the audience's knowledge of the subject? Does it seek to persuade, inform, or entertain them?
2. Focus: Does the introduction and the conclusion focus on the main point? Are all supporting arguments focused on the thesis?
3. Organization and paragraphing: Are there enough organizational cues to guide the reader? Are any paragraphs too long or too short?

4. Content: Is the supporting material persuasive? Are all ideas adequately developed? Is there any material that could be deleted?
5. Point of view: Is the draft free of distracting shifts in point of view? Is the point of view appropriate for the subject and intended audience?

Revising and editing sentences

Revising sentences is done to make writing more effective. Editing sentences is done to correct any errors. Revising sentences is usually best done on a computer, on which it is possible to try several versions easily. Some writers prefer to print out a hard copy and work with this for revisions. Each works equally well and depends on the individual preference.

Spelling and grammar checks on software are a great aid to a writer, but not a panacea. Many grammatical problems—such as faulty parallelism, mixed constructions, and misplaced modifiers—can slip past the programs. Even if errors are caught, the writing still must be evaluated for effectiveness. A combination of software programs and writer awareness is necessary to ensure an error-free manuscript.

Examples and illustrations

Examples are a common method of development and may be effectively used when a reader may ask, "For example?" Examples are selected instances, not an inclusive catalog. They may be used to suggest the validity of topic sentences.

Illustrations are extended examples, sometimes presented in story form for interest. They usually require several sentences each, so they are used sparingly. Well-selected illustrations can be a colorful and vivid way of developing a point. Stories that command reader interest, developed in a story form, can be powerful methods of emphasizing key points in an essay. Stories and illustrations should be specific and relate directly to a point or points being made in the text. They allow more colorful language and instill a sense of human interest in a subject. Used judiciously, illustrations and stories are excellent devices.

Narration, description, process, comparison, and contrast

A paragraph of narration tells a story or part of a story. It is usually arranged in chronological order but sometimes includes flashbacks, taking the story back to an earlier time.

A descriptive paragraph paints a verbal portrait of a person, place, or thing, using specific details that appeal to one or more of our senses: sight, sound, smell, taste, and touch. It conveys a real sense of being present and observing phenomena.

A process paragraph is related to time order, generally chronological. It usually describes a process or teaches readers how to perform the process.

Comparing two subjects draws attention to their similarities but can also indicate a consideration of differences. To contrast is to focus only on differences. Both comparisons and contrasts may be examined point by point or in succeeding paragraphs.

Analogies

Analogies draw comparisons between items that appear to have nothing in common. Analogies are employed by writers to attempt to provoke fresh thoughts and changed feelings about a subject. They may be used to make the unfamiliar more familiar, to clarify an abstract point, or to argue a point. Although analogies are effective literary devices, they should be used thoughtfully in arguments. Two things may be alike in some respects but completely different in others.

Cause and effect is an excellent device best used when the cause and effect are generally accepted as true. As a matter of argument, cause and effect is usually too complex and subject to other interpretations to be used successfully. A valid way of using cause and effect is to state the effect in the topic sentence of a paragraph and add the causes in the body of the paragraph. This adds logic and form to a paragraph and usually makes it more effective.

Classification, division, and definition

A grouping of items into categories based on some consistent criteria is called classification. The principle of classification a writer chooses will depend on the purpose of the classification. Most items can be classified by a number of criteria, and the selection of the specific classification will depend on the writer's aims in using this device.

Division, on the other hand, takes one item and divides it into parts. Just as with classification, the division must be based on a valid and consistent principle. For example, a body may be divided into various body systems easily but not as easily into body functions because the categories overlap.

Definition classifies a concept or word in a general group and then distinguishes it from other members of the class. Usually simple definitions can be provided in a sentence or two, whereas more complex ones may need a paragraph or two to adequately define them.

Transitions

Transitions are bridges between what has been read and what is about to be read. Transitions smooth the reader's path between sentences and inform the reader of major connections to new ideas forthcoming in the text. Transitional phrases should be used with care, selecting the appropriate phrase for a transition. Tone is another important consideration in using transitional phrases, varying the tone for different audiences. For example, in a scholarly essay, "in summary" would be preferable to the more informal "in short."

When working with transitional words and phrases, writers usually find a natural flow that indicates when a transition is needed. In reading a draft of the text, it should become apparent where the flow is uneven or rough. At this point, the writer can add transitional elements during the revision process. Revising can also afford an opportunity to delete transitional devices that seem heavy handed or unnecessary.

> ➤ **Review Video: <u>Transitions</u>**
> *Visit **mometrix.com/academy** and enter **Code: 707563***

- 52 -

Main point of a paragraph

A paragraph should be unified around a main point. A good topic sentence summarizes the paragraph's main point. A topic sentence is more general than subsequent supporting sentences are. Sometime the topic sentence will be used to close the paragraph if earlier sentences give a clear indication of the direction of the paragraph. Sticking to the main point means deleting or omitting unnecessary sentences that do not advance the main point.

The main point of a paragraph deserves adequate development, which usually means a substantial paragraph. A paragraph of two or three sentences often does not develop a point well enough, particularly if the point is a strong supporting argument of the thesis. An occasional short paragraph is fine, particularly if it is used as a transitional device. A choppy appearance should be avoided.

Making paragraphs coherent

A smooth flow of sentences and paragraphs without gaps, shifts, or bumps leads to paragraph coherence. Ties between old and new information can be smoothed by several strategies:
1. Linking ideas clearly, from the topic sentence to the body of the paragraph, is essential for a smooth transition. The topic sentence states the main point, and this should be followed by specific details, examples, and illustrations that support the topic sentence. The support may be direct or indirect. In indirect support, the illustrations and examples may support a sentence that in turn supports the topic directly.
2. The repetition of key words adds coherence to a paragraph. To avoid dull language, variations of the key words may be used.
3. Parallel structures are often used within sentences to emphasize the similarity of ideas and connect sentences giving similar information.
4. Maintaining a consistent verb tense throughout the paragraph helps. Shifting tenses affects the smooth flow of words and can disrupt the coherence of the paragraph.

Different lengths of paragraphs

The reader's comfort level is paragraphs of between 100 and 200 words. Shorter paragraphs cause too much starting and stopping, and give a choppy effect. Paragraphs that are too long often test the attention span of the reader. Two notable exceptions to this rule exist. In scientific or scholarly papers, longer paragraphs suggest seriousness and depth. In journalistic writing, constraints are placed on paragraph size by the narrow columns in a newspaper format.

The first and last paragraphs of a text will usually be the introduction and conclusion. These special-purpose paragraphs are likely to be shorter than paragraphs in the body of the work. Paragraphs in the body of the essay follow the subject's outline; one paragraph per point in short essays and a group of paragraphs per point in longer ones work. Some ideas require more development than others do, so it is good for a writer to remain flexible. A too-long paragraph may be divided, and shorter ones may be combined.

Beginning a new paragraph

Paragraph breaks are used for many reasons, usually as devices to improve the flow or content of the text. Some examples for beginning new paragraphs include the following:
1. To mark off the introduction and concluding paragraphs
2. To signal a shift to a new idea or topic
3. To indicate an important shift in time or place
4. To emphasize a point by repositioning a major sentence
5. To highlight a comparison, contrast, or cause-and-effect relationship
6. To signal a change in speaker, voice, or tense

Document design

Good document design promotes readability. Readability depends very much on the purpose and audience for the writing, as well as subject and length. All design choices should be made based on the particular writing assignment. Using a computer gives a writer multiple options for design.

Margins should be between 1 and 1.5 inches on all sides. Double spacing is advised to improve readability. A normal size font (10 to 12 points) and a fairly standard typeface are recommended. Left-justified text provides the best readability. Headings should be considered for longer texts. Brief and informative headings are best, and headings should be consistently formatted depending on the level of generalization. First-, second-, and third-level headings should be clearly and consistently highlighted. It is usually wise to be conservative in highlighting headings, lest the text look too busy and lack impact.

Adding visual elements to a document

Visual elements—such as charts, graphs, tables, photographs, maps, and diagrams—are useful in conveying information vividly and in a summary form.

Flow charts and pie charts are useful in helping readers follow a process or showing numerical information in graphic style. Tables are less stimulating but offer devices for summarizing information.

Diagrams are useful and sometimes necessary in scientific writing, to explain chemical formulas, for example.

Visual elements may be placed in a document close to the textual discussion or put in an appendix, labeled, and referred to in a text. Sometimes page layout makes it difficult to position visuals in optimum proximity to the corresponding text. In these cases, visuals may be placed later in the text, and readers told where they can find them. Software may be used to help the text flow around the visual for maximum impact.

Effective e-mail

E-mail has become so common in personal and business communication that it deserves its own conventions. Some guidelines for effective e-mail include the following:
1. The subject should be meaningful and concise and immediately clear to the reader.
2. The most important part of the message should appear on the first screen.
3. Summarize long messages in the first paragraph.

4. Write concisely in short, relevant paragraphs.
5. Use a mixture of capital and lower case letters for ease in reading.
6. Include the text of the attachment in the body of the e-mail if possible.
7. Proofread after using spell-check and grammar-check software.

Electronic documents will continue to grow in use and importance and writers must become skilled in this format.

Argumentative writing

In constructing a reasonable argument, the goal is not to win or have the last word but rather to reveal current understanding of the question and propose a solution to the perceived problem. The purpose of argument in a free society or a research field is to reach the best conclusion possible at the time.

Conventions of arguments vary from culture to culture. In America, arguments tend to be direct rather than subtle, carefully organized rather than discursive, spoken plainly rather than poetically. Evidence presented is usually specific and factual, and appeals to intuition or communal wisdom are rare.

Argumentative writing takes a stand on a debatable issue and seeks to explore all sides of the issue and reach the best possible solution. Argumentative writing should not be combative; at its strongest, it is assertive.

A prelude to argumentative writing is an examination of the issue's social and intellectual contexts.

Introduction to an argumentative essay

The introduction of an argumentative essay should end with a thesis sentence that states a position on the issue. A good strategy is to establish credibility with readers by showing both expert knowledge and fair-mindedness. Building common ground with undecided or neutral readers is helpful.

The thesis should be supported by strong arguments that support the stated position. The main lines of argument should have a cumulative effect of convincing readers that the thesis has merit. The sum of the main lines of argument will outline the overall argumentative essay. The outline will clearly illustrate the central thesis and subordinate claims that support it.

Evidence must be provided that supports both the thesis and supporting arguments. Evidence based on reading should be documented to show the sources. Readers must know how to check sources for accuracy and validity.

Supporting evidence

Most arguments must be supported by facts and statistics. Facts are something that is known with certainty and have been objectively verified. Statistics may be used selectively for partisan purposes. It is good to check statistics by reading authors writing on both sides of an issue. This will give a more accurate idea of the validity of the statistics cited.

Examples and illustrations add an emotional component to arguments, reaching readers in ways that facts and figures cannot. They are most effective when used in combination with objective information that can be verified.

Expert opinion can contribute to a position on a question. The source should be an authority whose credentials are beyond dispute. Sometimes it is necessary to provide the credentials of the expert. Expert testimony can be quoted directly or may be summarized by the writer. Sources must be well documented to ensure their validity.

Counterarguments

In addition to arguing a position, it is a good practice to review opposing arguments and attempt to counter them. This process can take place anywhere in the essay, but it is perhaps best placed after the thesis is stated. Objections can be countered on a point-by-point analysis or in a summary paragraph. Pointing out flaws in counterarguments is important, as is showing that the counterarguments have less weight than the supported thesis has.

Building common ground with neutral or opposed readers can make a strong case. Sharing values with undecided readers can allow people to switch positions without giving up what they feel is important. People who may oppose a position need to feel they can change their minds without compromising their intelligence or their integrity. This appeal to open-mindedness can be a powerful tool in arguing a position without antagonizing readers with opposing views.

Fallacious arguments

A number of unreasonable argumentative tactics are known as logical fallacies. Most fallacies are misguided uses of legitimate argumentative arguments.

Generalizing is drawing a conclusion from an array of facts using inductive reasoning. These conclusions are a probability, not a certainty. The fallacy known as a hasty generalization is a conclusion based on insufficient or unrepresentative evidence. Stereotyping is a hasty generalization about a group. This is common because of the human tendency to perceive selectively. Many observations are made through a filter of preconceptions, prejudices, and attitudes.

Analogies point out similarities between disparate things. When an analogy is unreasonable, it is called a false analogy. This usually consists of assuming if two things are alike in one respect, they must be alike in others. This, of course, may or may not be true. Each comparison must be independently verified to make the argument valid.

Post hoc fallacy

Tracing cause and effect can be a complicated matter. Because of the complexity involved, writers often oversimplify it. A common error is to assume that because one event follows another, the first is the cause of the second. This common fallacy is known as post hoc, from the Latin meaning "after this, therefore because of this."

A post hoc fallacy could run like this: "Since Abner Jones returned to the Giants lineup, the team has much better morale." The fact that Jones returned to the lineup may or may not have had an effect on team morale. The writer must show there is a cause and effect relationship between Jones's

- 56 -

return and team morale. It is not enough to note that one event followed another. It must be proved beyond a reasonable doubt that morale was improved by the return of Jones to the lineup. The two may be true but do not necessarily follow a cause-and-effect pattern.

Weighing options and making assumptions

When considering problems and solutions, the full range of possible options should be mentioned before recommending one solution above others. It is unfair to state there are only two alternatives when in fact there are more options. Writers who set up a choice between their preferred option and a clearly inferior one are committing the either ... or fallacy. All reasonable alternatives should be included in the possible solutions.

Assumptions are claims that are taken to be true without proof. If a claim is controversial, proof should be provided to verify the assumption. When a claim is made that few would agree with, the writer is guilty of a non sequitur (Latin for "does not follow") fallacy. Thus any assumption that is subject to debate cannot be accepted without supporting evidence.

Syllogism and the straw man fallacy

Deductive reasoning is constructed in a three-step method called a syllogism. The three steps are the major premise, the minor premise, and the conclusion. The major premise is a generalization, and the minor premise is a specific case. The conclusion is deduced from applying the generalization to the specific case. Deductive arguments fail if either the major or minor premise is not true, or if the conclusion does not logically follow from the premises. This means a deductive argument must stand on valid, verifiable premises, and the conclusion is a logical result of the premises.

The straw man fallacy consists of an oversimplification or distortion of opposing views. This fallacy is one of the most obvious and easily uncovered because it relies on gross distortions. The name comes from setting up a position so weak (the straw man) that it is easily refuted.

Tone and mood

Tone and mood in writing refer to the attitude the author displays toward the subject. Although tone is usually associated with attitude, it may not be identified with the writer. If the language is ambiguous, tone becomes very difficult to ascertain. A common tone in contemporary writing is irony. Tone is communicated by the writer's choice of language.

Tone is distinguished from mood, which is the feeling the writing evokes. Tone and mood may often be similar, but they also can be significantly different. Mood often depends on the manner in which words and language are employed by the writer. In a sense, tone and mood are two sides of a coin that color language and enliven the total approach of a writer to the subject. Mood and tone add richness and texture to words, bringing them alive in a deliberate strategy by the writer.

> ➢ **Review Video: <u>Style, Tone, and Mood</u>**
> Visit ***mometrix.com/academy*** *and enter **Code: 416961***

Point of view

Point of view is the perspective from which writing occurs. There are several possibilities:
1. First person is written so that the *I* of the story is a participant or observer.
2. Second person is a device to draw the reader in more closely. It is really a variation or refinement of the first-person narrative.
3. Third person, the most traditional form of point of view, is the omniscient narrator, in which the narrative voice, presumed to be the writer's, is presumed to know everything about the characters, plot, and action. Most novels use this point of view.
4. A multiple point of view is narration delivered from the perspective of several characters.
5. In modern writing, the stream-of-consciousness technique is often used. Developed fully by James Joyce, this technique uses an interior monologue that provides the narration through the thoughts, impressions, and fantasies of the narrator.

> ➤ **Review Video:** **Point of View**
> *Visit **mometrix.com/academy** and enter **Code: 383336**

Jargon and clichés

Jargon is a specialized language used among members of a trade, profession, or group. Jargon should be avoided and used only when the audience will be familiar with the language. Jargon includes exaggerated language usually designed to impress rather than inform. Sentences filled with jargon are both wordy and difficult to understand. Jargon is commonly used in such institutions as the military, politics, sports, and art.

Clichés are sentences and phrases that have been overused to the point of triviality. They have no creativity or originality and add very little to modern writing. Writers should avoid clichés whenever possible. When editing, the best solution for clichés is to delete them. If this does not seem easily accomplished, a cliché can be modified so that it is not predictable and trite. This often means adding phrases or sentences to change the cliché.

Slang and sexist language

Slang is an informal and sometimes private language that connotes the solidarity and exclusivity of a group, such as teenagers, sports fans, ethnic groups, or rock musicians. Slang has a certain vitality, but it is not always widely understood and should be avoided in most writing. An exception could be when the audience is a specialized group who understands the jargon and slang commonly used by the members.

Sexist language is language that stereotypes or demeans women, generally, or men occasionally. Such language is derived from stereotypical thinking, traditional pronoun use, and from words used to refer indefinitely to both sexes. Writers should avoid referring to a profession as being male or female, and using different conventions when referring to men and women. Pronouns *he, him,* and *his* should be avoided by using a pair of pronouns or revising the sentence to obviate the sexist language.

Pretentious language, euphemisms, and doublespeak

In an attempt to sound elegant, profound, poetic, or impressive, some writers embroider their sentences with flowery phrases, inflated language, and generally pretentious wordage. Pretentious language is often so ornate and wordy that it obscures the true meaning of the writing.

Euphemisms are pleasant-sounding words that replace language that seems overly harsh or ugly. Euphemisms are wordy and indirect, clouding meaning through pretty words. However, euphemisms are sometimes used as conventions when speaking about subjects such as death, bodily functions, and sex.

The term *doublespeak* was coined by George Orwell in his futuristic novel *1984*. It applies to any evasive or deceptive language, particularly favored by politicians. Doublespeak is evident in advertising, journalism, and political polemics. It should be avoided by serious writers.

Voice

Writers should find a voice that is appropriate for the subject, appeals to the intended audience, and conforms to the conventions of the genre to which the writing belongs. If there is doubt about the conventions of the genre—such as in lab reports, informal essays, research papers, and business memos— a writer may examine models of these works written by experts in the field. These models can serve as examples for form and style for a particular type of writing.

Voice can also include the writer's attitude toward the subject and audience. Care should be taken that the language and tone of the writing are considered in terms of the purpose of the writing and its intended audience.

Gauging the appropriate voice for a piece is part art, part science. It can be a crucial element in the ultimate effectiveness of the writing.

Choosing level of formality

In choosing a level of formality in writing, consider the subject and audience carefully. The subject may require a more dignified tone, or perhaps an informal style would be best. The relationship between writer and reader is important in choosing a level of formality. Is the audience one with which you can assume a close relationship, or should a more formal tone prevail?

Most student or business writing requires some degree of formality. Informal writing is appropriate for private letters, personal e-mails, and business correspondence between close associates. Vocabulary and language should be relatively simple.

It is important to be consistent in the level of formality in a piece of writing. Shifts in levels of formality can confuse readers and detract from the message of the writing.

Figures of speech

A figure of speech is an expression that uses words imaginatively rather than literally to make abstract ideas concrete. Figures of speech compare unlike things to reveal surprising similarities. The pitfall of using figures of speech is the failure of writers to think through the images they evoke.

The result can be a mixed metaphor, a combination of two or more images that do not make sense together.

In a simile, the writer makes an explicit comparison, usually by introducing it with *like* or *as.* An example would be "white as a sheet" or "my love is like a red, red, rose." Effective use of similes can add color and vivid imagery to language. Used carefully and sparingly, they provide a writer with an effective device to enhance meaning and style.

Figures of speech are particularly effective when used with discretion. Examples of figures of speech can be found in all genres of writing.

> **Review Video: <u>Figure of Speech</u>**
> Visit **mometrix.com/academy** *and enter* ***Code:*** **111295**

Allegory

Allegories are a type of narrative in which the story reflects at least one other meaning. Traditional allegory often employs personification, the use of human characters to represent abstract ideas. Early examples of the use of allegory are the medieval mystery plays in which abstractions such as Good, Evil, Penance, and Death appeared as characters.

Another type of allegory uses a surface story to refer to historical or political events. Jonathan Swift was a master at using allegory in this manner, particularly in his *Tale of a Tub* (1704), a satirical allegory of the Reformation.

Allegory has been largely replaced by symbolism by modern writers. Although they are sometimes confused, symbolism bears a natural relationship to the events in a story, whereas in allegory, the surface story is only an excuse for the secondary and more important meaning. Allegory has had a revival in postmodern writing and is seen in much contemporary literature.

Allusions

Allusions are references in writing to a person, place or thing outside the text itself. Allusions to events contemporary to the text are called topical allusions. Those referring to specific people are called personal illusions. An example of a topical allusion is the reference to the drunken porter in "Macbeth" which is an allusion to Father Henry Garnet, a Jesuit priest who was involved in the Gunpowder Plot of 1605. An example of a personal allusion is William Butler Yeat's reference to "golden thighed Pythagoras" in his poem "Among School Children."

Other uses of allusion are to summarize an important idea or to point to an ironic contrast between contemporary life and a heroic past (as in James Joyce's classic parallels in "Ulysses" (1922) to the heroic deeds in the "Odyssey" compared to the mundane details of everyday life in modern Dublin. Allusions are still a widely and effectively used literary device.

> **Review Video: <u>Allusion</u>**
> Visit **mometrix.com/academy** *and enter* ***Code:*** **294065**

Ambiguity

Historically, ambiguity in writing was generally viewed as an error or flaw. The word now means "a literary technique in which a word or phrase conveys two or more different meanings." William Empson defines ambiguity as "any verbal nuance, however slight, which gives room for alternative reactions to the same piece of language." Empson's chief purpose in defining ambiguity was to note how this device affects the interpretation of poetry. Empson identified seven types of ambiguity, including the traditional meaning. These seven types of ambiguity each provide a different view of possible interpretation of text in writing. Empson's *Seven Types of Ambiguity* was the first detailed analysis of the phenomenon of multiple meanings, sometimes called plurisignation. Ambiguity can be a useful device for some types of writing but does lend itself to informative or persuasive text.

Recursive nature

The process of writing is described as recursive. This means that the goals and parts of the writing process are often a seamless flow, constantly influencing each other without clear boundaries. The steps in the writing process occur organically, with planning, drafting, and revising all taking place simultaneously, in no necessary or orderly fashion. The writer rarely pays attention to the recursive patterns. The process unfolds naturally, without attention or dependence on a predetermined sequence. The writing process is a series of recursive activities, which rarely occur in a linear fashion, rather moving back and forth between planning, drafting, revising, more planning, more drafting, polishing until the writing is complete. Forthcoming topics will cover many parts of the process individually, but they go on together as a seamless flow.

Conventions

Conventions in writing are traditional assumptions or practices used by authors of all types of text. Some basic conventions have survived through the centuries, for example, the assumption that a first-person narrator in a work is telling the truth. Others, such as having characters in melodramas speak in asides to the audience, have become outmoded. Conventions are particularly important in specialized types of writing that demand specific formats and styles. This is true of scientific and research papers, as well as much of academic and business writing. This formality has relaxed somewhat in several areas but still holds true for many fields of technical writing. Conventions are particularly useful for writers working in various types of nonfiction writing, in which guidelines help the writer conform to the rules expected for that field. Conventions are part of the unspoken contract between writer and audience, and they should be respected.

Research

Research is a means of critical inquiry, investigations based on sources of knowledge. Research is the basis of scientific knowledge, inventions, scholarly inquiry, and many personal and general decisions. Much of work consists of research—finding something out and reporting on it. We can list five basic precepts about research.

1. Everyone does research. To buy a car, go to a film, to investigate anything is research. We all have experience in doing research.
2. Good research draws a person into a conversation about a topic. The results are gaining more knowledge about a subject, understanding different sides to issues, and being able to intelligently discuss nuances of the topic.
3. Research is always driven by a purpose. Reasons may vary from solving a problem to advocating a position, but research is almost always goal-oriented.
4. Research is shaped by purpose, and in turn the fruits of research refine the research further.
5. Research is usually not a linear process; it is modified and changed by the results it yields.

Free writing

Free writing is a form of brainstorming in a structured way. The method involves exploring a topic by writing about it for a certain period without stopping. A writer sets a time limit and begins writing in complete sentences everything that comes to mind about the topic. Writing continues without interruption until the set period expires. When time expires, read carefully everything that has been written down. Much of it may make little or no sense, but insights and observations may emerge that the free writer did not know existed in his or her mind. Writing has a unique quality of jogging loose ideas, and seeing a word or idea appear may trigger others. Free writing usually results in a fuller expression of ideas than brainstorming does because thoughts and associations are written more comprehensively. Both techniques can be used to complement one another and can yield much different results.

Economics

Economics

Economics is the study of the ways specific societies allocate resources to individuals and groups within that society. Also important are the choices society makes regarding what efforts or initiatives are funded and which are not. Since resources in any society are finite, allocation becomes a vivid reflection of that society's values.

In general, the economic system that drives an individual society is based on:
- What goods are produced
- How those goods are produced
- Who acquires the goods or benefits from them

Economics consists of two main categories, macroeconomics, which studies larger systems, and microeconomics, which studies smaller systems.

Market economy and planned economy

A market economy is based on supply and demand. Demand has to do with what customers want and need, as well as how quantity those consumers are able to purchase based on other economic factors. Supply refers to how much can be produced to meet demand, or how much suppliers are willing and able to sell. Where the needs of consumers meet the needs of suppliers is referred to as a market equilibrium price. This price varies depending on many factors, including the overall health of a society's economy, overall beliefs and considerations of individuals in society, and other factors.

In a market economy, supply and demand are determined by consumers.

In a planned economy, a public entity or planning authority makes the decisions about what resources will be produced, how they will be produced, and who will be able to benefit from them. The means of production, such as factories, are also owned by a public entity rather than by private interests.

In market socialism, the economic structure falls somewhere between the market economy and the planned economy. Planning authorities determine allocation of resources at higher economic levels, while consumer goods are driven by a market economy.

> ➤ **Review Video: Basics of Market Economy**
> Visit **mometrix.com/academy** and enter **Code: 791556**

Microeconomics

While economics generally studies how resources are allocated, microeconomics focuses on economic factors such as the way consumers behave, how income is distributed, and output and input markets. Studies are limited to the industry or firm level, rather than an entire country or society.

Among the elements studied in microeconomics are factors of production, costs of production, and factor income. These factors determine production decisions of individual firms, based on resources and costs.

> ➢ **Review Video: <u>Microeconomics</u>**
> Visit *mometrix.com/academy* and enter *Code:* **779207**

Classifying various markets

The conditions prevailing in a given market are used to classify markets. Conditions considered include:
- Existence of competition
- Number and size of suppliers
- Influence of suppliers over price
- Variety of available products
- Ease of entering the market

Once these questions are answered, an economist can classify a certain market according to its structure and the nature of competition within the market.

> ➢ **Review Video: <u>Classification of Markets</u>**
> Visit *mometrix.com/academy* and enter *Code:* **904798**

Market failure

When any of the elements for a successfully competitive market are missing, this can lead to a market failure. Certain elements are necessary to create what economists call "perfect competition." If one of these factors is weak or lacking, the market is classified as having "imperfect competition." Worse than imperfect competition, though, is a market failure.

There are five major types of market failure:
- Competition is inadequate
- Information is inadequate
- Resources are not mobile
- Negative externalities, or side effects
- Failure to provide public goods

Externalities are side effects of a market that affect third parties. These effects can be either negative or positive.

> ➢ **Review Video: <u>Market Failure</u>**
> Visit *mometrix.com/academy* and enter *Code:* **889023**

Production

Every good and service requires certain resources, or inputs. These inputs are referred to as factors of production. Every good and service requires four factors of production:
- Labor
- Land
- Capital
- Entrepreneurship

These factors can be fixed or variable and can produce fixed or variable costs. Examples of fixed costs include land and equipment. Variable costs include labor. The total of fixed and variable costs makes up the costs of production.

Factor income

Factors of production all have an associated factor income. Factors that earn income include:
- Labor—earns wages
- Capital—earns interest
- Land—earns rent
- Entrepreneurs—earn profit

Each factor's income is determined by its contribution. In a market economy, this income is not guaranteed to be equal. How scarce the factor is and the weight of its contribution to the overall production process determines the final factor income.

Market structures in an output market

1. Perfect competition—all existing firms sell an identical product. The firms are not able to control the final price. In addition, there is nothing that makes it difficult to become involved in or leave the industry. Anything that would prevent entering or leaving an industry is called a barrier to entry. An example of this market structure is agriculture.
2. Monopoly—a single seller controls the product and its price. Barriers to entry, such as prohibitively high fixed cost structures, prevent other sellers from entering the market.
3. Monopolistic competition—a number of firms sell similar products, but they are not identical, such as different brands of clothes or food. Barriers to entry are low.
4. Oligopoly—only a few firms control the production and distribution of products, such as automobiles. Barriers to entry are high, preventing large numbers of firms from entering the market.

Monopolies

1. Natural monopoly—occurs when a single supplier has a distinct advantage over the others
2. Geographic monopoly—only one business offers the product in a certain area
3. Technological monopoly—a single company controls the technology necessary to supply the product
4. Government monopoly—a government agency is the only provider of a specific good or service

The US government has passed several acts to regulate businesses, including:
- Sherman Antitrust Act (1890) — prohibited trusts, monopolies, and any other situations that eliminated competition.
- Clayton Antitrust Act (1914) — prohibited price discrimination.
- Robinson-Patman Act (1936) — strengthened provisions of the Clayton Antitrust Act.

The government has also taken other actions to ensure competition, including requirements for public disclosure. The Securities and Exchange Commission (SEC) requires companies that provide public stock to provide financial reports on a regular basis. Because of the nature of their business, banks are further regulated and required to provide various types of information to the government.

Marketing and utility

Marketing consists of all of the activity necessary to convince consumers to acquire goods. One major way to move products into the hands of consumers is to convince them that any single product will satisfy a need. The ability of a product or service to satisfy the need of a consumer is called utility.

There are four types of utility:
- Form utility—a product's desirability lies in its physical characteristics.
- Place utility—a product's desirability is connected to its location and convenience.
- Time utility—a product's desirability is determined by its availability at a certain time.
- Ownership utility—a product's desirability is increased because ownership of the product passes to the consumer.

Marketing behavior will stress any or all of the types of utility to the consumer to which the product is being marketed.

Marketing plan

1. Product—any elements pertaining directly to the product, including packaging, presentation, or services to include along with it.
2. Price—calculates cost of production, distribution, advertising, etc. as well as the desired profit to determine the final price.
3. Place—what outlets will be used to sell the product, whether traditional outlets such as brick and mortar stores or through direct mail or Internet marketing.
4. Promotion—ways to let consumers know the product is available, through advertising and other means.

Once these elements have all been determined, the producer can proceed with production and distribution of his product.

> ➤ **Review Video: Marketing Plan**
> *Visit **mometrix.com/academy** and enter **Code**: 379598*

Determining a product's market

Successful marketing depends not only on convincing customers they need the product, but also on focusing the marketing towards those who have a need or desire for the product. Before releasing a product into the general marketplace, many producers will test markets to determine which will be the most receptive to the product.

There are three steps usually taken to evaluate a product's market:
- Market research—researching a market to determine if the market will be receptive to the product.
- Market surveys—a part of market research, market surveys ask specific questions of consumers to help determine the marketability of a product to a specific group.
- Test marketing—releasing the product into a small geographical area to see how it sells. Often test marketing is followed by wider marketing if the product does well.

Distribution channels

Distribution channels determine the route a product takes on its journey from producer to consumer, and can also influenced the final price and availability of the product. There are two major forms of distributions: wholesale and retail. A wholesale distributor buys in large quantities and then resells smaller amounts to other businesses. Retailers sell directly to the consumers rather than to businesses.

In the modern marketplace, additional distribution channels have grown up with the rise of markets such as club warehouse stores as well as purchasing through catalogs or over the Internet. Most of these newer distribution channels bring products more directly to the consumer, eliminating the need for middlemen.

Distribution of income and poverty

Distribution of income in any society lies in a range from poorest to richest. In most societies, income is not distributed evenly. To determine income distribution, family incomes are ranked, lowest to highest. These rankings are divided into sections called quintiles, which are compared to each other. The uneven distribution of income is often linked to higher levels of education and ability in the upper classes, but can also be due to other factors such as discrimination and existing monopolies. The income gap in America continues to grow, largely due to growth in the service industry, changes in the American family unit and reduced influence of labor unions.

Poverty is defined by comparing incomes to poverty guidelines. Poverty guidelines determine the level of income necessary for a family to function. Those below the poverty line are often eligible for assistance from government agencies.

Macroeconomics

Macroeconomics examines economies on a much larger level than microeconomics. While microeconomics studies economics on a firm or industry level, macroeconomics looks at economic trends and structures on a national level. Variables studied in macroeconomics include:
- Output
- Consumption
- Investment
- Government spending
- Net exports

The overall economic condition of a nation is defined as the Gross Domestic Product, or GDP. GDP measures a nation's economic output over a limited time period, such as a year.

Consumer behavior as defined in macroeconomics

<u>Marginal propensity to consume</u> defines the tendency of consumers to increase spending in conjunction with increases in income. In general, individuals with greater income will buy more. As individuals increase their income through job changes or growth of experience, they will also increase spending.

<u>Utility</u> is a term that describes the satisfaction experienced by a consumer in relation to acquiring and using a good or service. Providers of goods and services will stress utility to convince consumers they want the products being presented.

Measuring the Gross Domestic Product of a country

1. The expenditures approach calculates the GDP based on how much money is spent in each individual sector.
2. The income approach calculates based on how much money is earned in each sector.

Both methods yield the same results and both of these calculation methods are based on four economic sectors that make up a country's macro economy:
- Consumers
- Business
- Government
- Foreign sector

Calculating GDP using the income approach

Several factors must be considered in order to accurately calculate the GDP using the incomes approach. Income factors are:
- Wages paid to laborers, or Compensation of Employees
- Rental income derived from land
- Interest income derived from invested capital
- Entrepreneurial income

Entrepreneurial income consists of two forms. Proprietor's Income is income that comes back to the entrepreneur himself. Corporate Profit is income that goes back into the corporation as a whole. Corporate profit is divided by the corporation into corporate profits taxes, dividends, and retained earnings. Two other figures must be subtracted in the incomes approach. These are indirect business taxes, including property and sales taxes, and depreciation.

Ideal balance to be obtained in an economy

Ideally, an economy functions efficiently, with the aggregate supply, or the amount of national output, equal to the aggregate demand, or the amount of the output that is purchased. In these cases, the economy is stable and prosperous.

However, economies more typically go through phases. These phases are:
- Boom—GDP is high and the economy prospers
- Recession—GDP falls, unemployment rises

- Trough—the recession reaches its lowest point
- Recovery—Unemployment lessens, prices rise, and the economy begins to stabilize again

These phases happen often, in cycles that are not necessarily predictable or regular.

Unemployment and inflation

When demand outstrips supply, prices are driven artificially high, or inflated. This occurs when too much spending causes an imbalance in the economy. In general, inflation occurs because an economy is growing too quickly.

When there is too little spending and supply has moved far beyond demand, a surplus of product results. Companies cut back on production, reduce the number of workers they employ, and unemployment rises as people lose their jobs. This imbalance occurs when an economy becomes sluggish.

In general, both these economic instability situations are caused by an imbalance between supply and demand. Government intervention is often necessary to stabilize an economy when either inflation or unemployment becomes too serious.

Forms of unemployment

1. Frictional—when workers change jobs and are unemployed while waiting for a new job.
2. Structural—when economical shifts reduce the need for workers.
3. Cyclical—when natural business cycles bring about loss of jobs.
4. Seasonal—when seasonal cycles reduce the need for certain jobs.
5. Technological—when advances in technology result in elimination of certain jobs.

Any of these factors can increase unemployment in certain sectors.

Inflation

Inflation is classified by the overall rate at which it occurs.
1. Creeping inflation—an inflation rate of about one to three percent annually.
2. Galloping inflation—a high inflation rate of 100 to 300 percent annually.
3. Hyperinflation—an inflation rate over 500 percent annually. Hyperinflation usually leads to complete monetary collapse in a society, as individuals become unable to generate sufficient income to purchase necessary goods.

Government intervention policies that can help mitigate inflation and unemployment

When an economy becomes too imbalanced, either due to excessive spending or not enough spending, government intervention often becomes necessary to put the economy back on track. Government Fiscal Policy can take several forms, including:
- Monetary policy
- Contractionary policies
- Expansionary policies

Contractionary policies help counteract inflation. These include increasing taxes and decreasing government spending to slow spending in the overall economy. Expansionary policies increase

- 69 -

government spending and lower taxes in order to reduce unemployment and increase the level of spending in the economy overall. Monetary policy can take several forms, and affects the amount of funds available to banks for making loans.

Population of a country and the Gross Domestic Product (GDP)

Changes in population can affect the calculation of a nation's GDP, particularly since GDP and GNP are generally measure per capita. If a country's economic production is low, but the population is high, the income per individual will be lower than if the income is high and the population is lower. Also, if the population grows quickly and the income grows slowly, individual income will remain low or even drop drastically.

Population growth can also affect overall economic growth. Economic growth requires both consumers to purchase goods and workers to produce them. A population that does not grow quickly enough will not supply enough workers to support rapid economic growth. Populations are studied by size, rates of growth due to immigration, the overall fertility rate, and life expectancy. For example, though the population of the United States is considerably larger than it was two hundred years ago, the rate of population growth has decreased greatly, from about three percent per year to less than one percent per year.

In the US, the fertility rate is fairly low, with most women choosing not to have large families, and life expectancy is high, creating a projected imbalance between older and younger people in the near future. In addition, immigration and the mixing of racially diverse cultures are projected to increase the percentages of Asian, Hispanic and African Americans.

Money

Money is used in three major ways:
1. As an accounting unit
2. As a store of value
3. As an exchange medium

In general, money must be acceptable throughout a society in exchange for debts or to purchase goods and services. Money should be relatively scarce, its value should remain stable, and it should be easily carried, durable, and easy to divide up.

There are three basic types of money: commodity, representative and fiat. Commodity money includes gems or precious metals. Representative money can be exchanged for items such as gold or silver which have inherent value. Fiat money, or legal tender, has no inherent value but has been declared to function as money by the government. It is often backed by gold or silver, but not necessarily on a one-to-one ratio.

Money in the US is not just currency. When economists calculate the amount of money available, they must take into account other factors such as deposits that have been placed in checking accounts, debit cards and "near moneys" such as savings accounts, that can be quickly converted into cash. Currency, checkable deposits and traveler's checks, referred to as M1, are added up, and then M2 is calculated by adding savings deposits, CDs and various other monetary deposits. The final result is the total quantity of available money.

Monetary policy and the role of the Federal Reserve System

The Federal Reserve System, also known as the Fed, implements all monetary policy in the US. Monetary policy regulates the amount of money available in the American banking system. The Fed can decrease or increase the amount of available money for loans, thus helping regulate the national economy.

Monetary policies implemented by the Fed are part of expansionary or contractionary monetary policies that help counteract inflation or unemployment. The Discount Rate is an interest rate charged by the Fed when banks borrow money from them. A lower discount rate leads banks to borrow more money, leading to increased spending. A higher discount rate has the opposite effect.

Banks

Banks earn their income by loaning out money and charging interest on those loans. If less money is available, fewer loans can be made, which affects the amount of spending in the overall economy. While banks function by making loans, they are not allowed to loan out all the money they hold in deposit. The amount of money they must maintain in reserve is known as the reserve ratio. If the reserve ratio is raised, less money is available for loans and spending decreases. A lower reserve ratio increases available funds and increases spending. This ratio is determined by the Federal Reserve System.

Open Market Operations

The Federal Reserve System can also expand or contract the overall money supply through Open Market Operations. In this case, the Fed can buy or sell bonds it has purchased from banks, or from individuals. When they buy bonds, more money is put into circulation, creating an expansionary situation to stimulate the economy. When the Fed sells bonds, money is withdrawn from the system, creating a contractionary situation to slow an economy suffering from inflation.

Because of international financial markets, however, American banks often borrow and lend money in markets outside the US. By shifting their attention to international markets, domestic banks and other businesses can circumvent whatever contractionary policies the Fed may have put into place in order to help a struggling economy.

International trade

International trade can take advantage of broader markets, bringing a wider variety of products within easy reach. By contrast, it can also allow individual countries to specialize in particular products that they can produce easily, such as those for which they have easy access to raw materials. Other products, more difficult to make domestically, can be acquired through trade with other nations.

International trade requires efficient use of native resources as well as sufficient disposable income to purchase native products and imported products. Many countries in the world engage extensively in international trade, but others still face major economic challenges.

Characteristics of a developing nation

1. Low GDP
2. Rapid growth of population
3. Economy that depends on subsistence agriculture
4. Poor conditions, including high infant mortality rates, high disease rates, poor sanitation, and insufficient housing
5. Low literacy rate

Developing nations often function under oppressive governments that do not provide private property rights and withhold education and other rights from women. They also often feature an extreme disparity between upper and lower classes, with little opportunity for lower classes to improve their position.

Economic development

Economic development occurs in three stages that are defined by the activities that drive the economy:
- Agricultural stage
- Manufacturing stage
- Service sector stage

In developing countries, it is often difficult to acquire the necessary funding to provide equipment and training to move into the advanced stages of economic development. Some can receive help from developed countries via foreign aid and investment or international organizations such as the International Monetary Fund or the World Bank. Having developed countries provide monetary, technical, or military assistance can help developing countries move forward to the next stage in their development.

Developing nations and economic growth

Developing nations typically struggle to overcome obstacles that prevent or slow economic development. Major obstacles can include:
- Rapid, uncontrolled population growth
- Trade restrictions
- Misused resources, often perpetrated by the nation's government
- Traditional beliefs that can slow or reject change.

Corrupt, oppressive governments often hamper the economic growth of developing nations, creating huge economic disparities and making it impossible for individuals to advance, in turn preventing overall growth. Governments sometimes export currency, called capital flight, which is detrimental to a country's economic development. In general, countries are more likely to experience economic growth if their governments encourage entrepreneurship and provide private property rights.

Problems with swift industrialization

Rapid growth throughout the world leaves some nations behind, and sometimes spurs their governments to move forward too quickly into industrialization and artificially rapid economic growth. While slow or nonexistent economic growth causes problems in a country, overly rapid industrialization carries its own issues.

Four major problems encountered due to rapid industrialization are:
- Use of technology not suited to the products or services being supplied
- Poor investment of capital
- Lack of time for the population to adapt to new paradigms
- Lack of time to experience all stages of development and adjust to each stage

E-commerce

The growth of the Internet has brought many changes to our society, not the least of which is the ways we do business. Where supply channels used to have to move in certain ways, many of these channels are now bypassed as e-commerce makes it possible for nearly any individual to set up a direct market to consumers, as well as direct interaction with suppliers. Competition is fierce. In many instances e-commerce can provide nearly instantaneous gratification, with a wide variety of products. Whoever provides the best product most quickly often rises to the top of a marketplace.

How this added element to the marketplace will affect the economy in the near and not-so-near future remains to be seen. Many industries are still struggling with the best ways to adapt to the rapid, continuous changes.

Knowledge economy

The knowledge economy is a growing sector in the economy of developed countries, and includes the trade and development of:
- Data
- Intellectual property
- Technology, especially in the area of communications

Knowledge as a resource is steadily becoming more and more important. What is now being called the Information Age may prove to bring about changes in life and culture as significant as those brought on by the Agricultural and Industrial Revolutions.

Cybernomics

Related to the knowledge economy is what has been dubbed "cybernomics," or economics driven by e-commerce and other computer-based markets and products. Marketing has changed drastically with the growth of cyber communication, allowing suppliers to connect one-on-one with their customers. Other issues coming to the fore regarding cybernomics include:

- Secure online trade
- Intellectual property rights
- Rights to privacy
- Bringing developing nations into the fold

As these issues are debated and new laws and policies developed, the face of many industries continues to undergo drastic change. Many of the old ways of doing business no longer work, leaving industries scrambling to function profitably within the new system.

Management

Basic management skills

- Planning skills: outline and analysis of goals, charting of specific objectives, creation of schedules, assessment of resources, and identification of individual responsibilities.
- Decision-making skills: assessments and evaluation of available options, followed by the making of well-considered choices.
- Meeting management skills: selection of the right participants, development of agendas, efficient time management, and effective meeting guidance.
- Delegation skills: effective distribution of tasks to those employees capable of performing them and comprehensive oversight of the delegated tasks

Essential management functions

- Planning: the establishment of long-term goals and the specific objectives that must be reached on the way to these goals.
- Organizing: the creation of the departments and structures for the accomplishment of goals; a manager may need to hire specific employees in order to accomplish goals.
- Leading: promotion of positive thinking and morale in an organization; good managers are able to inspire and encourage their employees.
- Controlling: oversight and evaluation of professional performance; the establishment of rules and procedures for conduct and task performance

Performance objectives

Established quality and time goals for the accomplishment of tasks are known as performance objectives. An effective manager establishes clear performance objectives so that employees will understand what is expected of them. Furthermore, it is a great idea to include employees in the creation of performance objectives. Employees, for instance, could be asked to create a first draft of the objectives, and then to modify the draft in consultation with the manager. This kind of system increases the employees' personal investment in performance objectives. In any case, performance objectives need to be directly related to job description. Employees should not be asked to perform tasks for which they have not been trained.

Delegation

Delegation is the distribution of responsibility and authority to subordinates. For instance, an upper manager might delegate the responsibility of running a meeting to a competent middle manager. Delegation occurs up and down the vertical hierarchy of an organization. In order for delegation to be effective, the subordinate employee must understand and be capable of completing the delegated task. This means that the employee should have enough authority to make the decisions required for task completion.

Once the delegated task is complete, the manager who delegated it should be capable of evaluating the report of the subordinate. In most organizations, final responsibility for a task lies with the manager who delegated it, rather than the subordinate who completed it.

When tasks are delegated, a manager has more time to devote to other, perhaps more important duties. Also, the subordinate who is assigned the task may improve his or her performance by gaining experience with new and more difficult tasks. Indeed, one way of determining whether employees deserve promotion is to evaluate their performance with delegated tasks. Research suggests that delegation can increase employee loyalty and innovation. Delegation can be viewed as a form of on-the-job training, which in the long run will empower employees.

Before a project can be effectively delegated, it must be defined in detail. The manager needs to be capable of fully explaining the task to the assigned employee. Also, the manager needs to be good at delegating tasks to those employees who are skilled and experienced enough to complete them. If there is any question about the employee's competence, the manager should be prepared to oversee the delegated task closely. Oftentimes, it is a good idea to ask the opinion of the subordinate before delegating the task. When a task is delegated, a manager should ensure that the employee has sufficient resources and time to complete it. The subordinate employee may need access to special equipment or to other employees. Regardless, the manager should check with the subordinate frequently, to see if any problems or questions have arisen.

Decision-making process

The first step in the decision-making process is to identify the problem to be solved. Next, a manager should make note of all the criteria related to the problem, as for instance the time, resources, and priority. The manager should place these decision criteria in order. Then, he or she can begin to generate options. Once the list is complete, all of the available options should be surveyed objectively, with due attention to advantages and disadvantages. After all of this information has been weighed, the manager should make the decision that creates the best possible outcome. The decision will then be implemented, after which point the manager should receive feedback and evaluate the success of his or her decision.

Individual decision-making

Individual decision-making depends on a number of different factors. Some of these enhance decision-making, while others are obstacles to effective choices:
- Individual values: for instance aesthetic, political, ethical, economic, or religious.
- Personality, gender, and social status: in some cases, a person's background can skew his or her perspective.
- Risk tolerance: the degree to which a manager can afford to make a risky decision. The assessment of risk will depend on the manager's evaluation of advantages and disadvantages.
- Cognitive dissonance: the difference between the situation as it is and the manager's perception of the situation. When there is a great degree of cognitive dissonance, decision-making tends to be poor.

Different decision-making styles

Just as managers all have different personalities, so do they have different decision-making styles. For instance, analytical decision-makers take a rational, measured approach. The focus of such a decision-maker is always obtaining as much information as possible. A directive decision-maker, on the other hand, assembles important information but emphasizes the necessity of making a quick decision. A directive decision-maker is not afraid to take risk. A conceptual decision-maker tends to create a mental model of the situation, and then to base his or her decision on this model's

- 76 -

predictions. Finally, a behavioral decision-maker concentrates on the effects of the decisions of other people. This kind of decision-maker is likely to ask for the opinions of others before making a decision.

Managerial decision-making

In general, managers find that they make better decisions when they have access to more information. However, it is also important for a manager to bring creativity, experience, and knowledge to the process of decision-making. Managers often draw a distinction between tactical decisions, which relate to the short term, and strategic decisions, which relate to the longer term. A particular decision may be characterized by certainty, uncertainty, or risk. That is, the decision-maker may have all of the necessary information, little of the necessary information, or some information but no guarantee of success.

One of the common characteristics of decisions made by managers is a lack of predetermined structure. In other words, managers are often called upon to solve problems without easy solutions. Many of the decisions made in an organization have preprogrammed answers, but managers are often required to create innovative solutions. For this reason, managerial decision-making entails a high degree of uncertainty. Managers are always at risk of making bad decisions. The best a manager can expect to do is minimize the amount of risk. A manager can expect to feel conflicted internally when making a difficult decision, and can expect negative feedback from others when making an unpopular decision.

Intuitive decision-making

When a manager bases a decision on his or her beliefs or emotions, he or she is engaging in intuitive decision-making. Often, experienced managers make correct decisions without exactly knowing why. They just have a certain intuition derived from long interaction with a given set of variables. It can be difficult to make a case in support of such a decision, however. There are certain personality issues that can lead to poor intuitive decision-making. For instance, a manager might become overly convinced of his or her intuition, to the extent that he or she ignores obvious counterarguments. A manager might become addicted to making risky decisions. On the other hand, a manager might be afraid to make controversial decisions because of a fear of failure.

Systematic decision-making

A manager who weighs the various alternatives before coming to a decision is engaging in a systematic decision-making process. One of the prerequisites for systematic decision-making is access to all relevant information. A manager needs to be able to isolate the information directly related to the decision, and must have access to employees who know a lot about the subject. A manager must be able to evaluate both sides of the issue and obtain more information when necessary. The manager should be able to construct logical counterarguments for his or her final decision. Also, the manager should know when to draw on the expertise of colleagues.

Rational decision model

In the rational decision model, the decision-maker uses all of the available data to select the most logical option. Of course, this is an idealized scenario; in real life, managers are always working with incomplete information. The rational decision model is most appropriate for programmed decisions and situations in which there is very little risk. Rational decision-making works better when decisions are made by a single person rather than a group. So long as the situation is predictable and all the advantages and disadvantages of various alternatives are clear, the rational decision model is the best.

Administrative decision model

Unlike other models of decision-making, the administrative model is more descriptive than prescriptive. According to the administrative model, perfect information is never available and no person is perfect at analysis. For this reason, decision-making is a process of inevitable risk. This decision-making model seems most appropriate for complex and uncertain decisions. It also seems to be a better descriptor of group decision-making than unitary executive decision-making. A manager is charged with making a satisfactory decision, not necessarily the best decision.

Political decision model

In the political decision model, the primary determinant is the anticipated reaction from those affected by the decision. The political decision model is most appropriate for decisions that need to create a consensus and minimize conflict. According to the political decision model, the best decision is not necessarily that which will achieve best results. In political life, sometimes the best decision is impossible because of the attitudes of constituents. This decision model takes into account the necessity of popular support for some decisions. This model is considered most appropriate for situations with ambiguous information and large groups of stakeholders.

Judgment errors that can occur in decision-making

Managers who become experienced at making decisions may develop some bad habits. For instance, managers often develop shortcuts, known as heuristics, which simplify the decision-making process. These are often helpful, but sometimes may lead to error. In the availability heuristic, for instance, a manager relies on his or her own memory rather than available information. The representative heuristic, on the other hand, is the use of similar precedents to determine a decision, rather than attention to the facts as they are. Some decision-makers rely on an anchoring and adjustment model, in which obtained information becomes the foundation for future decision-making. Finally, some managers tend to stick by their decisions even when the evidence suggests they should do otherwise. This is known as the escalation of commitment to heuristic.

Barriers to effective decision-making

There a number of psychological biases that can negatively impact decision-making. For instance, some managers have an illusion of control, which leads them to believe they have influence over uncontrollable factors. If a manager is suffering from the solution, he or she will be unlikely to adequately assess risk. Sometimes, a manager consistently makes bad decisions because he or she frames them incorrectly. In other words, the way information is presented can be as influential to decision-making as the content of the information. Some managers err by discounting the future, or overemphasizing short-term advantages at the expense of long-term factors. Finally, if a manager feels rushed, he or she is unlikely to make the best possible decision.

Plan, do, check, act (PDCA) cycle

One of the most common quality planning cycles used in business is called the plan, do, check, act (PDCA) cycle. As the title indicates, the PDCA cycle has four steps. First, the organization identifies the quality improvement changes that need to be made. Then, the organization tests these changes with a small sample run. Next, the employees determine whether the implemented changes had the desired effect. Finally, if the small sample run indicates that the changes were positive, the changes are implemented across the full range of production. Often, businesses will use the PDCA cycle in one production area to inspire changes in another.

Strategic planning process

The first step of the strategic planning process is to identify explicitly the purpose, mission, and values of the organization. Next, the planners need to determine goals and objectives for both the short and the long term. In doing this, the planners should identify the organization's core competencies and available resources, so that it can maximize their potential. Next, the planners should perform a detailed analysis of the business environment. After this, they can create a strategy for all departments and for the organization as a whole. The strategy should include performance expectations and target outcomes. The next step is to implement the plan and review the outcomes, for instance in terms of market share, product quality, and financial performance.

SWOT analysis

One simple tool for assessing the current health of a business is the SWOT analysis. SWOT stands for strengths, weaknesses, opportunities, and threats. The strengths of a business could be its resources, whether human or material. Experience and excellent training could be the strengths of a business. On the other hand, these same areas can be sources of weakness for a business. A lack of expertise in the production area is a definite weakness. The opportunities of a business are the ways in which it could improve its position. The threats to a business are all of the potential problems, such as malfeasance or a general decline in customer demand.

Recruitment and selection

Businesses use recruiting tactics to attract job applicants and manage their personnel needs. Large businesses need to plan hiring long in advance, so they hire special human resources employees to manage applications, interviews, and evaluations. The first step in the hiring process is a preliminary screening, during which candidates may be interviewed over the phone and resumes are reviewed. The next step is likely to be an in-person interview, which may be unstructured, semi-structured, or structured. A semi-structured interview uses some standard questions, while a structured interview uses a standard set of questions for all applicants.

Some businesses also administer aptitude, psychological, or personality tests. Next, a business will likely check the references of the remaining applicants, and may perform drug tests and background checks. Finally, candidates for management positions may be asked to participate in special leadership evaluations before hiring decisions are made.

Workplace compensation

Employee compensation is usually thought of in monetary terms, as some compensation is not directly financial. For instance, vacation days, use of company resources, and insurance are all

- 79 -

forms of indirect financial compensation. Compensation is handled differently depending on the employee's position: some employees receive a flat rate for the amount of time they work, while other employees are paid based on what they produce. Some employees receive a combination of a flat rate and an incentive rate.

Companies whose employees are members of a union typically receive a high flat rate established through collective bargaining. When employees are paid according to individual incentive, they get a certain amount for each unit produced. A straight piecework wage consists of an hourly rate plus a little more for each unit produced.

In a differential piece rate payment, the employer pays one rate for a low level of production, and a higher rate for greater production. In a production bonus system, the employee is given a flat rate payment and a bonus whenever their production is greater than a certain amount. Finally, a gain-sharing incentive plan gives employees a bonus when their group exceeds expectations.

Workplace benefits

The United States mandates that companies pay unemployment insurance, Social Security, and workers' compensation benefits. However, companies may also pay for vacation days, other forms of insurance, child care, and employee pensions. A pension plan is meant to supply retirement income. Some companies opt to contribute to an individual retirement account or 401(k) rather than a pension plan. Also, many companies pledge to match the employee's contribution to the retirement or pension plan. In a cafeteria or flexible benefit plan, employees agreed to set aside a portion of their wage they will spend on things like insurance or child care. This money is not entered into yearly total wages and is therefore not taxed as income.

Workplace training and development

Companies receive a number of benefits from continuously training and improving the skills of their employees. Production and efficiency tend to go up, and businesses often discover that some employees are capable of taking on more responsibility, which leads to less money spent on oversight. There's a slight distinction between training and development: training is learning how to perform a job for the first time, while development is learning how to perform an existing job better. Before training begins, employees are often given a needs assessment, so that their existing knowledge and skills can be assessed. Sometimes, performance on the needs assessment dictates the style of training. Businesses often provide basic orientation for new employees and diversity training so that employees harmoniously cooperate with colleagues from different cultures. For prospective managers, interpersonal training may be necessary. Some businesses have managers lead the training in what is known as coaching.

Job analysis, design, and redesign

Job analysis precedes job design. The fundamental point of job analysis is to determine how a particular job meshes with the organization as a whole. The job analyst will make a list of all the activities associated with a particular job, as well as the skills required to perform it. From this summary will come an outline of job descriptions and job specifications. Job design is the conscious construction of a professional role, with the aim of increasing employee satisfaction and efficiency. During job design, the designer is focused on specialization, range, and depth. Job redesign is the refinement of an already-existing job. It may involve the use of flex time, rotation, enlargement, or enrichment. More specialized jobs tend to have less range and depth, and vice versa.

Job enrichment

When employees feel that they do not have enough responsibility, are not growing professionally, and are not being recognized for their performance, they are more likely to perform below capacity or leave a job entirely. Job enrichment aims to reduce these occurrences by giving employees more autonomy and a broader set of skills. A job enrichment program can be expensive, however, so it is a good idea to determine whether an employee is willing before initiating one. An effective enrichment program will emphasize the following core areas:

- Skill variety: the employee is given a broader range of tasks to accomplish.
- Task identity: the employee is given charge of a task from its inception to its completion.
- Task significance: the employee is given more consequential tasks.
- Autonomy: the employee is given more freedom to pursue alternate methods.
- Feedback: the employee is given more response, both positive and negative, to his or her work.

Evaluating work performance

Performance evaluations may use graphic rating scales, ranking methods, or descriptive essays. They detail the strengths and weaknesses of an employee's work. Performance evaluations are used to determine employee placement, compensation, and training. Many managers use performance evaluations to motivate their employees, and this can be effective so long as the evaluations are perceived as fair. In a graphic rating scale, employee performance is assigned a rating from outstanding to poor. This descriptive method works best with small numbers of employees. Another way of expressing performance evaluations is with descriptive essays, but these are often hard to compare. It is easy for a manager's prejudice or particular judgments to skew an evaluation. For this reason, managers should be trained in the organization's particular methods. As much as possible, the performance evaluations should strive for specificity.

"Big Five" personality traits that appear to influence work behavior

The so-called "Big Five" personality traits related to work behavior are
1. Extraversion
2. Emotional stability
3. Openness to new experience
4. Conscientiousness
5. Agreeableness

The extent to which an employee will take responsibility for himself or herself is tied to his or her locus of control, which is his or her perception of personal determination. An "internal" is a person who believes he or she has control, while an "external" is a person who believes he or she has little control. An external tends to need more supervision. Employees can also be classified by whether they are Type A or Type B. A Type A personality feels the need to be superior to others, and tends to be aggressive. A Type B, on the other hand, is more mellow and inclined to wait and see. The Myers-Briggs personality classification system divides people into four cognitive styles: sensation-thinking, intuition-thinking, sensation-feeling, and intuition-feeling. The system also classifies people in terms of extroversion-introversion and a tendency towards judgment or perception.

Concepts of perceptual bias

- Selective perception: the conscious or unconscious removal of information that conflicts with a person's values or belief system.
- Stereotyping: an assumption about some other person based on his or her ethnicity, gender, religion, etc.; tends to cause misperceptions.
- Priming: excessive emphasis on first impression.
- Recency: excessive emphasis on the most recent impression.
- Halo effect: excessive emphasis on one trait of a person or situation; the selected trait may be positive or negative.

Managing a reinforcement and punishment program

In order to be consistent and effective, managers need to define the behaviors to be reinforced, rewarded, punished, and extinguished. All too often, a manager reinforces bad behavior by failing to identify successful deeds that were accomplished in the wrong way. The reinforcements should be appropriate to the individual employee. Money is not the only reinforcement in the workplace: managers can also use increased autonomy, personal recognition, and benefits to reward employee performance. Of course, managers and employees will inevitably make mistakes. If these mistakes are made in good faith, punishment should not be severe. Nevertheless, managers should implement disincentives and ensure that mistakes are dealt with constructively. The best way to run a reinforcement and punishment program is with consistent, detailed feedback.

Leadership and Management

Leadership is the development of an organizational vision, as well as the day-to-day guidance that encourages the team to work toward that vision. In business, a leader's vision is likely to include financial return for investors, quality products or services for customers, and efficient work within the organization. The theorists James Kouzes and Barry Posner outlined five important behaviors in a leader:
- Leaders question conventional beliefs and techniques.
- Leaders inspire others to a collective vision.
- Leaders provide their subordinates with information and autonomy.
- Leaders model the organizational vision in their own behavior.
- Leaders reward and appreciate their subordinates.

Leadership and management are similar, though management tends to be concerned with daily operations, while leadership has more to do with overall vision. Leaders establish the general direction of the organization, while managers create plans and budgets. Of course, the leader and the manager may be the same person. Nevertheless, a person in a leadership role needs to take a long-term, detached perspective. A manager, on the other hand, has to engage with the details of operations. Leadership can be described as supervisory or strategic. Supervisory leadership entails daily direction, support, and feedback. Strategic leadership, on the other hand, is more concerned with creating a climate of motivation and optimism within a company.

Leaders and followers

Managers have to be both leaders and followers, insofar as they direct the actions of subordinates and report to upper managers or executives. Some of the characteristics that make a good follower are also those that make a good leader. Both leaders and followers need to understand their job tasks, have some autonomy, and understand their position in the organization. Leaders are successful when their followers can manage themselves and enhance their own importance. In order for followers to improve themselves, they need feedback and training by managers. Performance evaluations are a good venue for this sort of improvement. Over time, leaders and followers will learn better how to deal with one another to create positive change.

Types of power for exerting authority

Legitimate power: the authority of a manager to issue commands to subordinates. In most organizations, the legitimate power of a manager is limited, so that he or she is only responsible for a defined range of employees and tasks.

Reward power: the authority of a manager to offer and distribute incentives, such as raises and bonuses.

Coercive power: the authority of a manager to discipline and punish subordinates.

Referent power: the authority of a manager that derives from his or her charisma, style, and other personal qualities.

Expert power: the authority of managers that derives from his or her exceptional training or knowledge of a certain subject.

Laws enacted in the United States that affect employment opportunities

Fair Labor Standards Act (1938): divided employees into exempt, who could not receive overtime pay, and non-exempt, who could.

Equal Pay Act (1963): outlawed pay discrimination based on gender.

Civil Rights Act (1964): outlawed employment discrimination based on race, sex, ethnicity, nationality, or religion; Title VII outlawed discrimination in recruiting, hiring, termination, promotion, compensation, and training.

Age Discrimination in Employment Act (1967): outlawed employment discrimination against those over 40 and limited mandatory retirement.

Vocational Rehabilitation Act (1973): enforced affirmative action for federal employers and contractors with respect to disability.

Americans with Disabilities Act (1990): outlawed employment discrimination against the disabled; definition of disability expanded to include cancer patients in remission, those afflicted with AIDS, alcoholics, and drug abusers.

Civil Rights Act (1991): strengthened anti-discriminatory legislation and redefined punishments for violators.

Family and Medical Leave Act (1991): asserted that employees with medical or family needs should receive twelve weeks unpaid leave without threat of termination.

Legal issues in compensation and benefits

Fair Labor Standards Act (FLSA), 1938: categorized exempt and non-exempt employees and established minimum wage, child labor, and maximum hour laws.

Equal Pay Act (EPA), 1963: outlawed pay discrimination based on gender, but allowed it in relation to merit, incentive systems, market demand, seniority, etc.

Comparable-worth doctrine: a woman who does work of equal worth to that of a man deserves to be paid as well as the man. There are no statutes requiring comparable-worth compensation, but some laws support this doctrine.

Employee Retirement Income Security Act (ERISA), 1974: employees who have earned the right to draw retirement benefits must be given them; bankrupt and defaulting companies will have their employee pensions paid by the government.

Pregnancy Discrimination Act (1978): categorized pregnancy as a disability and entitled pregnant women to the benefits afforded other disabled people.

Laws and legal concerns over health and safety

The Occupational Safety and Health Act (OSHA) asserts rules for workplace safety, as for instance mandatory onsite inspections and record-keeping related to deaths and injuries. Many professions remain dangerous. Coal miners, for instance, still die every year, although the numbers are greatly diminished from the hundreds of casualties suffered during the 1960s. To maintain workplace safety, it is essential for employees to speak up. There is legislation to protect workers who blow the whistle on unsafe working conditions. For instance, it is not legal for these employees to be fired for alerting authorities to conditions that could result in injury or death.

U.S. labor laws

National Labor Relations Act, otherwise known as the Wagner Act (1935): legalized labor unions, outlawed several employer practices related to labor, and created the National Labor Relations Board. This act basically unionized the country overnight and enabled collective bargaining to begin winning victories for workers, such as minimum wage and maternity leave.

Labor-Management Relations Act, otherwise known as the Taft-Hartley Act (1947): protected management by outlawing some labor union practices, allowing workers to decertify their union, and reinforcing free speech rights.

Labor-Management Reporting and Disclosure Act, otherwise known as the Landrum-Griffin Act (1959): created a bill of rights for union members, including union reporting requirements and control over union dues.

Psychology

Psychology studies human behavior and how the mind works. Some psychologists pursue scientific psychology, while others focus on applied psychology. Psychology correlates human behavior and can make use of this data to predict behavior or determine why a particular behavior has occurred. Psychologists also help work with people who have specific problems with relationships or with how they perceive the world. By observing patterns and recording them in detail, psychologists can apply these patterns to predictions about human behavior in individuals, groups, cultures, and even countries.

Techniques psychologists use in their research

Psychological researchers study their discipline in various ways. Based on what they are studying, they generally use one of the following methods.
1. Naturalistic observation—much as with sociological study, psychologists observe people and their natural behavior without interfering.
2. Survey method—surveys are distributed among a wide range of people and the answers are correlated.
3. Case studies—specific individuals or groups are studied in depth over a period of time, sometimes for many years.
4. Experimental method—involves experimental and control groups and use of specific experiments to prove or disprove a theory.
5. Correlational design—is concerned with relationships between variables, such as whether one factor causes or influences another.

Importance of Aristotle to the science of psychology

Aristotle is often cited as founding the science of psychology through his overall interest in the working of the human mind. His beliefs stated that the mind was part of the body, while the psyche functioned as a receiver of knowledge. He felt psychology's major focus was to uncover the soul. Later philosophers and scientists built on these ideas to eventually develop the modern science of psychology.

Contributions of 19th century intellectuals to the field of psychology

Johannes P. Muller and Hermann L.F. von Hemholtz, both German, conducted scientific, organized studies of sensation and perception. As the first psychologists to attempt this kind of study, they showed that it was possible to study actual physical processes that work to produce mental activity.

William James was the founder of the world's first psychology laboratory. William Wundt, also German, published the first experimental psychology journal. Together, James and Wundt helped bring psychology into its own, separating it from philosophy. The method of psychological study called introspection grew out of their work.

Significance and contributions of Sigmund Freud

An Austrian doctor, Freud developed a number of theories regarding human mental processes and behavior. He believed the subconscious to hold numerous repressed experiences and feelings that drove behavior without the individual being aware of it, and that these subconscious motivators could lead to severe personality problems and disorders. He particularly stressed sexual desire as a motivating force. He developed the method of psychoanalysis to help discover the hidden impulses driving individual behavior.

Freud's psychoanalytic theory proposed three major components to an individual's psychological makeup:
- Id—driven by instinct and basic drives.
- Ego—most conscious and producing self-awareness.
- Superego—strives for perfection and appropriate behavior.

The ego acts as mediator between the id and superego, which function in opposition to each other.

Theories developed by Carl Jung

A student of Freud, Jung eventually developed different theories regarding the workings of the human mind. With an intense interest in both Eastern and Western philosophy, he incorporated ideas from both into his psychological explorations. He developed the theories of extroversion and introversion, as well as proposing the existence of the collective unconscious and the occurrence of synchronicity.

Ivan Pavlov and B.F. Skinner

Ivan Pavlov and B.F. Skinner both built on the theories of John B. Watson, who developed the idea of behaviorism. This work came about largely as a counter to the growing importance of introspective techniques to psychological study.

Believing environment strongly influenced individual behavior, Pavlov and Skinner searched for connections between outside stimuli and behavioral patterns. Pavlov's experiments proved the existence of conditioned response. His most famous experiment conditioned dogs to salivate at the sound of a ringing bell.

Skinner went on to build further on these ideas, developing the "Skinner Box," a device used to develop and study conditioned response in rats.

Gestalt psychology, social psychology, and modern psychology

- Gestalt psychology is a theory developed by Max Wertheimer. In Gestalt theory, events are not considered individually, but as part of a larger pattern.
- Social psychology is the study of how social conditions affect individuals.
- Modern psychology, as it has developed, combines earlier schools of psychology, including Freudian, Jungian, behaviorism, cognitive, humanistic and stimulus-response theories.

Nativism

Nativism is a theory that states that there is a certain body of knowledge all people are born with. This knowledge requires no learning or experience on the part of the individual. Rene Descartes, a French philosopher, developed this concept. He believed the body and mind affected each other profoundly, largely because they are separate from each other. The physical site of this interaction took place in the pineal gland according to his theory. The pineal gland is a small gland in the brain. Descartes developed several theories in the field of philosophy and psychology that are still studied in modern universities.

Empiricism

Empiricism was in direct opposition to Descartes' theory of nativism. Nativism states that people are born with a certain body of knowledge that they do not have to learn. Empiricism theorizes that all knowledge is acquired through life experience, impressing itself on a mind and brain that are blank at the time of birth. Major proponents of empiricism were Thomas Hobbes, John Locke, David Hume and George Berkeley.

Behaviorism

John B. Watson, an American, developed the idea of behaviorism. In his theory, growth, learning and training would always win out over any possible inborn tendencies. He believed that any person, regardless of origin, could learn to perform any type of art, craft or enterprise with sufficient training and experience.

Divisions of the human lifespan used to classify behavior and growth

Development psychologists divide the human lifespan into stages, and list certain developmental milestones that generally take place during these stages.
1. Infancy and childhood—the most rapid period of human development during which, the child learns to experience its world, relate to other people, and perform tasks necessary to function in its native culture. Debate exists as to what characteristics are inborn and what are learned.
2. Adolescence—this period represents the shift from child to adult. Changes are rapid and can involve major physical and emotional shifts.
3. Adulthood—individuals take on new responsibilities, become self-sufficient, and often form their own families and other social networks.
4. Old age—priorities shift again as children become adults and no longer require support and supervision.

Types of learning identified and studied by psychologists

Psychologists define learning as a permanent change in behavior. They divide types of learning into three basic categories, depending upon on how the behavioral change is acquired.
1. Classical conditioning—a learning process in which a specific stimulus is associated with a specific response over time.
2. Operant conditioning—a learning process in which behavior is punished or rewarded, leading to a desired long-term behavior.
3. Social learning—learning based on observation of others and modeling others' behavior.

These three learning processes work together to produce the wide variety of human behavior.

Factors involved in social psychology

Social psychology studies the ways in which people interact as well as why and how they decide who to interact with. The ways people react with each other are defined in several ways, including:

1. Social perception—how we perceive others and their behavior as we make judgments based on our own experiences and prejudices.
2. Personal relationships—close relationships developed among people for various reasons, including the desire to reproduce and form a family unit.
3. Group behavior—people gather into groups with similar beliefs, needs, or other characteristics. Sometimes group behavior differs greatly from behavior that would be practiced by individuals alone.
4. Attitudes—individual attitudes toward others develop over time based on individual history, experience, knowledge, and other factors. Attitudes can change over time, but some are deeply ingrained and can lead to prejudice.

Important Terms

Affirmative action: a strategy for increasing the presence of minorities and underrepresented groups in business, by giving special preference to them in hiring.

Chain of command: the paths of authority in an organization, consisting of a series of superior-subordinate relationships.

Customer departmentalization: the process of sorting jobs according to the customers they serve, for instance, some manufacturers have different departments for dealing with corporate and private customers.

Departmentalization: the process of placing jobs in categories according to their customer base, geographical location, or function.

Equal employment opportunity (EEO): a foundation of business ethics in the United States, whereby all people are guaranteed an equal chance for employment, regardless of race, religion, gender, etc.

Functional departmentalization: the process of placing jobs in categories according to their function, such as marketing, manufacturing, and sales.

Geographic departmentalization: the sorting of jobs according to the geographical region served; this process is especially useful for very large international corporations.

Human resource management: the set of processes devoted to the hiring, training, and retention of employees, including preparation of compensation packages, performance evaluations, employee discipline, collective bargaining, arbitration, and terminations.

Human resource planning: process of predicting and planning for employee needs.

Job depth: the latitude or autonomy granted to a particular employee.

Job description: explicit verbal summary of the necessary skills, tasks, and equipment related to a job.

Job enlargement: an increase in the range of tasks performed by a single employee.

Job range: the span of different tasks to be performed by the same employee.

Job rotation: the movement of employees from position to position within an organization. Often, this strategy is employed to improve the skill base of each employee.

Job specialization: the degree to which an employee must perform different tasks; less-specialized jobs tend to have more range and depth.

Job specification: printed outline of the required knowledge and skills for a job.

Line position: any position within the chain of command that directly contributes to the completion of the organizational goals.

Product departmentalization: the process of sorting jobs according to their product line.

Staff position: any position that leads, assists, or supports the line positions.

Mathematics and Statistics

Basic mathematical operations

There are four basic mathematical operations:
Addition increases the value of one quantity by the value of another quantity. Example: 2 + 4 = 6; 8 + 9 = 17. The result is called the sum. With addition, the order does not matter. 4 + 2 = 2 + 4.

Subtraction is the opposite operation to addition; it decreases the value of one quantity by the value of another quantity. Example: 6 − 4 = 2; 17 − 8 = 9. The result is called the difference. Note that with subtraction, the order does matter. 6 − 4 ≠ 4 − 6.

> ➤ **Review Video: <u>Addition and Subtraction</u>**
> *Visit **mometrix.com/academy** and enter **Code: 521157***

Multiplication can be thought of as repeated addition. One number tells how many times to add the other number to itself. Example: 3 × 2 (three times two) = 2 + 2 + 2 = 6. With multiplication, the order does not matter. 2 × 3 (or 3 + 3) = 3 × 2 (or 2 + 2 + 2).

Division is the opposite operation to multiplication; one number tells us how many parts to divide the other number into. Example: 20 ÷ 4 = 5; if 20 is split into 4 equal parts, each part is 5. With division, the order of the numbers does matter. 20 ÷ 4 ≠ 4 ÷ 20.

> ➤ **Review Video: <u>Multiplication and Division</u>**
> *Visit **mometrix.com/academy** and enter **Code: 643326***

Order of Operations and PEMDAS

Order of Operations is a set of rules that dictates the order in which we must perform each operation in an expression so that we will evaluate at accurately. If we have an expression that includes multiple different operations, Order of Operations tells us which operations to do first. The most common mnemonic for Order of Operations is PEMDAS, or "Please Excuse My Dear Aunt Sally." PEMDAS stands for Parentheses, Exponents, Multiplication, Division, Addition, Subtraction. It is important to understand that multiplication and division have equal precedence, as do addition and subtraction, so those pairs of operations are simply worked from left to right in order.

Example: Evaluate the expression $5 + 20 \div 4 \times (2 + 3)^2 - 6$ using the correct order of operations.
P: Perform the operations inside the parentheses, (2 + 3) = 5.
E: Simplify the exponents, $(5)^2 = 25$.
The equation now looks like this: $5 + 20 \div 4 \times 25 - 6$.
MD: Perform multiplication and division from left to right, 20 ÷ 4 = 5; then 5 × 25 = 125.
The equation now looks like this: 5 + 125 − 6.
AS: Perform addition and subtraction from left to right, 5 + 125 = 130; then 130 − 6 = 124.

> ➤ **Review Video: <u>Order of Operations</u>**
> *Visit **mometrix.com/academy** and enter **Code: 259675***

Greatest common factor (GCF) and least common multiple (LCM)

The greatest common factor (GCF) is the largest number that is a factor of two or more numbers. For example, the factors of 15 are 1, 3, 5, and 15; the factors of 35 are 1, 5, 7, and 35. Therefore, the greatest common factor of 15 and 35 is 5.

> ➢ **Review Video: Greatest Common Factor**
> *Visit **mometrix.com/academy** and enter Code:* **838699**

The least common multiple (LCM) is the smallest number that is a multiple of two or more numbers. For example, the multiples of 3 include 3, 6, 9, 12, 15, etc.; the multiples of 5 include 5, 10, 15, 20, etc. Therefore, the least common multiple of 3 and 5 is 15.

> ➢ **Review Video: Least Common Multiple**
> *Visit **mometrix.com/academy** and enter Code:* **946579**

Manipulating fractions

Fractions can be manipulated by multiplying or dividing (but not adding or subtracting) both the numerator and denominator by the same number, without changing the value of the fraction. If you divide both numbers by a common factor, you are reducing or simplifying the fraction. Two fractions that have the same value, but are expressed differently are known as equivalent fractions. For example, $\frac{2}{10}, \frac{3}{15}, \frac{4}{20}$, and $\frac{5}{25}$ are all equivalent fractions. They can also all be reduced or simplified to $\frac{1}{5}$.

When two fractions are manipulated so that they have the same denominator, this is known as finding a common denominator. The number chosen to be that common denominator should be the least common multiple of the two original denominators. Example: $\frac{3}{4}$ and $\frac{5}{6}$; the least common multiple of 4 and 6 is 12. Manipulating to achieve the common denominator: $\frac{3}{4} = \frac{9}{12}; \frac{5}{6} = \frac{10}{12}$.

Relationships between percentages, fractions, and decimals

Percentages can be thought of as fractions that are based on a whole of 100; that is, one whole is equal to 100%. The word percent means "per hundred." Fractions can be expressed as percents by finding equivalent fractions with a denomination of 100. Example: $\frac{7}{10} = \frac{70}{100} = 70\%; \frac{1}{4} = \frac{25}{100} = 25\%$.

To express a percentage as a fraction, divide the percentage number by 100 and reduce the fraction to its simplest possible terms. Example: $60\% = \frac{60}{100} = \frac{3}{5}; 96\% = \frac{96}{100} = \frac{24}{25}$.

Converting decimals to percentages and percentages to decimals is as simple as moving the decimal point. To convert from a decimal to a percent, move the decimal point two places to the right. To convert from a percent to a decimal, move it two places to the left. Example: 0.23 = 23%; 5.34 = 534%; 0.007 = 0.7%; 700% = 7.00; 86% = 0.86; 0.15% = 0.0015.

It may be helpful to remember that the percentage number will always be larger than the equivalent decimal number.

> ➤ **Review Video:** <u>Converting Decimals to Fractions and Percentages</u>
> Visit *mometrix.com/academy* and enter *Code:* **986765**

Percentage problems and the process to be used for solving them

A percentage problem can be presented three main ways:
1. Find what percentage of some number another number is. Example: What percentage of 40 is 8?
2. Find what number is some percentage of a given number. Example: What number is 20% of 40?
3. Find what number another number is a given percentage of. Example: What number is 8 20% of?

The three components in all of these cases are the same: a whole (W), a part (P), and a percentage (%). These are related by the equation:
- P = W × %. This is the form of the equation you would use to solve problems of type (2). To solve types (1) and (3), you would use these two forms: % = P/W and W = P/%.

The thing that frequently makes percentage problems difficult is that they are often also word problems, so a large part of solving them is figuring out which quantities are what. Example: In a school cafeteria, 7 students choose pizza, 9 choose hamburgers, and 4 choose tacos. Find the percentage that chooses tacos. To find the whole, you must first add all of the parts: 7 + 9 + 4 = 20. The percentage can then be found by dividing the part by the whole (% = P/W): $\frac{4}{20} = \frac{20}{100} = 20\%$

Improper fractions and mixed numbers

A fraction whose denominator is greater than its numerator is known as a proper fraction, while a fraction whose numerator is greater than its denominator is known as an improper fraction. Proper fractions have values less than one and improper fractions have values greater than one.

A mixed number is a number that contains both an integer and a fraction. Any improper fraction can be rewritten as a mixed number. Example: $\frac{8}{3} = \frac{6}{3} + \frac{2}{3} = 2 + \frac{2}{3} = 2\frac{2}{3}$. Similarly, any mixed number can be rewritten as an improper fraction. Example: $1\frac{3}{5} = 1 + \frac{3}{5} = \frac{5}{5} + \frac{3}{5} = \frac{8}{5}$.

> ➤ **Review Video:** <u>Proper and Improper Fractions and Mixed Numbers</u>
> Visit *mometrix.com/academy* and enter *Code:* **211077**

Adding, subtracting, multiplying, and dividing fractions

If two fractions have a common denominator, they can be added or subtracted simply by adding or subtracting the two numerators and retaining the same denominator. Example: $\frac{1}{2} + \frac{1}{4} = \frac{2}{4} + \frac{1}{4} = \frac{3}{4}$. If the two fractions do not already have the same denominator, one or both of them must be manipulated to achieve a common denominator before they can be added or subtracted.

> ➤ **Review Video: <u>Adding and Subtracting Fractions</u>**
> *Visit mometrix.com/academy and enter Code:* **378080**

Two fractions can be multiplied by multiplying the two numerators to find the new numerator and the two denominators to find the new denominator. Example: $\frac{1}{3} \times \frac{2}{3} = \frac{1 \times 2}{3 \times 3} = \frac{2}{9}$.

Two fractions can be divided flipping the numerator and denominator of the second fraction and then proceeding as though it were a multiplication. Example: $\frac{2}{3} \div \frac{3}{4} = \frac{2}{3} \times \frac{4}{3} = \frac{8}{9}$.

> ➤ **Review Video: <u>Multiplying and Dividing Fractions</u>**
> *Visit mometrix.com/academy and enter Code:* **150485**

Exponents and parentheses

An exponent is a superscript number placed next to another number at the top right. It indicates how many times the base number is to be multiplied by itself. Exponents provide a shorthand way to write what would be a longer mathematical expression. Example: a² = a × a; 2⁴ = 2 × 2 × 2 × 2. A number with an exponent of 2 is said to be "squared," while a number with an exponent of 3 is said to be "cubed."

The value of a number raised to an exponent is called its power. So, 8⁴ is read as "8 to the 4th power," or "8 raised to the power of 4." A negative exponent is the same as the reciprocal of a positive exponent. Example: a⁻² = 1/a².

> ➤ **Review Video: <u>Exponents</u>**
> *Visit mometrix.com/academy and enter Code:* **600998**

Parentheses are used to designate which operations should be done first when there are multiple operations. Example: 4 – (2 + 1) = 1; the parentheses tell us that we must add 2 and 1, and then subtract the sum from 4, rather than subtracting 2 from 4 and then adding 1 (this would give us an answer of 3).

Laws of exponents

The laws of exponents are as follows:
1. Any number to the power of 1 is equal to itself: $a^1 = a$.
2. The number 1 raised to any power is equal to 1: $1^n = 1$.
3. Any number raised to the power of 0 is equal to 1: $a^0 = 1$.
4. Add exponents to multiply powers of the same base number: $a^n \times a^m = a^{n+m}$.
5. Subtract exponents to divide powers of the same number: $a^n \div a^m = a^{n-m}$.
6. Multiply exponents to raise a power to a power: $(a^n)^m = a^{n \times m}$.

- 93 -

7. If multiplied or divided numbers inside parentheses are collectively raised to a power, this is the same as each individual term being raised to that power: $(a \times b)^n = a^n \times b^n$; $(a \div b)^n = a^n \div b^n$.

Note: Exponents do not have to be integers. Fractional or decimal exponents follow all the rules above as well. Example: $5^{\frac{1}{4}} \times 5^{\frac{3}{4}} = 5^{\frac{1}{4}+\frac{3}{4}} = 5^1 = 5$.

Roots

A root, such as a square root, is another way of writing a fractional exponent. Instead of using a superscript, roots use the radical symbol ($\sqrt{}$) to indicate the operation. A radical will have a number underneath the bar, and may sometimes have a number in the upper left: $\sqrt[n]{a}$, read as "the nth root of a." The relationship between radical notation and exponent notation can be described by this equation: $\sqrt[n]{a} = a^{1/n}$. The two special cases of n = 2 and n = 3 are called square roots and cube roots. If there is no number to the upper left, it is understood to be a square root (n = 2). Nearly all of the roots you encounter will be square roots. A square root is the same as a number raised to the one-half power. When we say that a is the square root of b (a = $\sqrt{b}$), we mean that a multiplied by itself equals b: (a × a = b).

A perfect square is a number that has an integer for its square root. There are 10 perfect squares from 1 to 100: 1, 4, 9, 16, 25, 36, 49, 64, 81, 100 (the squares of integers 1 through 10).

> ➤ **Review Video: Roots**
> *Visit **mometrix.com/academy** and enter **Code: 795655***

Scientific notation

Scientific notation is a way of writing large numbers in a shorter form. The form a × 10^n is used in scientific notation, where a is greater than or equal to 1, but less than 10, and n is the number of places the decimal must move to get from the original number to a.

Example: The number 230,400,000 is cumbersome to write. To write the value in scientific notation, place a decimal point between the first and second numbers, and include all digits through the last non-zero digit (a = 2.304). To find the appropriate power of 10, count the number of places the decimal point had to move (n = 8). The number is positive if the decimal moved to the left, and negative if it moved to the right. We can then write 230,400,000 as 2.304 × 10^8.

If we look instead at the number 0.00002304, we have the same value for a, but this time the decimal moved 5 places to the right (n = -5). Thus, 0.00002304 can be written as 2.304 × 10^{-5}. Using this notation makes it simple to compare very large or very small numbers. By comparing exponents, it is easy to see that 3.28 × 10^4 is smaller than 1.51×10^5, because 4 is less than 5.

> ➤ **Review Video: Scientific Notation**
> *Visit **mometrix.com/academy** and enter **Code: 976454***

Ratio and proportion

A ratio is a comparison of two quantities in a particular order. Example: if there are 14 computers in a lab, and the class has 20 students, there is a student to computer ratio of 20 to 14, commonly written as 20:14.

> ➤ **Review Video:** <u>Ratios</u>
> *Visit **mometrix.com/academy** and enter Code:* **996914**

A proportion is a relationship between two quantities that dictates how one changes when the other changes. A direct proportion describes a relationship in which a quantity increases by a set amount for every increase in the other quantity, or decreases by that same amount for every decrease in the other quantity. Example: For every 1 sheet cake, 18 people can be served cake. The number of sheet cakes, and the number of people that can be served from them is directly proportional.

Inverse proportion is a relationship in which an increase in one quantity is accompanied by a decrease in the other, or vice versa. Example: the time required for a car trip decreases as the speed increases, and increases as the speed decreases, so the time required is inversely proportional to the speed of the car.

> ➤ **Review Video:** <u>Proportions</u>
> *Visit **mometrix.com/academy** and enter Code:* **505355**

Integers, prime, composite, even, and odd

Numbers are the basic building blocks of mathematics. Specific features of numbers are identified by the following terms:
- Integers – The set of positive and negative numbers, including zero. Integers do not include fractions ($\frac{1}{3}$), decimals (0.56), or mixed numbers ($7\frac{3}{4}$).
- Prime number – A whole number greater than 1 that has only two factors, itself and 1; that is, a number that can be divided evenly only by 1 and itself.
- Composite number – A whole number greater than 1 that has more than two different factors; in other words, any whole number that is not a prime number. For example: The composite number 8 has the factors of 1, 2, 4, and 8.
- Even number – Any integer that can be divided by 2 without leaving a remainder. For example: 2, 4, 6, 8, and so on.
- Odd number – Any integer that cannot be divided evenly by 2. For example: 3, 5, 7, 9, and so on.

Rational, irrational, and real numbers

Rational, irrational, and real numbers can be described as follows:

Rational numbers include all integers, decimals, and fractions. Any terminating or repeating decimal number is a rational number.

> ➤ **Review Video:** <u>Rational Numbers</u>
> *Visit **mometrix.com/academy** and enter Code:* **280645**

Irrational numbers cannot be written as fractions or decimals because the number of decimal places is infinite and there is no recurring pattern of digits within the number. For example, pi (π) begins with 3.141592 and continues without terminating or repeating, so pi is an irrational number.

> ➢ **Review Video: <u>Irrational Numbers on a Number Line</u>**
> *Visit **mometrix.com/academy** and enter **Code: 433866***

Real numbers are the set of all rational and irrational numbers.

> ➢ **Review Video: <u>Real Numbers and the Number Line</u>**
> *Visit **mometrix.com/academy** and enter **Code: 816439***

Factors

Factors are numbers that are multiplied together to obtain a product. For example, in the equation $2 \times 3 = 6$, the numbers 2 and 3 are factors. A prime number has only two factors (1 and itself), but other numbers can have many factors.

A common factor is a number that divides exactly into two or more other numbers. For example, the factors of 12 are 1, 2, 3, 4, 6, and 12, while the factors of 15 are 1, 3, 5, and 15. The common factors of 12 and 15 are 1 and 3.

A prime factor is also a prime number. Therefore, the prime factors of 12 are 1, 2, and 3. For 15, the prime factors are 1, 3, and 5.

> ➢ **Review Video: <u>Factors</u>**
> *Visit **mometrix.com/academy** and enter **Code: 920086***

Fractions, numerators, and denominators

A fraction is a number that is expressed as one integer written above another integer, with a dividing line between them ($\frac{x}{y}$). It represents the quotient of the two numbers "x divided by y." It can also be thought of as x out of y equal parts.

The top number of a fraction is called the numerator, and it represents the number of parts under consideration. The 1 in $\frac{1}{4}$ means that 1 part out of the whole is being considered in the calculation. The bottom number of a fraction is called the denominator, and it represents the total number of equal parts. The 4 in $\frac{1}{4}$ means that the whole consists of 4 equal parts.

A fraction cannot have a denominator of zero; this is referred to as "undefined."

Decimal, decimal point, and decimal place

The decimal, or base 10, system is a number system that uses ten different digits (0, 1, 2, 3, 4, 5, 6, 7, 8, 9). An example of a number system that uses something other than ten digits is the binary, or base 2, number system, used by computers, which uses only the numbers 0 and 1. It is thought that the decimal system originated because people had only their 10 fingers for counting.

Decimal – a number that uses a decimal point to show the part of the number that is less than one. Example: 1.234.

Decimal point – a symbol used to separate the ones place from the tenths place in decimals or dollars from cents in currency.

Decimal place – the position of a number to the right of the decimal point. In the decimal 0.123, the 1 is in the first place to the right of the decimal point, indicating tenths; the 2 is in the second place, indicating hundredths; and the 3 is in the third place, indicating thousandths.

> **Review Video: <u>Decimals</u>**
Visit *mometrix.com/academy* and enter *Code:* **837268**

Measure of central tendency

A *Measure of Central Tendency* is a statistical value that gives a general tendency for the center of a group of data. There are several different ways of describing the measure of central tendency. Each one has a unique way it is calculated, and each one gives a slightly different perspective on the data set. Whenever you give a measure of central tendency, always make sure the units are the same. If the data has different units, such as hours, minutes, and seconds, convert all the data to the same unit, and use the same unit in the measure of central tendency. If no units are given in the data, do not give units for the measure of central tendency.

Statistical mean

The statistical mean of a group of data is the same as the arithmetic average of that group. To find the mean of a set of data, first convert each value to the same units, if necessary. Then find the sum of all the values, and count the total number of data values, making sure you take into consideration each individual value. If a value appears more than once, count it more than once. Divide the sum of the values by the total number of values and apply the units, if any. Note that the mean does not have to be one of the data values in the set, and may not divide evenly.

$$\text{mean} = \frac{\text{sum of the data values}}{\text{quantity of data values}}$$

Disadvantages of using the mean as the only measure of central tendency

While the *Mean* is relatively easy to calculate and averages are understood by most people, the mean can be very misleading if used as the sole measure of central tendency. If the data set has outliers (data values that are unusually high or unusually low compared to the rest of the data values), the mean can be very distorted, especially if the data set has a small number of values. If unusually high values are countered with unusually low values, the mean is not affected as much. For example, if five of twenty students in a class get a 100 on a test, but the other 15 students have an average of 60 on the same test, the class average would appear as 70. Whenever the mean is skewed by outliers, it is always a good idea to include the median as an alternate measure of central tendency.

- 97 -

Median

The statistical *Median* is the value in the middle of the set of data. To find the median, list all data values in order from smallest to largest or from largest to smallest. Any value that is repeated in the set must be listed the number of times it appears. If there are an odd number of data values, the median is the value in the middle of the list. If there is an even number of data values, the median is the arithmetic mean of the two middle values.

The statistical *Mode* is the data value that occurs the most number of times in the data set. It is possible to have exactly one mode, more than one mode, or no mode. To find the mode of a set of data, arrange the data like you do to find the median (all values in order, listing all multiples of data values). Count the number of times each value appears in the data set. If all values appear an equal number of times, there is no mode. If one value appears more than any other value, that value is the mode. If two or more values appear the same number of times, but there are other values that appear fewer times and no values that appear more times, all of those values are the modes.

> ➤ **Review Video: Mean, Median, and Mode**
> *Visit mometrix.com/academy and enter Code:* **286207**

Disadvantages of using the median or the mode as the only measure of central tendency

The main disadvantage of using the median as a measure of central tendency is that is relies solely on a value's relative size as compared to the other values in the set. When the individual values in a set of data are evenly dispersed, the median can be an accurate tool. However, if there is a group of rather large values or a group of rather small values that are not offset by a different group of values, the information that can be inferred from the median may not be accurate because the distribution of values is skewed.

The main disadvantage of the mode is that the values of the other data in the set have no bearing on the mode. The mode may be the largest value, the smallest value, or a value anywhere in between in the set. The mode only tells which value or values, if any, occurred the most number of times. It does not give any suggestions about the remaining values in the set.

Measure of dispersion

A *Measure of Dispersion* is a single value that helps to "interpret" the measure of central tendency by providing more information about how the data values in the set are distributed about the measure of central tendency. The measure of dispersion helps to eliminate or reduce the disadvantages of using the mean, median, or mode as a single measure of central tendency, and give a more accurate picture of the data set as a whole. To have a measure of dispersion, you must know or calculate the range, standard deviation, or variance of the data set.

Range

The *Range* of a set of data is the difference between the greatest and lowest values of the data in the set. To calculate the range, you must first make sure the units for all data values are the same, and then identify the greatest and lowest values. Use the formula range = highest value – lowest value. If there are multiple data values that are equal for the highest or lowest, just use one of the values in the formula. Write the answer with the same units as the data values you used to do the calculations.

Standard deviation

Standard Deviation is a measure of dispersion that compares all the data values in the set to the mean of the set to give a more accurate picture. To find the standard deviation of a population, use the formula:

$$\sigma = \sqrt{\frac{\sum_{i=1}^{n}(x_i - \bar{x})^2}{n}}$$

where σ is the standard deviation of a population, x represents the individual values in the data set, $\bar{x}$ is the mean of the data values in the set, and n is the number of data values in the set. The higher the value of the standard deviation is, the greater the variance of the data values from the mean.

Variance

The *Variance* of a population, or just variance, is the square of the standard deviation of that population. While the mean of a set of data gives the average of the set and gives information about where a specific data value lies in relation to the average, the variance of the population gives information about the degree to which the data values are spread out and tell you how close an individual value is to the average compared to the other values. The units associated with variance are the same as the units of the data values.

Percentiles and quartiles

Percentiles and Quartiles are other methods of describing data within a set. *Percentiles* tell what percentage of the data in the set fall below a specific point. For example, achievement test scores are often given in percentiles. A score at the 80th percentile is one which is equal to or higher than 80 percent of the scores in the set. In other words, 80 percent of the scores were lower than that score.

Quartiles are percentile groups that make up quarter sections of the data set. The first quartile is the 25th percentile. The second quartile is the 50th percentile; this is also the median of the data set. The third quartile is the 75th percentile.

5-number summary and box-and-whiskers plot

The *5-Number Summary* of a set of data gives a very informative picture of the set. The five numbers in the summary include the minimum value, maximum value, and the three quartiles. This information gives the reader the range and median of the set, as well as an indication of how the data is spread about the median.

A *Box-and-Whiskers Plot* is a graphical representation of the 5-number summary. To draw a box-and-whiskers plot, plot the points of the 5-number summary on a number line. Draw a box whose ends are through the points for the first and third quartiles. Draw a vertical line in the box through the median to divide the box in half. Draw a line segment from the first quartile point to the minimum value, and from the third quartile point to the maximum value.

Simple regression

In statistics, *Simple Regression* is using an equation to represent a relation between an independent and dependent variables. The independent variable is also referred to as the explanatory variable or the predictor, and is generally represented by the variable x in the equation. The dependent variable, usually represented by the variable y, is also referred to as the response variable. The equation may be any type of function – linear, quadratic, exponential, etc. The best way to handle this task is to use the regression feature of your graphing calculator. This will easily give you the curve of best fit and provide you with the coefficients and other information you need to derive an equation.

Scatter plots

Scatter plots are useful in determining the type of function represented by the data and finding the simple regression. Linear scatter plots may be positive or negative. Nonlinear scatter plots are generally exponential or quadratic. These are some common types of scatter plots:

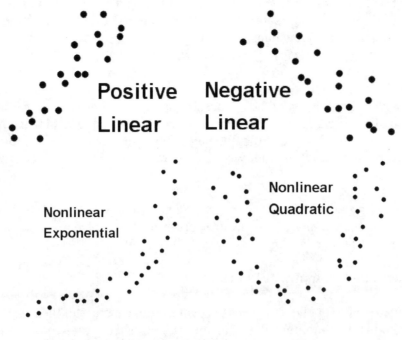

➢ **Review Video:** <u>Scatter Plots</u>
*Visit **mometrix.com/academy** and enter Code:* **596526**

Line of best fit

In a scatter plot, the *Line of Best Fit* is the line that best shows the trends of the data. The line of best fit is given by the equation $\hat{y} = ax + b$, where 'a' and 'b' are the regression coefficients. The regression coefficient 'a' is also the slope of the line of best fit, and 'b' is also the y-coordinate of the point at which the line of best fit crosses the x-axis. Not every point on the scatter plot will be on the line of best fit. The differences between the y-values of the points in the scatter plot and the corresponding y-values according to the equation of the line of best fit are the residuals. The line of best fit is also called the least-squares regression line because it is also the line that has the lowest sum of the squares of the residuals.

Correlation coefficient

The *Correlation Coefficient* is the numerical value that indicates how strong the relationship is between the two variables of a linear regression equation. A correlation coefficient of –1 is a perfect negative correlation. A correlation coefficient of +1 is a perfect positive correlation. Correlation coefficients close to –1 or +1 are very strong correlations. A correlation coefficient equal to zero indicates there is no correlation between the two variables. This test is a good indicator of whether or not the equation for the line of best fit is accurate. The formula for the correlation coefficient is

$$r = \frac{\sum_{i=1}^{n}(x_i - \bar{x})(y_i - \bar{y})}{\sqrt{\sum_{i=1}^{n}(x_i - \bar{x})^2}\sqrt{\sum_{i=1}^{n}(y_i - \bar{y})^2}}$$

where r is the correlation coefficient, n is the number of data values in the set, (x_i, y_i) is a point in the set, and $\bar{x}$ and $\bar{y}$ are the means.

68-95-99.7 rule

The *68–95–99.7 Rule* describes how a normal distribution of data should appear when compared to the mean. This is also a description of a normal bell curve. According to this rule, 68 percent of the data values in a normally distributed set should fall within one standard deviation of the mean (34 percent above and 34 percent below the mean), 95 percent of the data values should fall within two standard deviations of the mean (47.5 percent above and 47.5 percent below the mean), and 99.7 percent of the data values should fall within three standard deviations of the mean, again, equally distributed on either side of the mean. This means that only 0.3 percent of all data values should fall more than three standard deviations from the mean

Z-scores

A *Z-score* is an indication of how many standard deviations a given value falls from the mean. To calculate a z-score, use the formula $= \frac{x-\mu}{\sigma}$, where x is the data value, μ is the mean of the data set, and σ is the standard deviation of the population. If the z-score is positive, the data value lies above the mean. If the z-score is negative, the data value falls below the mean. These scores are useful in interpreting data such as standardized test scores, where every piece of data in the set has been counted, rather than just a small random sample. In cases where standard deviations are calculated from a random sample of the set, the z-scores will not be as accurate.

Population and parameter

In statistics, the *Population* is the entire collection of people, plants, etc., that data can be collected from. For example, a study to determine how well students in the area schools perform on a standardized test would have a population of all the students enrolled in those schools, although a study may include just a small sample of students from each school. A *Parameter* is a numerical value that gives information about the population, such as the mean, median, mode, or standard deviation. Remember that the symbol for the mean of a population is μ and the symbol for the standard deviation of a population is σ.

Sample and statistic

A *Sample* is a portion of the entire population. Whereas a parameter helped describe the population, a *Statistic* is a numerical value that gives information about the sample, such as mean, median, mode, or standard deviation. Keep in mind that the symbols for mean and standard deviation are different when they are referring to a sample rather than the entire population. For a sample, the symbol for mean is $\bar{x}$ and the symbol for standard deviation is s. The mean and standard deviation of a sample may or may not be identical to that of the entire population due to a sample only being a subset of the population. However, if the sample is random and large enough, statistically significant values can be attained. Samples are generally used when the population is too large to justify including every element or when acquiring data for the entire population is impossible.

Inferential statistics and sampling distribution

Inferential Statistics is the branch of statistics that uses samples to make predictions about an entire population. This type of statistics is often seen in political polls, where a sample of the population is questioned about a particular topic or politician to gain an understanding about the attitudes of the entire population of the country. Often, exit polls are conducted on election days using this method. Inferential statistics can have a large margin of error if you do not have a valid sample.

Statistical values calculated from various samples of the same size make up the sampling distribution. For example, if several samples of identical size are randomly selected from a large population and then the mean of each sample is calculated, the distribution of values of the means would be a *Sampling Distribution*.

Sampling distribution of the mean

The *Sampling Distribution of the Mean* is the distribution of the sample mean, $\bar{x}$, derived from random samples of a given size. It has three important characteristics. First, the mean of the sampling distribution of the mean is equal to the mean of the population that was sampled. Second, assuming the standard deviation is non-zero, the standard deviation of the sampling distribution of the mean equals the standard deviation of the sampled population divided by the square root of the sample size. This is sometimes called the standard error. Finally, as the sample size gets larger, the sampling distribution of the mean gets closer to a normal distribution via the Central Limit Theorem.

Central Limit Theorem

According to the *Central Limit Theorem*, regardless of what the original distribution of a sample is, the distribution of the means tends to get closer and closer to a normal distribution as the sample size gets larger and larger (this is necessary because the sample is becoming more all-encompassing of the elements of the population). As the sample size gets larger, the distribution of the sample mean will approach a normal distribution with a mean of the population mean and a variance of the population variance divided by the sample size.

Survey studies

A *Survey Study* is a method of gathering information from a small group in an attempt to gain enough information to make accurate general assumptions about the population. Once a survey study is completed, the results are then put into a summary report. Survey studies are generally in the format of surveys, interviews, or questionnaires as part of an effort to find opinions of a particular group or to find facts about a group. It is important to note that the findings from a survey study are only as accurate as the sample chosen from the population.

Correlational studies

Correlational Studies seek to determine how much one variable is affected by changes in a second variable. For example, correlational studies may look for a relationship between the amount of time a student spends studying for a test and the grade that student earned on the test or between student scores on college admissions tests and student grades in college. It is important to note that correlational studies cannot show a cause and effect, but rather can show only that two variables are or are not potentially correlated.

Experimental studies

Experimental Studies take correlational studies one step farther, in that they attempt to prove or disprove a cause-and-effect relationship. These studies are performed by conducting a series of experiments to test the hypothesis. For a study to be scientifically accurate, it must have both an experimental group that receives the specified treatment and a control group that does not get the treatment. This is the type of study pharmaceutical companies do as part of drug trials for new medications. Experimental studies are only valid when proper scientific method has been followed. In other words, the experiment must be well-planned and executed without bias in the testing process, all subjects must be selected at random, and the process of determining which subject is in which of the two groups must also be completely random.

Observational studies

Observational Studies are the opposite of experimental studies. In observational studies, the tester cannot change or in any way control all of the variables in the test. For example, a study to determine which gender does better in math classes in school is strictly observational. You cannot change a person's gender, and you cannot change the subject being studied. The big downfall of observational studies is that you have no way of proving a cause-and-effect relationship because you cannot control outside influences. Events outside of school can influence a student's performance in school, and observational studies cannot take that into consideration.

Samples

A sample is a piece of the entire population that is selected for a particular study in an effort to gain knowledge or information about the entire population. For most studies, a *Random Sample* is necessary to produce valid results. Random samples should not have any particular influence to cause sampled subjects to behave one way or another. The goal is for the random sample to be a *Representative Sample*, or a sample whose characteristics give an accurate picture of the characteristics of the entire population. To accomplish this, you must make sure you have a proper *Sample Size*, or an appropriate number of elements in the sample.

Bias and extraneous variables

In statistical studies, biases must be avoided. *Bias* is an error that causes the study to favor one set of results over another. For example, if a survey to determine how the country views the president's job performance only speaks to registered voters in the president's party, the results will be skewed because a disproportionately large number of responders would tend to show approval, while a disproportionately large number of people in the opposite party would tend to express disapproval.

Extraneous Variables are, as the name implies, outside influences that can affect the outcome of a study. They are not always avoidable, but could trigger bias in the result.

Frequency curves

The five general shapes of frequency curves are *Symmetrical*, *U-shaped*, *Skewed*, *J-shaped*, and *Multimodal*. Symmetrical curves are also known as bell curves or normal curves. Values equidistant from the median have equal frequencies. U-shaped curves have two maxima – one at each end. Skewed curves have the maximum point off-center. Curves that are negative skewed, or left skewed, have the maximum on the right side of the graph so there is longer tail and lower slope on the left side. The opposite is true for curves that are positive skewed, or right skewed. J-shaped curves have a maximum at one end and a minimum at the other end. Multimodal curves have multiple maxima. For example, if the curve has exactly two maxima, it is called a bimodal curve.

United States Government

Political science

Political science focuses on studying different governments and how they compare to each other, general political theory, ways political theory is put into action, how nations and governments interact with each other, and a general study of governmental structure and function. Other elements of political science include the study of elections, governmental administration at various levels, development and action of political parties, and how values such as freedom, power, justice and equality are expressed in different political cultures.

Political science also encompasses elements of other disciplines, including:
- History—how historical events have shaped political thought and process
- Sociology—the effects of various stages of social development on the growth and development of government and politics
- Anthropology—the effects of governmental process on the culture of an individual group and its relationships with other groups
- Economics—how government policies regulate distribution of products and how they can control and/or influence the economy in general

Political theory

1. Ensuring national security—the government protects against international, domestic and terrorist attack and also ensures ongoing security through negotiating and establishing relationships with other governments.
2. Providing public services—government should "promote the general welfare," as stated in the Preamble to the US Constitution, by providing whatever is needed to its citizens.
3. Ensure social order—the government supplies means of settling conflicts among citizens as well as making laws to govern the nation, state, or city.
4. Make decisions regarding the economy—laws help form the economic policy of the country, regarding both domestic and international trade and related issues. The government also has the ability to distribute goods and wealth among its citizens.

Theories regarding the origin of the state

Evolutionary—the state evolved from the family, with the head of state the equivalent of the family's patriarch or matriarch.

Force—one person or group of people brought everyone in an area under their control, forming the first government.

Divine Right—certain people were chosen by the prevailing deity to be the rulers of the nation, which is itself created by the deity or deities.

Social Contract—there is no natural order. The people allow themselves to be governed to maintain social order, while the state in turn promises to protect the people they govern. If the government fails to protect its people, the people have the right to seek new leaders.

Influences of philosophers on political study

Ancient Greek philosophers Aristotle and Plato believed political science would lead to order in political matters, and that this scientifically organized order would create stable, just societies.

Thomas Aquinas adapted the ideas of Aristotle to a Christian perspective. His ideas stated that individuals should have certain rights, but also certain duties, and that these rights and duties should determine the type and extent of government rule. In stating that laws should limit the role of government, he laid the groundwork for ideas that would eventually become modern constitutionalism.

Niccolò Machiavelli, author of *The Prince*, was a proponent of politics based solely on power.

Philosophical ideas of Thomas Hobbes and John Locke

Thomas Hobbes, author of *Leviathan* (1651), believed that individual's lives were focused solely on a quest for power, and that the state must work to control this urge. Hobbes felt that people were completely unable to live harmoniously without the intervention of government.

John Locke wrote *Two Treatises of Civil Government* in 1690. This work argued against the ideas of Thomas Hobbes. He put forth the theory of *tabula rasa*—that people are born with minds that are a blank slate. Experience molds individual minds, not innate knowledge or intuition. He also believed that all men are essentially good, as well as independent and equal. Many of Locke's ideas found their way into the Constitution of the United States.

Montesquieu and Rousseau

These two French philosophers heavily influenced the French Revolution (1789-1815). They believed government policies and ideas should change to alleviate existing problems, an idea referred to as "liberalism." Rousseau in particular directly influenced the Revolution with writings such as *The Social Contract* (1762), *Declaration of the Rights of Man,* and *The Citizen* (1789). Other ideas Rousseau and Montesquieu espoused included:
- Individual freedom and community welfare are of equal importance
- Man's innate goodness leads to natural harmony
- Reason develops with the rise of civilized society
- Individual citizens carry certain obligations to the existing government

Political ideologies of 18th and 19th century philosophers

Hume and Bentham believed politics should have as its main goal maintaining "the greatest happiness of the greatest number." Hume also believed in empiricism, or that ideas should not be believed until the proof has been observed. He was a natural skeptic, as well, and always sought out the truth of matters himself rather than believing what he was told.

John Stuart Mill, a British philosopher as well as an economist, believed in progressive policies such as women's suffrage, emancipation, and the development of labor organizations and farming cooperatives. Fichte and Hegel were eighteenth century German philosophers who supported a form of liberalism grounded largely in socialism and a sense of nationalism.

Political orientations

Liberal—believes government should work to increase equality, even at the expense of some freedoms. Government should assist those in need of help. Focus on enforced social justice and free education for everyone.

Conservative—believes government should be limited in most cases. Government should allow its citizens to help one another and solve their own problems rather than enforcing solutions. Business should not be overregulated, allowing a free market.

Moderate—incorporates some liberal and some conservative values, generally falling somewhere in between in overall belief.

Libertarian—believes government's role should be limited to protecting the life and liberty of citizens. Government should not be involved in any citizen's life unless that citizen is encroaching upon the rights of another.

Principles of government as outlined in the United States Constitution

Federalism—the power of the government does not belong entirely to the national government, but is divided between national and state governments.

Popular sovereignty—the government is determined by the people, and gains its authority and power from the people.

Separation of powers—the government is divided into three branches, executive, legislative and judicial, with each branch having its own set of powers.

Judicial review—courts at all levels of government can declare laws invalid if they contradict the constitutions of individual states, or the US Constitution, with the Supreme Court serving as the final judicial authority on decisions of this kind.

Checks and balances—no single branch can act without input from another, and each branch has the power to "check" any other, as well as balance other branches' powers.

Limited government—governmental powers are limited and certain individual rights are defined as inviolable by the government.

Federalism

Debate on how federalism should function in practice has gone on since the period when the Constitution was being written. There were—and still are—two main factions regarding this issue:
1. States' rights—those favoring the states' rights position feel that the state governments should take the lead in performing local actions to manage various problems.
2. Nationalist—those favoring a nationalist position feel the national government should take the lead to deal with those same matters.

The flexibility of the Constitution has allowed US government to shift and adapt as the needs of the country have changed. Power has often shifted from the state governments to the national government and back again, and both levels of government have developed various ways to influence each other.

Federalism has three major effects on public policy in the US.
1. Determining whether the local, state or national government originates policy
2. Affecting how policies are made
3. Ensuring policy-making functions under a set of limitations

Federalism also influences the political balance of power in the US by:
1. making it difficult if not impossible for a single political party to seize total power.
2. ensuring that individuals can participate in the political system at various levels.
3. making it possible for individuals working within the system to be able to affect policy at some level, whether local or more widespread.

Powers delegated to the national government by the US Constitution

The structure of the US government divides powers between national and state governments. Powers delegated to the national government by the Constitution are:
1. Expressed powers—powers directly defined in the Constitution, including power to declare war, regulate commerce, make money, and collect taxes.
2. Implied powers—powers the national government must have in order to carry out the expressed powers.
3. Inherent powers—powers inherent to any government. These powers are not expressly defined in the constitution.

Some of these powers, such as collection and levying of taxes, are also granted to the individual state governments.

Branches of the US Federal government

Legislative Branch—consists of the two Houses of Congress: the House of Representatives and the Senate. All members of the Legislative Branch are elected officials.

Executive Branch—consists of the President, Vice President, presidential advisors, and other various cabinet members. These advisors are appointed by the President, but must be approved by Congress.

Judicial Branch—is made up of the federal court system, headed by the Supreme Court.

> ➤ **Review Video: <u>The Three Branches of the Federal Government</u>**
> Visit ***mometrix.com/academy*** *and enter* ***Code: 718704***

Responsibilities of the three branches of the Federal government

The Legislative Branch is largely concerned with law-making. All laws must be approved by Congress before they go into effect. They are also responsible for regulating money and trade, approving presidential appointments, and establishing organizations like the postal service and federal courts. Congress can also propose amendments to the Constitution, and can impeach, or bring charges against, the president. Only Congress can declare war.

The Executive Branch carries out laws, treaties, and war declarations enacted by Congress. The President can also veto bills approved by Congress, and serves as commander-in-chief of the US military. The president appoints cabinet members, ambassadors to foreign countries, and federal judges.

The Judicial Branch makes decisions on challenges as to whether laws passed by Congress meet the requirements of the US Constitution. The Supreme Court may also choose to review decisions made by lower courts to determine their constitutionality.

Qualifications of a US citizen

Anyone born in the US, born abroad to a US citizen, or who has gone through a process of naturalization to become a citizen, is considered a citizen of the United States. It is possible to lose US citizenship as a result of conviction of certain crimes such as treason. Citizenship may also be lost if a citizen pledges an oath to another country or serves in the military of a country engaged in hostilities with the US. A US citizen can also choose to hold dual citizenship, work as an expatriate in another country without losing US citizenship, or even to renounce citizenship if he or she so chooses.

Rights, duties and responsibilities of citizens of the United States

Citizens are granted certain rights under the US government. The most important of these are defined in the Bill of Rights, and include freedom of speech, religion, assembly, and a variety of other rights the government is not allowed to remove.

Duties of a US citizen include:
1. Paying taxes
2. Loyalty to the government, though the US does not prosecute those who criticize or seek to change the government
3. Support and defend the Constitution
4. Serve in the Armed Forces as required by law
5. Obeying laws as set forth by the various levels of government.

Responsibilities of a US citizen include:
1. Voting in elections
2. Respecting one another's rights and not infringing upon them
3. Staying informed about various political and national issues
4. Respecting one another's beliefs

Bill of Rights

The first ten amendments of the US Constitution are known as the Bill of Rights. These amendments prevent the government from infringing upon certain freedoms that the founding fathers felt were natural rights that already belonged to all people. These rights included freedom of speech, freedom of religion, right to bear arms, and freedom of assembly. Many of the rights were formulated in direct response to the way the colonists felt they had been mistreated by the British government.

The first ten amendments were passed by Congress in 1789. Three-fourths of the existing thirteen states had ratified them by December of 1791, making them official additions to the Constitution.

- First Amendment—grants freedom of religion, speech, freedom of the press, and the right to assemble.
- Second Amendment—right to bear arms.
- Third Amendment—Congress cannot force individuals to house troops.
- Fourth Amendment—protection from unreasonable search and seizure.
- Fifth Amendment—no individual is required to testify against himself, and no individual may be tried twice for the same crime.
- Sixth Amendment—right to criminal trial by jury, right to legal counsel.
- Seventh Amendment—right to civil trial by jury.
- Eighth Amendment—no excessive bail, no cruel and unusual punishment.
- Ninth Amendment—prevents the absence of rights not explicitly named in the Constitution from being interpreted as a reason to have them taken away.
- Tenth Amendment—any rights not directly delegated to the national government, or not directly prohibited, belong to the states or to the people

Instances for restrictions on First Amendment freedoms

In some cases, the government restricts certain elements of First Amendment rights. Some examples include:
- Freedom of religion—when a religion espouses activities that are otherwise illegal, the government often restricts these forms of religious expression. Examples include polygamy, animal sacrifice, and use of illicit drugs or illegal substances.
- Freedom of speech—can be restricted if exercise of free speech endangers other people.
- Freedom of the press—laws prevent the press from publishing falsehoods.

In emergency situations such as wartime, stricter restrictions are sometimes placed on these rights, especially rights to free speech and assembly, and freedom of the press, in order to protect national security.

Rights of those accused of crimes as addressed by the Constitution

The US Constitution makes allowances for the rights of criminals, or anyone who has transgressed established laws. There must be laws to protect citizens from criminals, but those accused of crimes must also be protected and their basic rights as individuals preserved. In addition, the Constitution protects individuals from the power of authorities who act in case of transgressions to prevent police forces and other enforcement organizations from becoming oppressive.

The Fourth, Fifth, Sixth and Eighth amendments specifically address these issues:
- No unreasonable search and seizure (Fourth Amendment)
- No self-incrimination or double jeopardy—being tried for the same crime more than once (Fifth Amendment)
- Right to trial by jury and right to legal counsel (Sixth Amendment)
- No cruel or unusual punishment (Eighth Amendment)

Supreme Court

When the Founding Fathers wrote in the Declaration of Independence that "all men are created equal," they meant "men," and, in fact, defined citizens as white men who owned land. However, as the country has developed and changed, the definition has expanded to more wholly include all people.

"Equality" does not mean all people are inherently the same, but it does mean they all should be granted the same rights and should be treated the same by the government. Amendments to the Constitution have granted citizenship and voting rights to all Americans. The Supreme Court evaluates various laws and court decisions to determine if they properly represent the idea of equal protection. One sample case was Brown v. Board of Education, in 1954, which declared separate-but-equal to be unconstitutional.

Civil liberties and civil rights

While the terms civil liberties and civil rights are often used synonymously, in actuality their definitions are slightly different. The two concepts work together, however, to define the basics of a free state.
1. "Civil liberties" defines the role of the state in providing equal rights and opportunities to individuals within that state. An example is non-discrimination policies with regards to granting citizenship.
2. "Civil rights" defines the limitations of state rights, describing those rights that belong to individuals and which cannot be infringed upon by the government. Examples of these rights include freedom of religion, political freedom, and overall freedom to live how we choose.

Current political discussions on civil liberty challenges

The civil rights movements of the 1960s and ongoing struggle for women's rights and rights of other minorities have led to challenges to existing law. In addition, debate has raged over how much information the government should be required to divulge to the public. Major issues in today's political climate include:
*   Continued debate over women's rights, especially as regards equal pay for equal work
*   Debate over affirmative action to encourage hiring of minorities
*   Debate over civil rights of homosexuals, including marriage and military service
*   Decisions as to whether any minorities should be compensated for past discriminatory practices
*   Balance between the public's right to know and the government's need to maintain national security
*   Balance between the public's right to privacy and national security

Suffrage and franchise

Suffrage and franchise are both terms referring to the right to vote. Which individuals actually have the right to vote has changed as the US has developed as a nation.

In the early years, only white male landowners were granted suffrage. By the nineteenth century, most states had franchised, or granted the right to vote to, all adult white males. The Fifteenth

Amendment of 1870 granted suffrage to former slaves. The Nineteenth Amendment gave women the right to vote, and in 1971 the Twenty-sixth Amendment expanded voting rights to include any US citizen over the age of eighteen. However, those who have not been granted full citizenship and citizens who have committed certain crimes do not have voting rights.

Changes in the voting process

The first elections in the US were held by public ballot. However, election abuses soon became common, since public ballot made it easy to intimidate, threaten, or otherwise influence the votes of individuals or groups of individuals. New practices were put into play, including registering voters before elections took place, and using a secret or Australian ballot.

In 1892, the introduction of the voting machine further privatized the voting process, since it allowed voters to vote in complete privacy. Even today debate continues about the accuracy of various voting methods, including high-tech voting machines and even low tech punch cards.

Political parties

George Washington was adamantly against the establishment of political parties, based on the abuses perpetrated by such parties in Britain. However, political parties developed in US politics almost from the beginning. Major parties throughout US History have included:
- Federalists and Democratic-Republicans—formed in the late 1700s and disagreed on the balance of power between national and state government
- Democrats and Whigs—developed before the Civil War, based on disagreements about various issues such as slavery
- Democrats and Republicans—developed after the Civil War, with issues centering on the treatment of the post-war South.

While third parties sometimes enter the picture in US politics, the government is basically a two-party system, dominated by the Democrats and Republicans.

Different types and numbers of political parties can have a significant effect on how a government is run. If there is a single party, or a one-party system, the government is defined by that one party, and all policy is based on that party's beliefs. In a two-party system, two parties with different viewpoints compete for power and influence. The US is basically a two-party system, with checks and balances to make it difficult for one party to gain complete power over the other. There are also multi-party systems, with three or more parties. In multiparty systems, various parties will often come to agreements in order to form a majority and shift the balance of power.

Political parties form organizations at all levels of government. Activities of individual parties include:
- Recruiting and backing candidates for offices
- Discussing various issues with the public, increasing public awareness
- Working toward compromise on difficult issues
- Staffing government offices and providing administrative support

At the administrative level, parties work to ensure that viable candidates are available for elections and that offices and staff are in place to support candidates as they run for office and afterwards, when they are elected.

Processes of selecting political candidates

Historically, in the quest for political office, a potential candidate has followed one of the following four processes:

1. Nominating conventions—an official meeting of the members of a party for the express purpose of nominating candidates for upcoming elections. The Democratic National Convention and the Republican National Convention, convened to announce candidates for presidency, are examples of this kind of gathering.
2. Caucuses—a meeting, usually attended by a party's leaders. Some states still use caucuses, but not all.
3. Primary elections—the most common method of choosing candidates today, the primary is a publicly held election to choose candidates.
4. Petitions—signatures are gathered to place a candidate on the ballot. Petitions can also be used to place legislation on a ballot.

Ways to participate in the political process

In addition to voting for elected officials, American citizens are able to participate in the political process through several other avenues. These include:

- Participating in local government
- Participating in caucuses for large elections
- Volunteering to help political parties
- Running for election to local, state, or national offices

Individuals can also donate money to political causes, or support political groups that focus on specific causes such as abortion, wildlife conservation or women's rights. These groups often make use of representatives who lobby legislators to act in support of their efforts.

Funding political campaign

Political campaigns are very expensive ventures. In addition to the basic necessities of a campaign office, including office supplies, office space, etc., a large quantity of the money that funds a political campaign goes toward advertising. Television advertising in particular is quite costly.

Money to fund a political campaign can come from several sources including:

- The candidate's personal funds
- Donations by individuals
- Special interest groups

The most significant source of campaign funding is special interest groups. Groups in favor of certain policies will donate money to candidates they believe will support those policies. Special interest groups also do their own advertising in support of candidates they endorse.

Free press and the media

The right to free speech guaranteed in the first amendment to the Constitution allows the media to report on government and political activities without fear of retribution. Because the media has access to information about the government, its policies and actions, as well as debates and discussions that occur in Congress, it can ensure that the people are informed about the inner workings of the government. The media can also draw attention to injustices, imbalances of power, and other transgressions the government or government officials might commit.

However, media outlets may, like special interest groups, align themselves with certain political viewpoints and skew their reports to fit that viewpoint. The rise of the Internet has made media reporting even more complex, as news can be found from an infinite variety of sources, both reliable and unreliable.

Anarchism, communism and dictatorship

Anarchists believe that all government should be eliminated and that individuals should rule themselves. Historically, anarchists have used violence and assassination to further their beliefs.

Communism is based on class conflict, revolution and a one-party state. Ideally, a communist government would involve a single government for the entire world. Communist government controls the production and flow of goods and services rather than leaving this to companies or individuals.

Dictatorship involves rule by a single individual. If rule is enforced by a small group, this is referred to as an oligarchy. Few malevolent dictatorships have existed. Dictators tend to rule with a violent hand, using a highly repressive police force to ensure control over the populace.

Fascism and monarchy

Fascism centers on a single leader and is, ideologically, an oppositional belief to Communism. Fascism includes a single party state and centralized control. The power of the fascist leader lies in the "cult of personality," and the fascist state often focuses on expansion and conquering of other nations.

Monarchy was the major form of government for Europe through most of its history. A monarchy is led by a king or a queen. This position is hereditary, and the rulers are not elected. In modern times, constitutional monarchy has developed, where the king and queen still exist but most of the governmental decisions are made by democratic institutions such as a parliament.

Presidential System and Socialism

A Presidential System, like a parliamentary system, has a legislature and political parties, but there is no difference between the head of state and the head of government. Instead of separating these functions, an elected president performs both. Election of the president can be direct or indirect, and the president may not necessarily belong to the largest political party.

In Socialism, the state controls production of goods, though it does not necessarily own all means of production. The state also provides a variety of social services to citizens and helps guide the economy. A democratic form of government often exists in socialist countries.

Totalitarian and authoritarian systems of government

A totalitarian system believes everything should be under the control of the government, from resource production to the press to religion and other social institutions. All aspects of life under a totalitarian system must conform to the ideals of the government.

Authoritarian governments practices widespread state authority, but do not necessarily dismantle all public institutions. If a church, for example, exists as an organization but poses no threat to the authority of the state, an authoritarian government might leave it as it is. While all totalitarian governments are by definition authoritarian, a government can be authoritarian without becoming totalitarian.

> ➤ **Review Video: <u>Authoritarian and Totalitarian Government</u>**
> *Visit **mometrix.com/academy** and enter **Code: 553715***

Parliamentary and democratic systems of government

In a parliamentary system, government involves a legislature and a variety of political parties. The head of government, usually a Prime Minister, is typically the head of the dominant party. A head of state can be elected, or this position can be taken by a monarch, such as in Great Britain's constitutional monarchy system.

In a democratic system of government, the people elect their government representatives. The term democracy is a Greek term that means "for the rule of the people." There are two forms of democracy—direct and indirect. In a direct democracy, each issue or election is decided by a vote where each individual is counted separately. An indirect democracy employs a legislature that votes on issues that affect large number of people whom the legislative members represent. Democracy can exist as a Parliamentary system or a Presidential system. The US is a presidential, indirect democracy.

Realism, liberalism, institutionalism and constructivism

The theory of realism states that nations are by nature aggressive, and work in their own self-interest. Relations between nations are determined by military and economic strength. The nation is seen as the highest authority.

Liberalism believes states can cooperate, and that they act based on capabilities rather than power. This term was originally coined to describe Woodrow Wilson's theories on international cooperation.

In institutionalism, institutions provide structure and incentive for cooperation among nations. Institutions are defined as a set of rules used to make international decisions. These institutions also help distribute power and determine how nations will interact.

Constructivism, like liberalism, is based on international cooperation, but recognizes that perceptions countries have of each other can affect their relations.

Foreign policy

Foreign policy is a set of goals, policies and strategies that determine how an individual nation will interact with other countries. These strategies shift, sometimes quickly and drastically, according to actions or changes occurring in the other countries. However, a nation's foreign policy is often based on a certain set of ideals and national needs.

Examples of US foreign policy include isolationism versus internationalism. In the 1800s, the US leaned more toward isolationism, exhibiting a reluctance to become involved in foreign affairs. The World Wars led to a period of internationalism, as the US entered these wars in support of other countries and joined the United Nations.

Today's foreign policy tends more toward interdependence, or globalism, recognizing the widespread affects of issues like economic health. US foreign policy is largely determined by Congress and the president, influenced by the secretary of state, secretary of defense, and the national security adviser. Executive officials actually carry out policies. The main departments in charge of these day-to-day issues are the US Department of State, also referred to as the State Department.

The Department of State carries out policy, negotiates treaties, maintains diplomatic relations, assists citizens traveling in foreign countries, and ensures that the president is properly informed of any international issues. The Department of Defense, the largest executive department in the US, supervises the armed forces and provides assistance to the president in his role as commander in chief.

International organizations

Intergovernmental organizations (IGOs). These organizations are made up of members from various national governments. The UN is an example of an intergovernmental organization. Treaties among the member nations determine the functions and powers of these groups.

Nongovernmental organizations (NGOs). An NGO lies outside the scope of any government and are usually supported through private donations. An example of an NGO is the International Red Cross, which works with governments all over the world when their countries are in crisis, but is formally affiliated with no particular country or government.

Diplomats

Diplomats are individuals who reside in foreign countries in order to maintain communications between that country and their home country. They help negotiate trade agreements, environmental policies, and convey official information to foreign governments. They also help resolve conflicts between the countries, often working to sort out issues without making the conflicts official in any way. Diplomats, or ambassadors, are appointed in America by the president. Appointments must be approved by Congress.

United Nations

The United Nations (UN) helps form international policies by hosting representatives of various countries who then provide input into policy decisions. Countries who are members of the UN must agree to abide by all final UN resolutions, but this is not always the case in practice, as dissent is not uncommon. If countries do not follow UN resolutions, the UN can decide on sanctions against those countries, often economic sanctions, such as trade restriction. The UN can also send military forces to problem areas, with "peace keeping" troops brought in from member nations. An example of this function is the Korean War, the first war in which an international organization played a major role.

United States Society and Culture

Well-known Native Americans

Squanto, an Algonquian, helped early English settlers survive the hard winter by teaching them the native methods of planting corn, squash, and pumpkins.

Pocahontas, also Algonquian, became famous as a liaison with John Smith's Jamestown colony in 1607.

Sacagawea, a Shoshone, served a vital role in the Lewis and Clark expedition when the two explorers hired her as their guide in 1805.

Crazy Horse and Sitting Bull led Sioux and Cheyenne troops in the Battle of the Little Bighorn in 1876, soundly defeating George Armstrong Custer.

Chief Joseph, a leader of the Nez Perce who supported peaceful interaction with white settlers, attempted to relocate his tribe to Canada rather than move them to a reservation.

Regional Native American groups

The Algonquians in the eastern part of the United States lived in wigwams. The northern tribes subsisted on hunting and gathering, while those who were farther south grew crops such as corn.

The Iroquois, also an east coast tribe, spoke a different language from the Algonquians, and lived in rectangular longhouses.

The Plains tribes lived between the Mississippi River and the Rocky Mountains. Nomadic tribes, they lived in teepees and followed the buffalo herds. Plains tribes included the Sioux, Cheyenne, Comanche and Blackfoot.

Pueblo tribes included the Zuni, Hope, and Acoma. They lived in the Southwest deserts in homes made of stone or adobe. They domesticated animals and cultivated corn and beans.

On the Pacific coast, tribes such as the Tlingit, Chinook and Salish lived on fish as well as deer, native berries and roots. Their rectangular homes housed large family groups, and they used totem poles.

In the far north, the Aleuts and Inuit lived in skin tents or igloos. Talented fishermen, they built kayaks and umiaks and also hunted caribou, seals, whales and walrus.

Age of Exploration

The Age of Exploration is also called the Age of Discovery. It is generally considered to have begun in the early fifteenth century, and continued into the seventeenth century. Major developments of the Age of Exploration included technological advances in navigation, mapmaking and shipbuilding.

These advances led to expanded European exploration of the rest of the world. Explorers set out from several European countries, including Portuguese, Spain, France and England, seeking new routes to Asia. These efforts led to the discovery of new lands, as well as colonization in India, Asia, Africa, and North America.

Technological advances in navigation and seafaring

For long ocean journeys, it was important for sailors to be able to find their way home even when their vessels sailed far out to sea, well out of sight of land. A variety of navigational tools enabled them to launch ambitious journeys over long distances. The compass and astrolabe were particularly important advancements. The magnetic compass had been used by Chinese navigators for some time, and knowledge of the astrolabe came to Europe from Arab navigators and traders who had refined designs developed by the ancient Greeks.

The Portuguese developed a ship called a caravel in the 1400s that incorporated navigational advancements with the ability to make long sea journeys. Equipped with this advanced vessel, the Portuguese achieved a major goal of the Age of Exploration by discovering a sea route from Europe to Asia in 1498.

Voyage of Christopher Columbus

In 1492, Columbus, a Genoan explorer, obtained financial backing from King Ferdinand and Queen Isabella of Spain to seek a sea route to Asia. He sought a trade route with the Asian Indies to the west. With three ships, the *Niña*, the *Pinta* and the *Santa Maria*, he eventually landed in the West Indies. While Columbus failed in his effort to discover a western route to Asia, he is credited with the discovery of the Americas.

> ➤ **Review Video:** <u>Christopher Columbus</u>
> *Visit* **mometrix.com/academy** *and enter* ***Code:* 496598**

Goals of the French, Spanish, Dutch and British in the colonization of the Americas

Initial French colonies were focused on expanding the fur trade. Later, French colonization led to the growth of plantations in Louisiana which brought numerous African slaves to the New World.

Spanish colonists came to look for wealth, and to converting the natives to Christianity. For some, the desire for gold led to mining in the New World, while others established large ranches.

The Dutch were also involved in the fur trade, and also imported slaves as the need for laborers increased.

British colonists arrived with various goals. Some were simply looking for additional income, while others were fleeing Britain to escape religious persecution.

New England colonies

The New England colonies were: New Hampshire, Connecticut, Rhode Island and Massachusetts.

The colonies in New England were founded largely to escape religious persecution in England. The beliefs of the Puritans, who migrated to America in the 1600s, significantly influenced the development of these colonies.

Situated in the northeast coastal areas of America, the New England colonies featured numerous harbors as well as dense forest. The soil, however, is rocky and, with a very short growing season, was not well suited for agriculture.

The economy of New England during the colonial period centered around fishing, shipbuilding and trade along with some small farms and lumber mills. Although some groups congregated in small farms, life centered largely on towns and cities where merchants largely controlled the trade economy. Coastal cities such as Boston grew and thrived.

Middle Atlantic Colonies

The Middle or Middle Atlantic Colonies were: New York, New Jersey, Pennsylvania and Delaware. Unlike the New England colonies, where most colonists were from England and Scotland, the Middle Colonies founders were from various countries including the Netherlands, Holland and Sweden. Various factors led these colonists to America.

More fertile than New England, the Middle Colonies became major producers of crops included rye, oats, potatoes, wheat, and barley. Some particularly wealthy inhabitants owned large farms and/or businesses. Farmers in general were able to produce enough to have a surplus to sell. Tenant farmers also rented land from larger land owners.

Southern Colonies

The Southern Colonies were Maryland, Virginia, North Carolina, South Carolina and Georgia. Of the Southern Colonies, Virginia was the first permanent English colony and Georgia the last. The warm climate and rich soil of the south encouraged agriculture, and the growing season was long. As a result, economy in the south was based largely on labor-intensive plantations. Crops included tobacco, rice and indigo, all of which became valuable cash crops. Most land in the south was controlled by wealthy plantation owners and farmers. Labor on the farms came in the form of indentured servants and African slaves. The first of these African slaves arrived in Virginia in 1619, starting a long, unpleasant history of slavery in the American colonies.

Navigation Acts

Enacted in 1651, the Navigation Acts were an attempt by Britain to dominate international trade. Aimed largely at the Dutch, the Acts banned foreign ships from transporting goods to the British colonies, and from transporting goods to Britain from elsewhere in Europe. While the restrictions on trade angered some colonists, these Acts were helpful to other American colonists who, as members of the British Empire, were legally able to provide ships for Britain's growing trade interests and use the ships for their own trading ventures. By the time the French and Indian War had ended, one-third of British merchant ships were built in the American colonies. Many colonists amassed fortunes in the shipbuilding trade.

French and Indian Wars

The British defeat of the Spanish Armada in 1750 led to the decline of Spanish power in Europe. This in turn led the British and French into battle over several wars between 1689 and 1748. These wars were:

- King William's War, or the Nine Years War, 1689-1697. This war was fought largely in Flanders.
- The War of Spanish Succession, or Queen Anne's War, 1702-1713
- War of Austrian Succession, or King George's War, 1740-1748

The fourth and final, the French and Indian War, was fought largely in the North American territory, and resulted in the end of France's reign as a colonial power in North America. Although the French held many advantages, including more cooperative colonists and numerous Indian allies, the strong leadership of William Pitt eventually led the British to victory. Costs incurred during the wars eventually led to discontent in the colonies. This helped spark the American Revolution.

> **Review Video: French and Indian War**
> *Visit mometrix.com/academy and enter Code: 502183*

Reasons that Britain extensively taxed the American colonies

The French and Indian War created circumstances for which the British desperately needed more revenue. These included:

- The need to pay off the war debt.
- The need for funds to defend the expanding empire
- The need for funds to govern Britain's thirty-three far-flung colonies, including the American colonies

These needs led the British to pass additional laws to increase revenues from the colonies. Because they had spent so much money to defend the American colonies, the British felt it was appropriate to collect considerably higher taxes from them. The colonists felt this was unfair, and many were led to protest the increasing taxes. Eventually, protest led to violence.

Triangular trade

Triangular trade began in the Colonies with ships setting off for Africa carrying rum. In Africa, the rum was traded for gold or slaves. Ships then went from Africa to the West Indies, trading slaves for sugar, molasses, or money. To complete the triangle, the ships returned to the colonies with sugar or molasses to make more rum, as well as stores of gold and silver.

This trade triangle violated the Molasses Act of 1733, which required the colonists to pay high duties to Britain on molasses acquired from French, Dutch, and Spanish colonies. The colonists ignored these duties, and the British government adopted a policy of salutary neglect by not enforcing them.

> **Review Video: Triangular Trade**
> *Visit mometrix.com/academy and enter Code: 415470*

Effects of new laws on British-Colonial relations

While earlier revenue-generating acts such as the Navigation Acts brought money to the colonists, the new laws after 1763 required colonists to pay money back to Britain. The British felt this was fair since the colonists were British subjects and since they had incurred debt protecting the Colonies. The colonists felt it was not only unfair, but illegal.

The development of local government in America had given the colonists a different view of the structure and role of government. This made it difficult for the British to understand colonist's protests against what the British felt was a fair and reasonable solution to the mother country's financial problems.

Factors that led to increasing discontent in the American colonies

More and more colonists had been born on American soil, decreasing any sense of kinship with the far away British rulers. Their new environment had led to new ideas of government and a strong view of the colonies as a separate entity from Britain.

Colonists were allowed to self-govern in domestic issues, but Britain controlled international issues. In fact, the American colonies were largely left to form their own local government bodies, giving them more freedom than any other colonial territory. This gave the colonists a sense of independence which led them to resent control from Britain.

Threats during the French and Indian War led the colonists to call for unification in order to protect themselves.

Differences between colonial government and British government

As new towns and other legislative districts developed in America, the colonists began to practice representative government. Colonial legislative bodies were made up of elected representatives chosen by male property owners in the districts. These individuals represented interests of the districts from which they had been elected.

By contrast, in Britain the Parliament represented the entire country. Parliament was not elected to represent individual districts. Instead, they represented specific classes. Because of this drastically different approach to government, the British did not understand the colonists' statement that they had no representation in the British Parliament.

Acts of British Parliament that occurred after the French and Indian Wars

The Quartering Act, 1765. This act required colonists to provide accommodations and supplies for British troops. In addition, colonists were prohibited from settling west of the Appalachians until given permission by Britain.

The Sugar Act, 1764. This act not only required taxes to be collected on molasses brought into the colonies, but gave British officials the right to search the homes of anyone suspected of violating it.

The Stamp Act, 1765. The Stamp Act taxed printed materials such as newspapers and legal documents. Protests led the Stamp Act to be repealed in 1766, but the repeal also included the Declaratory Act, which stated that Parliament had the right to govern the colonies.

The Townshend Acts, 1767. These acts taxed paper, paint, lead and tea that came into the colonies. Colonists led boycotts in protest, and in Massachusetts leaders like Samuel and John Adams began to organize resistance against British rule.

Boston Massacre

With the passage of the Stamp Act, nine colonies met in New York to demand its repeal. Elsewhere, protest arose in New York City, Philadelphia, Boston and other cities. These protests sometimes escalated into violence, often targeting ruling British officials.

The passage of the Townshend Acts in 1767 led to additional tension in the colonies. The British sent troops to New York City and Boston. On March 5, 1770, protesters began to taunt the British troops, throwing snowballs. The soldiers responded by firing into the crowd. This clash between protesters and soldiers led to five deaths and eight injuries, and was christened the Boston Massacre. Shortly thereafter, Britain repealed the majority of the Townshend Acts.

Tea Act and the Boston Tea Party

The majority of the Townshend Acts were repealed after the Boston Massacre in 1770, but Britain kept the tax on tea. In 1773, the Tea Act was passed. This allowed the East India Company to sell tea for much lower prices, and also allowed them to bypass American distributors, selling directly to shopkeepers instead. Colonial tea merchants saw this as a direct assault on their business. In December of 1773, 150 merchants boarded ships in Boston Harbor and dumped 342 chests of tea into the sea in protest of the new laws. This act of protest came to be known as the Boston Tea Party.

Coercive Acts

The Coercive Acts passed by Britain in 1774 were meant to punish Massachusetts for defying British authority. The four Coercive Acts:
1. Shut down ports in Boston until the city paid back the value of the tea destroyed during the Boston Tea Party.
2. Required that local government officials in Massachusetts be appointed by the governor rather than being elected by the people.
3. Allowed trials of British soldiers to be transferred to Britain rather than being held in Massachusetts.
4. Required locals to provide lodging for British soldiers any time there was a disturbance, even if lodging required them to stay in private homes.

These Acts led to the assembly of the First Continental Congress in Philadelphia on September 5, 1774. Fifty-five delegates met, representing 12 of the American colonies. They sought compromise with England over England's increasingly harsh efforts to control the colonies.

First Continental Congress

The First Continental Congress met in Philadelphia on September 5, 1774. Their goal was to achieve a peaceful agreement with Britain. Made up of delegates from 12 of the 13 colonies, the Congress affirmed loyalty to Britain and the power of Parliament to dictate foreign affairs in the colonies. However, they demanded that the Intolerable Acts be repealed, and instituted a trade embargo with Britain until this came to pass.

In response, George III of Britain declared that the American colonies must submit or face military action. The British sought to end assemblies opposing their policies. These assemblies gathered weapons and began to form militias. On April 19, 1775, the British military was ordered to disperse a meeting of the Massachusetts Assembly. A battle ensued on Lexington Common as the armed colonists resisted. The resulting battles became the Battle of Lexington and Concord—the first battles of the American Revolution.

Second Continental Congress

The Second Continental Congress met in Philadelphia on May 10, 1775, a month after Lexington and Concord. Their discussions centered on defense of the American colonies and how to conduct the growing war, as well as local government. The delegates also discussed declaring independence from Britain, with many members in favor of this drastic move. They established an army, and on June 15, named George Washington as its commander in chief.

By 1776, it was obvious that there was no turning back from full-scale war with Britain. The colonial delegates of the Continental Congress drafted the Declaration of Independence on July 4, 1776.

> ➤ **Review Video:** <u>**The First and Second Continental Congress**</u>
> *Visit **mometrix.com/academy** and enter **Code:** **835211***

Declaration of Independence

Penned by Thomas Jefferson and signed on July 4, 1776, the Declaration of Independence stated that King George III had violated the rights of the colonists and was establishing a tyrannical reign over them.

Many of Jefferson's ideas of natural rights and property rights were shaped by seventeenth century philosopher John Locke. Jefferson focused on natural rights, as demonstrated by the assertion of people's rights to "life, liberty and the pursuit of happiness." Locke's comparable idea asserted "life, liberty, and private property." Both felt that the purpose of government was to protect the rights of the people, and that individual rights were more important than individuals' obligations to the state.

> ➤ **Review Video:** <u>Declaration of Independence</u>
> *Visit **mometrix.com/academy** and enter **Code:** **256838***

Five battles of the Revolutionary War

1. The Battle of Lexington and Concord (April, 1775) is considered the first engagement of the Revolutionary War.
2. The Battle of Bunker Hill, in June of 1775, was one of the bloodiest of the entire war. Although American troops withdrew, about half the British army was lost. The colonists proved they could stand against professional British soldiers. In August, Britain declared that the American colonies were officially in a state of rebellion.
3. The first colonial victory occurred in Trenton, New Jersey, when Washington and his troops crossed the Delaware River on Christmas Day, 1776 for a December 26, surprise attack on British and Hessian troops.
4. The Battle of Saratoga effectively ended a plan to separate the New England colonies from their Southern counterparts. The surrender of British general John Burgoyne led to France joining the war as allies of the Americans, and is generally considered a turning point of the war.
5. On October 19, 1781, General Cornwallis surrendered after a defeat in the Battle of Yorktown, Virginia, ending the Revolutionary War.

> ➤ **Review Video: Revolutionary War**
> Visit **mometrix.com/academy** and enter **Code: 935282**

Treaty of Paris

The Treaty of Paris was signed on September 3, 1783, bringing an official end to the Revolutionary War. In this document, Britain officially recognized the United States of America as an independent nation. The treaty established the Mississippi River as the country's western border. The treaty also restored Florida to Spain, while France reclaimed African and Caribbean colonies seized by the British in 1763. On November 24, 1783, the last British troops departed from the newly born United States of America.

Articles of Confederation

A precursor to the Constitution, the Articles of Confederation represented the first attempt of the newly independent colonies to establish the basics of independent government. The Continental Congress passed the Articles on November 15, 1777. They went into effect on March 1, 1781, following ratification by the thirteen states.

The Articles prevented a central government from gaining too much power, instead giving power to a Congressional body made up of delegates from all thirteen states. However, the individual states retained final authority.

Without a strong central executive, though, this weak alliance among the new states proved ineffective in settling disputes or enforcing laws. The idea of a weak central government needed to be revised. Recognition of these weaknesses eventually led to the drafting of a new document, the Constitution.

> ➤ **Review Video: Articles of Confederation**
> Visit **mometrix.com/academy** and enter **Code: 927401**

Process by which the Constitution was initially proposed and drafted

Delegates from twelve of the thirteen states (Rhode Island was not represented) met in Philadelphia in May of 1787, initially intending to revise the Articles of Confederation. However, it quickly became apparent that a simple revision would not provide the workable governmental structure the newly formed country needed.

After vowing to keep all the proceedings secret until the final document was completed, the delegates set out to draft what would eventually become the Constitution of the United States of America. By keeping the negotiations secret, the delegates were able to present a completed document to the country for ratification, rather than having every small detail hammered out by the general public.

Virginia Plan, the New Jersey Plan, and the Great Compromise

The delegates agreed that the new nation required a strong central government, but that its overall power should be limited. The various branches of the government should have balanced power, so that no one group could control the others. Final power belonged with the citizens who voted officials into office based on who would provide the best representation.

Disagreement immediately occurred between delegates from large states and those from smaller states. The governor of Virginia, Edmond Randolph, felt that representation in Congress should be based on state population. This was the Virginia Plan. The New Jersey Plan, presented by William Paterson, from New Jersey, proposed each state have equal representation.

Finally, Roger Sherman from Connecticut formulated the Connecticut Compromise, also called the Great Compromise. The result was the familiar structure we have today. Each state has the equal representation of two Senators in the Senate, with the number of representatives in the House of Representatives based on population. This is called a bicameral Congress. Both houses may draft bills, but financial matters must originate in the House of Representatives.

Three-fifths compromise

During debate on the U.S. Constitution, a disagreement arose between the Northern and Southern states involving how slaves should be counted when determining a state's quota of representatives. In the South large numbers of slaves were commonly used to run plantations. Delegates wanted slaves to be counted to determine the number of representatives, but not counted to determine the amount of taxes the states would pay. The Northern states wanted exactly the opposite arrangement. The final decision was to count three-fifths of the slave population both for tax purposes and to determine representation. This was called the three-fifths compromise.

Commerce Compromise

The Commerce Compromise also resulted from a North/South disagreement. In the North the economy was centered on industry and trade. The Southern economy was largely agricultural. The Northern states wanted to give the new government the ability to regulate exports as well as trade between the states. The South opposed this plan. Another compromise was in order. In the end, Congress received regulatory power over all trade, including the ability to collect tariffs on exported goods. In the South, this raised another red flag regarding the slave trade, as they were concerned about the effect on their economy if tariffs were levied on slaves. The final agreement allowed importing slaves to continue for twenty years without government intervention. Import taxes on slaves were limited, and after the year 1808, Congress could decide whether to allow continued imports of slaves.

Initial concerns for the Constitution

Once the Constitution was drafted, it was presented for approval by the states. Nine states needed to approve the document for it to become official. However, debate and discussion continued. Major concerns included:
- The lack of a bill of rights to protect individual freedoms.
- States felt too much power was being handed over to the central government.
- Voters wanted more control over their elected representatives.

Discussion about necessary changes to the Constitution divided roughly into two camps: Federalists and Anti-Federalists. Federalists wanted a strong central government. Anti-Federalists wanted to prevent a tyrannical government from developing if a central government held too much power.

Federalist and Anti-Federalist camps

Major Federalist leaders included Alexander Hamilton, John Jay and James Madison. They wrote a series of letters, called the Federalist Papers, aimed at convincing the states to ratify the Constitution. These were published in New York papers.

Anti-Federalists included Thomas Jefferson and Patrick Henry. They argued against the Constitution as it was originally drafted in arguments called the Anti-Federalist Papers.

The final compromise produced a strong central government controlled by checks and balances. A Bill of Rights was also added, becoming the first ten amendments to the Constitution. These amendments protected rights such as freedom of speech, freedom of religion, and other basic rights. Aside from various amendments added throughout the years, the United States Constitution has remained unchanged.

Members of the first administration of the new government

George Washington was elected as the first President of the United States in 1789.

John Adams, who finished second in the election, became the first Vice President.

Thomas Jefferson was appointed by Washington as Secretary of State.

Alexander Hamilton was also appointed Secretary of the Treasury.

Alien and Sedition Acts

When John Adams became president, a war was raging between Britain and France. While Adams and the Federalists backed the British, Thomas Jefferson and the Republican Party supported the French. The United States nearly went to war with France during this time period, while France worked to spread its international standing and influence under the leadership of Napoleon Bonaparte.

The Alien and Sedition Acts grew out of this conflict, and made it illegal to speak in a hostile fashion against the existing government. They also allowed the president to deport anyone in the U.S. who was not a citizen and who was suspected of treason or treasonous activity.

When Jefferson became the third president in 1800, he repealed these four laws and pardoned anyone who had been convicted under them.

Development of political parties in early U.S. government

Many in the U.S. were against political parties after seeing the way parties, or factions, functioned in Britain. The factions in Britain were more interested in personal profit than the overall good of the country, and they did not want this to happen in the U.S.

However, the differences of opinion between Thomas Jefferson and Alexander Hamilton led to formation of political parties. Hamilton favored a stronger central government, while Jefferson felt more power should remain with the states. Jefferson was in favor of strict Constitutional interpretation, while Hamilton believed in a more flexible approach. As various others joined the separate camps, Hamilton backers began to term themselves Federalists while those supporting Jefferson became identified as Democratic-Republicans.

Whig Party, the Democratic Party, and the Republican Party

Thomas Jefferson was elected president in 1800 and again in 1804. The Federalist Party began a decline, and its major figure, Alexander Hamilton, died in a duel with Aaron Burr in 1804. By 1816, the Federalist Party virtually disappeared.

New parties sprang up to take its place. After 1824, the Democratic-Republican Party suffered a split. The Whigs arose, backing John Quincy Adams and industrial growth. The new Democratic Party formed, in opposition to the Whigs, and their candidate, Andrew Jackson, was elected as president in 1828.

By the 1850s, issues regarding slavery led to the formation of the Republican Party, which was anti-slavery, while the Democratic Party of the time, with a larger interest in the South, favored slavery. This Republican/Democrat division formed the basis of today's two-party system.

Marbury v. Madison

The main duty of the Supreme Court today is judicial review. This power was largely established by Marbury v. Madison.

When John Adams was voted out of office in 1800, he worked, during his final days in office, to appoint Federalist judges to Supreme Court positions, knowing Jefferson, his replacement, held opposing views. As late as March 3, the day before Jefferson was to take office, Adams made last-minute appointments referred to as "Midnight Judges."

One of the late appointments was William Marbury. The next day, March 4, Jefferson ordered his Secretary of State, James Madison, not to deliver Marbury's commission. This decision was backed by Chief Justice Marshall, who determined that the Judiciary Act of 1789, which granted the power to deliver commissions, was illegal in that it gave the Judicial Branch powers not granted in the Constitution.

This case set precedent for the Supreme Court to nullify laws it found to be unconstitutional.

> **Review Video: <u>Marbury v. Madison</u>**
> Visit *mometrix.com/academy* and enter *Code:* **573964**

McCulloch v Maryland

Judicial review was further exercised by the Supreme Court in McCulloch v Maryland. When Congress chartered a national bank, the Second Bank of the United States, Maryland voted to tax any bank business dealing with banks chartered outside the state, including the federally chartered bank. Andrew McCulloch, an employee of the Second Bank of the US in Baltimore, refused to pay this tax. The resulting lawsuit from the State of Maryland went to the Supreme Court for judgment.

John Marshall, Chief Justice of the Supreme Court, stated that Congress was within its rights to charter a national bank. In addition, the State of Maryland did not have the power to levy a tax on the federal bank or on the federal government in general. In cases where state and federal government collided, precedent was set for the federal government to prevail.

Affect of Treaty of Paris on Native Americans

After the Revolutionary War, the Treaty of Paris, which outlined the terms of surrender of the British to the Americans, granted large parcels of land to the U.S. that were occupied by Native Americans. The new government attempted to claim the land, treating the natives as a conquered people. This approached proved unenforceable.

Next, the government tried purchasing the land from the Indians via a series of treaties as the country expanded westward. In practice, however, these treaties were not honored, and Native Americans were simply dislocated and forced to move farther and farther west as American expansion continued, often with military action.

Indian Removal Act of 1830 and the Treaty of New Echota

The Indian Removal Act of 1830 gave the new American government power to form treaties with Native Americans. In theory, America would claim land east of the Mississippi in exchange for land west of the Mississippi, to which the natives would relocate voluntarily. In practice, many tribal leaders were forced into signing the treaties, and relocation at times occurred by force.

The Treaty of New Echota was supposedly a treaty between the US government and Cherokee tribes in Georgia. However, the treaty was not signed by tribal leaders, but rather by a small portion of the represented people. The leaders protested by refusing to be removed, but President, Martin Van Buren, enforced the treaty by sending soldiers. During their forced relocation, more than 4,000 Cherokee Indians died on what became known as the Trail of Tears.

Economic trends that developed in different areas of the country

In the Northeast, the economy mostly depended on manufacturing, industry and industrial development. This led to a dichotomy between rich business owners and industrial leaders and the much poorer workers who supported their businesses.

The South continued to depend on agriculture, especially large-scale farms or plantations worked mostly by slaves and indentured servants.

In the West, where new settlement had begun to develop, the land was largely wild. Growing communities were essentially agricultural; growing crops and raising livestock. The differences between regions led each to support different interests both politically and economically.

Louisiana Purchase

With tension still high between France and Britain, Napoleon was in need of money to support his continuing war efforts. To secure necessary funds, he decided to sell the Louisiana Territory to the U.S. At the same time President Thomas Jefferson wanted to buy New Orleans, feeling U.S. trade was made vulnerable to both Spain and France at that port. Instead, Napoleon sold him the entire territory for the bargain price of fifteen million dollars. The Louisiana Territory was larger than all the rest of the United States put together, and it eventually became fifteen additional states.

Federalists in Congress were opposed to the purchase. They feared that the Louisiana Purchase would extend slavery, and that further western growth would weaken the power of the northern states.

> **Review Video:** <u>The Louisiana Purchase</u>
> Visit *mometrix.com/academy* and enter *Code:* **920513**

Major ideas driving American foreign policy during its early years

Isolationism – the early US government did not intend to establish colonies, though they did plan to grow larger within the bounds of North America.

No entangling alliances – both George Washington and Thomas Jefferson were opposed to forming any permanent alliances with other countries or becoming involved in other countries' internal issues.

Nationalism –a positive patriotic feeling about the United States blossomed quickly among its citizens, particularly after the War of 1812, when the U.S. once again defeated Britain. The Industrial Revolution also sparked increased nationalism by allowing even the most far-flung areas of the U.S. to communicate with each other via telegraph and the expanding railroad.

War of 1812

The War of 1812 grew out of the continuing tension between France and Great Britain. Napoleon continued to strive to conquer Britain, while the U.S. continued trade with both countries, but favoring France and the French colonies. Because of what Britain saw as an alliance between America and France, they determined to bring an end to trade between the two nations.

With the British preventing U.S. trade with the French and the French preventing trade with the British, James Madison's presidency introduced acts to regulate international trade. If either Britain or France removed their restrictions, America would not trade with the other. Napoleon acted first, and Madison prohibited trade with England. England saw this as the U.S. formally siding with the French, and war ensued in 1812.

The War of 1812 has been called the Second American Revolution. It established the superiority of the U.S. naval forces and reestablished U.S. independence from Britain and Europe.

Two major naval battles, at Lake Erie and Lake Champlain, kept the British from invading the U.S. via Canada. American attempts to conquer Canadian lands were not successful.

In another memorable British attack, the British invaded Washington DC and burned the White House. Legend has it that Dolly Madison, the First Lady, salvaged the American flag from the fire.

On Christmas Eve, 1814, the Treaty of Ghent officially ended the war. However, Andrew Jackson, unaware that the war was over, managed another victory at New Orleans on January 8, 1815. This victory upped American morale and led to a new wave of nationalism and national pride known as the "Era of Good Feelings."

Britian's efforts to prevent America from trading with France

The British had two major objections to America's continued trade with France. First, they saw the US as helping France's war effort by providing supplies and goods. Second, the United States had grown into a competitor, taking trade and money away from British ships and tradesmen.

In its attempts to end American trade with France, the British put into effect the Orders in Council, which made any and all French-owned ports off-limits to American ships. They also began to seize American ships and conscript their crews, a practice greatly offensive to the U.S.

Monroe Doctrine

On December 2, 1823, President Monroe delivered a message to Congress in which he introduced the Monroe Doctrine. In this address, he stated that any attempts by European powers to establish new colonies on the North American continent would be considered interference in American politics. The U.S. would stay out of European matters, and expected Europe to offer America the same courtesy. This approach to foreign policy stated in no uncertain terms that America would not tolerate any new European colonies in the New World, and that events occurring in Europe would no longer influence the policies and doctrines of the U.S.

Lewis and Clark Expedition

The purchase of the Louisiana Territory from France in 1803 more than doubled the size of the United States. President Thomas Jefferson wanted to have the area mapped and explored, since much of the territory was wilderness. He chose Meriwether Lewis and William Clark to head an expedition into the Louisiana Territory. After two years, Lewis and Clark returned, having traveled all the way to the Pacific Ocean. They brought maps, detailed journals, and various types of knowledge and information about the wide expanse of land they had traversed. The Lewis and Clark Expedition opened up the west in the Louisiana Territory and beyond for further exploration and settlement.

> ➤ **Review Video: The Lewis and Clark Expedition**
> *Visit **mometrix.com/academy** and enter **Code: 570657***

Manifest Destiny

In the 1800s, many believed America was destined by God to expand west, bringing as much of the North American continent as possible under the umbrella of U.S. government. With the Northwest Ordinance and the Louisiana Purchase, over half of the continent became American. However, the rapid and relentless expansion brought conflict with the Native Americans, Great Britain, Mexico and Spain.

One result of "Manifest Destiny" was the Mexican-American War, which occurred from 1846-1848. By the end of the war, Texas, California and a large portion of what is now the American Southwest joined the growing nation. Conflict also arose over the Oregon country, shared by the US and Britain. In 1846, President James Polk resolved this problem by compromising with Britain, establishing a U.S. boundary south of the 49th parallel.

> **Review Video: Manifest Destiny**
> Visit *mometrix.com/academy* and enter *Code:* **957409**

Mexican-American War

Spain had held colonial interests in America since the 1540s—earlier even than Great Britain. In 1821, Mexico revolted against Spain and became a free nation. Likewise, this was followed by Texas, who after an 1836 revolution declared its independence.

In 1844, the Democrats pressed President Tyler to annex Texas. Unlike his predecessor, Andrew Jackson, Tyler agreed to admit Texas into the Union. In 1845, Texas became a state.

During Mexico's war for independence, they had incurred $4.5 million in war debts to the U.S. Polk offered to forgive the debts in return for New Mexico and Upper California, but Mexico refused. In 1846, war was declared in response to a Mexican attack on American troops along the southern border of Texas.

Additional conflict arose in Congress over the Wilmot Proviso, which stated that any territory the U.S. acquired from Mexico should be legally open to slavery. The war ended in 1848.

> **Review Video: Mexican-American War**
> Visit *mometrix.com/academy* and enter *Code:* **271216**

Gadsden Purchase

After the Mexican-American war, a second treaty in 1853 determined hundreds of miles of America's southwest borders. In 1854, the Gadsden Purchase was finalized, providing even more territory to aid in the building of the transcontinental railroad. This purchase added what would eventually become the southernmost regions of Arizona and New Mexico to the growing nation. The modern outline of the United States was by this time nearly complete.

The American System's influence on the American economy

Spurred by the trade conflicts of the War of 1812, and supported by Henry Clay and others, the American System set up tariffs to help protect American interests from competition with products from overseas. Reducing competition led to growth in employment and an overall increase in American industry. The higher tariffs also provided funds for the government to pay for various improvements. Congress passed high tariffs in 1816 and also chartered a federal bank. The Second Bank of the United States was given the job of regulating America's money supply.

Jacksonian Democracy

Jacksonian Democracy is largely seen as a shift from politics favoring the wealthy to politics favoring the common man. All free white males were given the right to vote, not just property owners, as had been the case previously. Jackson's approach favored the patronage system, Laissez faire economics, and relocation of the Indian tribes from the Southeast portion of the country. Jackson opposed the formation of a federal bank, and allowed the Second Band of the United States to collapse by vetoing a bill to renew the charter.

Jackson also faced the challenge of the "null and void" or nullification theory when South Carolina claimed that it could ignore or nullify any federal law it considered unconstitutional. Jackson sent troops to the state to enforce the protested tariff laws, and a compromise engineered by Henry Clay in 1833 settled the matter for the time being.

Attitudes on education in the early nineteenth century

Horace Mann, among others, felt that public schooling could help children become better citizens, keep them away from crime, prevent poverty, and help American society become more unified. His *Common School Journal* brought his ideas of the importance of education into the public consciousness. Increased literacy led to increased awareness of current events, Western expansion, and other major developments of the time period. Public interest and participation in the arts and literature also increased. By the end of the 19th century, all children had access to a free public elementary education.

Developments in transportation

As America expanded its borders, it also developed new technology to travel the rapidly growing country. Roads and railroads traversed the nation, with the Transcontinental Railroad eventually allowing travel from one coast to the other. Canals and steamboats simplified water travel and made shipping easier and less expensive. The Erie Canal (1825) connected the Great Lakes with the Hudson River. Other canals connected other major water ways, further facilitating transportation and the shipment of goods.

With growing numbers of settlers moving into the West, wagon trails developed, including the Oregon Trail, California Trail and the Santa Fe Trail. The most common vehicles seen along these westbound trails were covered wagons, also known as prairie schooners.

Industrial activity before and after 1800

During the eighteenth century, goods were often manufactured in houses or small shops. With increased technology allowing for the use of machines, factories began to develop. In factories a large volume of salable goods could be produced in a much shorter amount of time. Many Americans, including increasing numbers of immigrants, found jobs in these factories, which were in constant need of labor.

Another major invention was the cotton gin, which significantly decreased the processing time of cotton, and was a major factor in the rapid expansion of cotton production in the South.

Development of labor movements

In 1751, a group of bakers held a protest in which they stopped baking bread. This was technically the first American labor strike. In the 1830s and 1840s, labor movements began in earnest. Boston's masons, carpenters and stoneworkers protested the length of the workday, fighting to reduce it to ten hours. In 1844, a group of women in the textile industry also fought to reduce their workday to ten hours, forming the Lowell Female Labor Reform Association. Many other protests occurred and organizations developed through this time period with the same goal in mind.

Second Great Awakening

Led by Protestant evangelical leaders, the Second Great Awakening occurred between 1800 and 1830. Several missionary groups grew out of the movement, including the American Home Missionary Society, which formed in 1826. The ideas behind the Second Great Awakening focused on personal responsibility, both as an individual and in response to injustice and suffering. The American Bible Society and the American Tract Society provided literature, while various traveling preachers spread the word. New denominations arose, including the Latter Day Saints and Seventh-Day Adventists.

Another movement associated with the Second Great Awakening was the temperance movement, focused on ending the production and use of alcohol. One major organization behind the temperance movement was the Society for the Promotion of Temperance, formed in 1826 in Boston, Massachusetts.

Women's rights movement

The women's rights movement began in the 1840s with leaders including Elizabeth Cady Stanton, Ernestine Rose and Lucretia Mott. Later, in 1869, the National Woman Suffrage Association, fighting for women's right to vote, came into being. It was led by Susan B. Anthony, Ernestine Rose and Elizabeth Cady Stanton.

> **Review Video:** Elizabeth Cady Stanton
> Visit *mometrix.com/academy* and enter *Code:* **987734**

In 1848 in Seneca Falls, the first women's rights convention was held, with about three hundred attendees. The Seneca Falls Convention brought to the floor the issue that women could not vote or run for office. The convention produced a "Declaration of Sentiments" which outlined a plan for women to attain the rights they deserved. Frederick Douglass supported the women's rights movement, as well as the abolition movement. In fact, women's rights and abolition movements often went hand-in-hand through this time period.

Conflicts between the Northern and Southern States

The conflict between North and South coalesced around the issue of slavery, but other elements contributed to the growing disagreement. Though most farmers in the South worked small farms with little or no slave labor, the huge plantations run by the South's rich depended on slaves or indentured servants to remain profitable. They had also become more dependent on cotton, with slave populations growing in concert with the rapid increase in cotton production.

In the North, a more diverse agricultural economy and the growth of industry made slaves rarer. The abolitionist movement grew steadily, with Harriet Beecher Stowe's *Uncle Tom's Cabin* giving many an idea to rally around. A collection of anti-slavery organizations formed, with many actively working to free slaves in the South, often bringing them North.

Anti-slavery organizations

1. American Colonization Society—protestant churches formed this group, aimed at returning black slaves to Africa. Former slaves subsequently formed Liberia, but the colony did not do well, as the region was not well-suited for agriculture.
2. American Anti-Slavery Society—William Lloyd Garrison, a Quaker, was the major force behind this group and its newspaper, *The Liberator.*
3. Female Anti-Slavery Society—a women-only group formed by Margaretta Forten because women were not allowed to join the Anti-Slavery Society formed by her father.
4. Anti-Slavery Convention of American Women—This group continued meeting even after pro-slavery factions burned down their original meeting place.
5. Female Vigilant Society—an organization that raised funds to help the Underground Railroad, as well as slave refugees.

Missouri Compromise

By 1819, the United States had developed a tenuous balance between slave and free states, with exactly twenty-two senators in Congress from each faction. However, Missouri was ready to join the union as a state. As a slave state, it would tip the balance in Congress. To prevent this imbalance, the Missouri Compromise brought the northern part of Massachusetts into the union as Maine, established as a free state. Maine's admission balanced the admission of Missouri as a slave state, maintaining the status quo. In addition, the remaining portion of the Louisiana Purchase was to remain free north of latitude 36° 30'. Since cotton did not grow well this far north, this limitation was acceptable to congressmen representing the slave states.

However, the proposed Missouri constitution presented a problem, as it outlawed immigration of free blacks into the state. Another compromise was in order, this time proposed by Henry Clay. Clay earned his title of the Great Compromiser by stating that the U.S. Constitution overruled Missouri's.

> ➤ **Review Video: Missouri Compromise**
> *Visit **mometrix.com/academy** and enter Code: **848091***

Popular sovereignty and the Compromise of 1850

In addition to the pro-slavery and anti-slavery factions, a third group rose who felt that each individual state should decide whether to allow or permit slavery within its borders. This idea was referred to as popular sovereignty.

When California applied to join the union in 1849, the balance of congressional power was again threatened. The Compromise of 1850 introduced a group of laws meant to bring an end to the conflict.

These laws included:
- California being admitted as a free state.
- Slave trade in Washington, D.C. being outlawed.
- An increase in efforts to capture escaped slaves.
- New Mexico and Utah territories would decide individually whether or not to allow slavery.

- 134 -

In spite of these measures, debate raged each time a new state prepared to enter the union.

Kansas-Nebraska Act

With the creation of the Kansas and Nebraska territories in 1854, another debate began. Congress allowed popular sovereignty in these territories, but slavery opponents argued that the Missouri Compromise had already made slavery illegal in this region. In Kansas, two separate governments arose, one pro- and one anti-slavery. Conflict between the two factions rose to violence, leading Kansas to gain the nickname of "Bleeding Kansas."

Dred Scott Decision

Abolitionist factions coalesced around the case of Dred Scott, using his case to test the country's laws regarding slavery. Scott, a slave, had been taken by his owner from Missouri, which was a slave state. He then traveled to Illinois, a free state, then on to the Minnesota Territory, also free based on the Missouri Compromise. Then, he returned to Missouri. The owner subsequently died. Abolitionists took Scott's case to court, stating that Scott was no longer a slave but free, since he had lived in free territory. The case went to the Supreme Court.

> ➤ **Review Video: Dred Scott**
> *Visit* **mometrix.com/academy** *and enter* **Code: 364838**

The Supreme Court stated that, because Scott, as a slave, was not a U.S. citizen, his time in free states did not change his status. He also did not have the right to sue. In addition, the Court determined that the Missouri Compromise was unconstitutional, saying Congress had overstepped its bounds by outlawing slavery in the territories.

Harper's Ferry and John Brown

John Brown, an abolitionist, had participated in several anti-slavery actions, including killing five pro-slavery men in retaliation, after Lawrence, Kansas, an anti-slavery town, was sacked. He and other abolitionists also banded together to pool their funds and build a runaway slave colony.

In 1859, Brown seized a federal arsenal in Harper's Ferry, located in what is now West Virginia. Brown intended to seize guns and ammunition and lead a slave rebellion. Robert E. Lee captured Brown and 22 followers, who were subsequently tried and hanged. While Northerners took the executions as an indication that the government supported slavery, Southerners were of the opinion that most of the North supported Brown and were, in general, anti-slavery.

Presidential candidates for the 1860 election

The 1860 Presidential candidates represented four different parties, each with a different opinion on slavery.
- John Breckenridge, representing the Southern Democrats, was pro-slavery.
- Abraham Lincoln, of the Republican Party, was anti-slavery.
- Stephen Douglas, of the Northern Democrats, felt that the issue should be determined locally, on a state-by-state basis.
- John Bell, of the Constitutional Union Party, focused primarily on keeping the Union intact.

In the end, Abraham Lincoln won both the popular and electoral election. Southern states, who had sworn to secede from the Union if Lincoln was elected did so, led by South Carolina. Shortly thereafter, the Civil War began when shots were fired on Fort Sumter in Charleston.

Advantages of the North and South in the Civil War

The Northern states had significant advantages, including:
- Larger population. The North consisted of 24 states to the South's 11.
- Better transportation and finances. With railroads primarily in the North, supply chains were much more dependable, as was trade coming from overseas.
- More raw materials. The North held the majority of America's gold, as well as iron, copper and other minerals vital to wartime.

The South's advantages included:
- Better-trained military officers. Many of the Southern officers were West Point trained and had commanded in the Mexican and Indian wars.
- More familiar with weapons. The climate and lifestyle of the South meant most of the people were well versed in both guns and horses. The industrial North had less extensive experience
- Defensive position. The South felt victory was guaranteed, since they were protecting their own lands, while the North would be invading.
- Well-defined goals. The South was fighting a war to be allowed to govern themselves and preserve their way of life.

Emancipation Proclamation

The Emancipation Proclamation, issued by President Lincoln in 1863, freed all slaves in Confederate States that did not return to the Union by the beginning of the year. While the original proclamation did not free any slaves actually under Union control, it did set a precedent for the emancipation of slaves as the war progressed.

The Emancipation Proclamation worked in the Union's favor as many freed slaves and other black troops joined the Union Army. Almost 200,000 blacks fought in the Union army, and over 10,000 served in the navy. By the end of the war, over 4 million slaves had been freed, and in 1865 slavery was banned by Constitutional amendment.

> ➢ **Review Video:** <u>Emancipation Proclamation</u>
> *Visit **mometrix.com/academy** and enter **Code: 181778***

Major battles of the Civil War

The Battle of Bull Run, July 21, 1861. The First Battle of Bull Run, was the first major land battle of the war. Observers, expecting to enjoy an entertaining skirmish, set up picnics nearby. Instead, they found themselves witness to a bloodbath. Union forces were defeated, and the battle set the course of the Civil War as long, bloody and costly.

The Capture of Fort Henry by Ulysses S. Grant. This battle in February of 1862 marked the Union's first major victory.

The Battle of Gettysburg, July 1-3, 1863. Often seen as the turning point of the war, Gettysburg also saw the largest number of casualties of the war, with over 50,000 dead. Robert E. Lee was defeated, and the Confederate army, significantly crippled, withdrew.

The Overland Campaign, 1864. Grant, now in command of all the Union armies, led this high casualty campaign that eventually positioned the Union for victory.

Sherman's March to the Sea. William Tecumseh Sherman, in May of 1864, conquered Atlanta. He then continued to Savannah, destroying indiscriminately as he went.

Following Lee's defeat at the Appomattox Courthouse, General Grant accepted Lee's surrender in the home of Wilmer McLean, Appomattox, Virginia on April 9, 1865.

Lincoln's assassination

The Civil War ended with the surrender of the South on April 9, 1865. Five days later, Lincoln and his wife, Mary, attended the play *Our American Cousin* at the Ford Theater. John Wilkes Booth, unaware that the war was over, performed his part in a conspiracy to aid the Confederacy by shooting Lincoln in the back of the head. Booth was tracked down and killed by Union soldiers 12 days later. Lincoln, carried from the theater to a nearby house, died the next morning.

Thirteenth, Fourteenth and Fifteenth Amendments

The Thirteenth Amendment was passed on December 18, 1865. This amendment prohibited slavery in the United States.

> **Review Video: 13th Amendment**
> Visit *mometrix.com/academy* and enter *Code:* **800185**

The Fourteenth Amendment overturned the Dred Scott decision, and was ratified July 9, 1868. American citizenship was redefined, with all citizens guaranteed equal legal protection by all states. It also guaranteed citizens the right to file a lawsuit or serve on a jury.

> **Review Video: 14th Amendment**
> Visit *mometrix.com/academy* and enter *Code:* **851325**

The Fifteenth Amendment was ratified February 3, 1870. It states that no citizen of the United States can be denied the right to vote based on race, color, or previous status as a slave.

> **Review Video: 15th Amendment**
> Visit *mometrix.com/academy* and enter *Code:* **287199**

Reconstruction and the Freedmen's Bureau

In the aftermath of the Civil War, the South was left in chaos. From 1865 to 1877, government on all levels worked to help restore order to the South, ensure civil rights to the freed slaves, and bring the Confederate states back into the Union. In 1866, Congress passed the Reconstruction Acts, putting former Confederate states under military rule.

The Freedmen's Bureau was formed to help freedmen and give assistance to whites in the South who needed basic necessities like food and clothing. Many in the South felt the Freedmen's Bureau worked to set freed slaves against their former owners. The Bureau was intended to help former

- 137 -

slaves become self-sufficient, and to keep them from falling prey to those who would take advantage of them.

Phases of Reconstruction

Presidential Reconstruction – largely driven by President Andrew Johnson's policies, the Presidential phase of Reconstruction was lenient on the South and allowed continued discrimination against and control over blacks.

Congressional Reconstruction – Congress, controlled largely by Radical Republicans, took a different stance, providing a wider range of civil rights for blacks and greater control over Southern government. Congressional Reconstruction is marked by military control of the former Confederate States.

Redemption – Gradually, the Confederate states were readmitted into the union. During this time, white Democrats took over the government of most of the South. Troops finally departed the South in 1877.

> **Review Video: <u>Reconstruction</u>**
> Visit *mometrix.com/academy* and enter *Code*: **790561**

Radical and Moderate Republicans

The Radical Republicans wished to treat the South quite harshly after the war. Thaddeus Stephens, the House Leader, suggested that the Confederate States be treated as if they were territories again, with ten years of military rule and territorial government before they would be readmitted. They also wanted to give all black men the right to vote. Former Confederate soldiers would be required to swear they had not fought against the Union in order to be granted full rights as American citizens.

By contrast, the moderate Republicans wanted only black men who were literate or who had served as Union troops to be able to vote. All Confederate soldiers except troop leaders would also be able to vote. Before his death, Lincoln had favored a more moderate approach to Reconstruction, hoping this approach might bring some states back into the Union before the end of the war.

Black Codes and the Civil Rights bill

The Black Codes were proposed to control freed slaves. They would not be allowed to bear arms, assemble, serve on juries, or testify against whites. Schools would be segregated, and unemployed blacks could be arrested and forced to work.

The Civil Rights bill countered these codes, providing much wider rights for the freed slaves.

Andrew Johnson, who became president after Lincoln's death, supported the Black Codes, and vetoed the Civil Rights bill. Congress overrode his veto and impeached Johnson, the culmination of tensions between Congress and the president. He came within a single vote of being convicted.

Carpetbaggers and Scalawags

The chaos in the south attracted a number of people seeking to fill the power vacuums and take advantage of the economic disruption.

Scalawags were southern Whites who aligned with Freedmen to take over local governments. Many in the South who could have filled political offices refused to take the necessary oath required to grant them the right to vote, leaving many opportunities for Scalawags and others.

Carpetbaggers were northerners who traveled to the South for various reasons. Some provided assistance, while others sought to make money or to acquire political power during this chaotic period.

Transcontinental railroad

In 1869, the Union Pacific Railroad completed the first section of a planned transcontinental railroad. This section went from Omaha, Nebraska to Sacramento, California. With the rise of the railroad, products were much more easily transported across country. While this was positive overall for industry throughout the country, it was often damaging to family farmers, who found themselves paying high shipping costs for smaller supply orders while larger companies received major discounts.

Ninety percent of the workers constructing the railroad were Chinese, working in very dangerous conditions for very low pay.

Limits on immigration in the 19th century

In 1870, the Naturalization Act put limits on U.S. citizenship, allowing full citizenship only to whites and those of African descent. The Chinese Exclusion Act of 1882 put limits on Chinese immigration. The Immigration Act of 1882 taxed immigrants, charging fifty cents per person. These funds helped pay administrative costs for regulating immigration. Ellis Island opened in 1892 as a processing center those arriving in New York. 1921 saw the Emergency Quota Act passed, also known as the Johnson Quota Act, which severely limited the number of immigrants allowed into the country.

Agriculture as a result of technological advances

During the mid 1800s, irrigation techniques improved significantly. Advances occurred in cultivation and breeding, as well as fertilizer use and crop rotation. In the Great Plains, also known as the Great American Desert, the dense soil was finally cultivated with steel plows. In 1892, gasoline-powered tractors arrived, and were widely used by 1900.

Other advancements in agriculture's tool set included barbed wire fences, combines, silos, deep-water wells, and the cream separator.

Major legislation for improving agriculture

The Department of Agriculture came into being in 1862, working for the interests of farmers and ranchers across the country.

The Morrill Land-Grant Acts were passed in 1862, allowing land-grant colleges.

In conjunction with land-grant colleges, the Hatch Act of 1887 brought agriculture experimental stations into the picture, helping discover new farming techniques.

In 1914, the Smith-Lever Act provided cooperative programs to help educate people about food, home economics, community development and agriculture. Related agriculture extension programs helped farmers increase crop production to feed the rapidly growing nation.

Major inventors from the 1800s

1. Alexander Graham Bell—the telephone
2. Orville and Wilbur Wright—the airplane
3. Richard Gatling—the machine gun
4. Walter Hunt, Elias Howe and Isaac Singer—the sewing machine
5. Nikola Tesla—alternating current
6. George Eastman—the camera
7. Thomas Edison—light bulbs, motion pictures, the phonograph
8. Samuel Morse—the telegraph
9. Charles Goodyear—vulcanized rubber
10. Cyrus McCormick—the reaper
11. George Westinghouse—the transformer, the air brake

This was an active period for invention, with about 700,000 patents registered between 1860 and 1900.

Gilded Age

The time period from the end of the Civil War to the beginning of the First World War is often referred to as the Gilded Age, or the Second Industrial Revolution. The U.S. was changing from an agriculturally based economy to an industrial economy, with rapid growth accompanying the shift. In addition, the country itself was expanding, spreading into the seemingly unlimited West.

This time period saw the beginning of banks, department stores, chain stores, and trusts—all familiar features of our modern-day landscape. Cities also grew rapidly, and large numbers of immigrants arrived in the country, swelling the urban ranks.

Populist Party

A major recession struck the United States during the 1890s, with crop prices falling dramatically. Drought compounded the problems, leaving many American farmers in crippling debt. The Farmers Alliance formed, drawing the rural poor into a single political entity.

Recession also affected the more industrial parts of the country. The Knights of Labor, formed in 1869 by Uriah Stephens, was able to unite workers into a union to protect their rights. Dissatisfied by views espoused by industrialists, these two groups, the Farmers Alliance and the Knights of Labor, joined to form the Populist Party.

Some of the elements of the party's platform included:
- National currency
- Income tax
- Government ownership of railroads, telegraph and telephone systems
- Secret ballot for voting
- Immigration restriction
- Term limits for President and Vice-President

The Populist Party was in favor of decreasing elitism and making the voice of the common man more easily heard in the political process.

Growth of the labor movement through the late nineteenth century

The first large, well-organized strike occurred in 1892. Called the Homestead Strike, it occurred when the Amalgamated Association of Iron and Steel Works struck against the Carnegie Steel Company. Gunfire ensued, and Carnegie was able to eliminate the plant's union.

In 1894, workers, led by Eugene Debs, initiated the Pullman Strike after the Pullman Palace Car Co. cut their wages by 28 percent. President Grover Cleveland called in troops to break up the strike on the grounds that it interfered with mail delivery.

Mary Harris Jones, also known as Mother Jones, organized the Children's Crusade to protest child labor. A protest march proceeded to the home of President Theodore Roosevelt in 1902. Jones also worked with the United Mine Workers of America, and helped found the Industrial Workers of the World.

Panic of 1893

Far from a U.S.-centric event, the Panic of 1893 was an economic crisis that affected most of the globe. As a response to the Panic, President Grover Cleveland repealed the Sherman Silver Purchase Act, afraid it had caused the downturn rather than boosting the economy as intended.

The Panic led to bankruptcies, with railroads going under and factory unemployment rising as high as 25 percent. In the end, the Republican Party regained power due to the economic crisis.

Progressive Era

From the 1890s to the end of the First World War, Progressives set forth an ideology that drove many levels of society and politics. The Progressives were in favor of workers' rights and safety, and wanted measures taken against waste and corruption. They felt science could help improve society, and that the government could—and should—provide answers to a variety of social problems.

Progressives came from a wide variety of backgrounds, but were united in their desire to improve society.

> ➤ **Review Video: Progressive Era**
> Visit *mometrix.com/academy* and enter *Code:* **722394**

Muckrakers

"Muckrakers" was a term used to identify aggressive investigative journalists who brought to light scandals, corruption, and many other wrongs being perpetrated in late nineteenth century society. Among these intrepid writers were:
- Ida Tarbell—he exposed the Standard Oil Trust.
- Jacob Riis—a photographer, he helped improve the lot of the poor in New York.
- Lincoln Steffens—he worked to expose political corruption.
- Upton Sinclair—his book *The Jungle* led to reforms in the meat packing industry.

Through the work of these journalists, many new policies came into being, including workmen's compensation, child labor laws, and trust-busting.

Sixteenth, Seventeenth, Eighteenth and Nineteenth Amendments

The early twentieth century saw several amendments made to the U.S. Constitution. These included:

- Sixteenth Amendment, 1913 established a graduated income tax.
- Seventeenth Amendment, 1913 allowed direct election of Senators.
- Eighteenth Amendment, 1919 prohibited the sale, production and importation of alcohol. This amendment was later repealed by the Twenty-first Amendment.
- Nineteenth Amendment, 1920 gave women the right to vote.

These amendments largely grew out of the Progressive Era, as many citizens worked to improve American society.

Federal Trade Commission

Muckrakers such as Ida Tarbell and Lincoln Steffens brought to light the damaging trend of trusts—huge corporations working to monopolize areas of commerce and so control prices and distribution. The Sherman Act and the Clayton Antitrust Act set out guidelines for competition among corporations and set out to eliminate these trusts. The Federal Trade Commission was formed in order to enforce antitrust measures and ensure companies were operated fairly and did not create controlling monopolies.

Government dealings with Native Americans in the late 19th century

America's westward expansion led to conflict and violent confrontations with Native Americans such as the Battle of Little Bighorn. In 1876, the American government ordered all Indians to relocate to reservations. Lack of compliance led to the Dawes Act in 1887, which ordered assimilation rather than separation. This act remained in effect until 1934. Reformers also forced Indian children to attend Indian Boarding Schools, where they were not allowed to speak their native language and were forced to accept Christianity. Children were often abused in these schools, and were indoctrinated to abandon their identity as Native Americans.

In 1890, the massacre at Wounded Knee, accompanied by Geronimo's surrender, led the Native Americans to work to preserve their culture rather than fight for their lands.

Spanish-American War

Spain had controlled Cuba since the fifteenth century. Over the centuries, the Spanish had quashed a variety of revolts. In 1886, slavery ended in Cuba, and another revolt was rising.

In the meantime, the US had expressed interest in Cuba, offering Spain $130 million for the island in 1853, during Franklin Pierce's presidency. In 1898, the Cuban revolt was underway. In spite of various factions supporting the Cubans, the US President, William McKinley, refused to recognize the rebellion, preferring negotiation over involvement in war. Then The Maine, a US battleship in Havana Harbor, was blown up, costing nearly 300 lives. The US declared war two months later, and the war ended four months later with a Spanish surrender.

The Spanish-American war, 1898-1902, saw a number of Native Americans serving with Teddy Roosevelt in the Rough Riders. Apache scouts accompanied General John J. Pershing to Mexico, hoping to find Pancho Villa. More than 17,000 Native Americans were drafted into service for World War I, though at the time they were not considered as legal citizens. In 1924, Indians were finally granted official citizenship by the Indian Citizenship Act.

After decades of relocation, forced assimilation and outright genocide the number of Native Americans in the U.S. has greatly declined. Though many Native Americans have chosen—or have been forced—to assimilate, about 300 reservations exist today, with most of their inhabitants living in abject poverty.

Panama Canal

Initial work began on the Panama Canal in 1880, though the idea had been discussed since the 1500s. The Canal greatly reduces the length and time needed to sail from one ocean to the other by connecting the Atlantic to the Pacific through the Isthmus of Panama, which joins South America to North America. Before the Canal was built, travelers had to sail all the way around South America to reach the West Coast of the US.

The French began the work in 1880, after successfully completing the Suez Canal, connecting the Mediterranean Sea to the Red Sea. However, their efforts quickly fell apart. The US moved in to take over, completing the complex canal in 1914.

The Panama Canal was constructed as a lock-and-lake canal, with ships actually lifted on locks to travel from one lake to another over the rugged, mountainous terrain. In order to maintain control of the Canal Zone, the US assisted Panama in its battle for independence from Columbia.

Roosevelt's "Big Stick Diplomacy"

Theodore Roosevelt's famous quote, "Speak softly and carry a big stick," is supposedly of African origins, at least according to Roosevelt. He used this proverb to justify expanded involvement in foreign affairs during his tenure as President. The US military was deployed to protect American interests in Latin America. Roosevelt also worked to maintain an equal or greater influence in Latin America than those held by European interests.

As a result, the US Navy grew larger, and the US generally became more involved in foreign affairs. Roosevelt felt that if any country was left vulnerable to control by Europe, due to economic issues or political instability, the US had not only a right to intervene, but was obligated to do so. This led to US involvement in Cuba, Nicaragua, Haiti and the Dominican Republic over several decades leading into the First and Second World Wars.

William Howard Taft's "Dollar Diplomacy"

During William Howard Taft's presidency, Taft instituted "Dollar Diplomacy." This approach was used as a description of American efforts to influence Latin America and East Asia through economic rather than military means. Taft saw past efforts in these areas to be political and warlike, while his efforts focused on peaceful economic goals. His justification of the policy was to protect the Panama Canal, which was vital to US trade interests.

In spite of Taft's assurance that Dollar Diplomacy was a peaceful approach, many interventions proved violent. During Latin American revolts, such as those in Nicaragua, the US sent troops to settle the revolutions. Afterwards, bankers moved in to help support the new leaders through loans. Dollar Diplomacy continued until 1913, when Woodrow Wilson was elected President.

International diplomacy of Woodrow Wilson

Turning away from Taft's "Dollar Diplomacy", Wilson instituted a foreign policy he referred to as "moral diplomacy." This approach still influences American foreign policy today.

Wilson felt that representative government and democracy in all countries would lead to worldwide stability. Democratic governments, he felt, would be less likely to threaten American interests.

He also saw the US and Great Britain as the great role models in this area, as well as champions of world peace and self-government. Free trade and international commerce would allow the US to speak out regarding world events.

Main elements of Wilson's policies included:
1. Maintaining a strong military
2. Promoting democracy throughout the world
3. Expanding international trade to boost the American economy

First World War

The First World War occurred from 1914 to 1918 and was fought largely in Europe. Triggered by the assassination of Austrian Archduke Francis Ferdinand, the war rapidly escalated. At the beginning of the conflict, Woodrow Wilson declared the US neutral. Major events influencing US involvement included:

Sinking of the Lusitania
The British passenger liner RMS Lusitania was sunk by a German U-boat in 1915. Among the 1,000 civilian victims were 100 Americans. Outraged by this act, many Americans began to push for US involvement in the war, using the Lusitania as a rallying cry.

German U-boat aggression
Wilson continued to keep the US out of the war, with his 1916 reelection slogan, "He kept us out of war." While he continued to work toward an end of the war, German U-boats began to indiscriminately attack American and Canadian merchant ships carrying supplies to Germany's enemies in Europe.

Zimmerman Note
The final event that brought the US into World War I was the interception of the Zimmerman Note. In this telegram, Germany communicated with the Mexican government its intentions to invade the US with Mexico's assistance.

> ➤ **Review Video: World War I**
> *Visit **mometrix.com/academy** and enter **Code: 947845***

US support toward WWI

American railroads came under government control in December 1917. The widespread system was consolidated into a single system, with each region assigned a director. This greatly increased the efficiency of the railroad system, allowing the railroads to supply both domestic and military needs. Control returned to private ownership in 1920. In 1918, telegraph, telephone and cable services also came under Federal control, to be returned to private management the next year.

The American Red Cross supported the war effort by knitting clothes for Army and Navy troops. They also helped supply hospital and refugee clothing and surgical dressings. Over eight million people participated in this effort.

To generate wartime funds, the US government sold Liberty Bonds. In four issues, they sold nearly $25 billion—more than one fifth of Americans purchased them. After the war, Liberty Bonds were replaced with Victory Bonds.

Wilson's Fourteen Points

President Woodrow Wilson proposed Fourteen Points as the basis for a peace settlement to end the war. Presented to the US Congress in January 1918, the Fourteen Points included:
- Five points outlining general ideals
- Eight points to resolve immediate problems of political and territorial nature
- One point proposing an organization of nations with the intent of maintaining world peace

In November of that same year, Germany agreed to an armistice, assuming the final treaty would be based on the Fourteen Points. However, during the peace conference in Paris 1919, there was much disagreement, leading to a final agreement that punished Germany and the other Central Powers much more than originally intended. Henry Cabot Lodge, who had become the Foreign Relations Committee chairman in 1918, wanted an unconditional surrender from Germany.

A League of Nations was included in the Treaty of Versailles at Wilson's insistence. The Senate rejected the Treaty of Versailles, and in the end Wilson refused to concede to Lodge's demands. As a result, the US did not join the League of Nations.

> **Review Video:** Woodrow Wilson's 14 Points
> Visit *mometrix.com/academy* and enter *Code:* 335789

America in the 1920s

The post-war '20s saw many Americans moving from the farm to the city, with growing prosperity in the US. The Roaring Twenties, or the Jazz Age, was driven largely by growth in the automobile and entertainment industries. Individuals like Charles Lindbergh, the first aviator to make a solo flight cross the Atlantic Ocean, added to the American admiration of individual accomplishment. Telephone lines, distribution of electricity, highways, the radio, and other inventions brought great changes to everyday life.

The Harlem Renaissance saw a number of African American artists settling in Harlem, New York City. This community produced a number of well-known artists and writers, including Langston Hughes, Nella Larson, Zora Neale Hurston, Claude McKay, Countee Cullen and Jean Toomer.

The growth of jazz, also largely driven by African Americans, defined the Jazz Age. Its unconventional, improvisational style matched the growing sense of optimism and exploration of the decade. Originating as an offshoot of the blues, jazz began in New Orleans. Some significant jazz musicians were Duke Ellington, Louis Armstrong and Jelly Roll Morton.

Big Band and Swing Jazz also developed in the 1920s. Well-known musicians of this movement included Bing Crosby, Frank Sinatra, Count Basie, Benny Goodman, Billie Holiday, Ella Fitzgerald and The Dorsey Brothers.

National Origins Act of 1924

The National Origins Act (Johnson-Reed Act) placed limitations on immigration. The number of immigrants allowed into the US was based on the population of each nationality of immigrants who were living in the country in 1890. Only two percent of each nationality's 1890 population numbers were allowed to immigrate. This led to great disparities between immigrants from various nations, and Asian immigration was not allowed at all.

Some of the impetus behind the Johnson-Reed Act came as a result of paranoia following the Russian Revolution. Fear of communist influences in the US led to a general fear of immigrants.

Red Scare

World War I created many jobs, but after the war ended these jobs disappeared, leaving many unemployed. In the wake of these employment changes the International Workers of the World and the Socialist Party, headed by Eugene Debs, became more and more visible. Workers initiated strikes in an attempt to regain the favorable working conditions that had been put into place before the war. Unfortunately, many of these strikes became violent, and the actions were blamed on "Reds," or Communists, for trying to spread their views into America. With the Bolshevik Revolution being recent news in Russia, many Americans feared a similar revolution might occur here. The Red Scare ensued, with many individuals jailed for supposedly holding communist, anarchist or socialist beliefs.

Growth of civil rights for African Americans

Marcus Garvey founded the Universal Negro Improvement Association, which became a large and active organization focused on building black nationalism. In 1911, the National Association for the Advancement of Colored People (NAACP) came into being, working to defeat Jim Crow laws. The NAACP also helped prevent racial segregation from becoming federal law, fought against lynchings, helped black soldiers in WWI become officers, and helped defend the Scottsboro Boys, who were unjustly accused of rape.

Ku Klux Klan

In 1866, Confederate Army veterans came together to fight against Reconstruction in the South, forming a group called the Ku Klux Klan (KKK). With white supremacist beliefs, including anti-Semitism, nativism, anti-Catholicism, and overt racism, this organization relied heavily on violence to get its message across. In 1915, they grew again in power, using a film called *The Birth of a Nation*, by D.W. Griffith, to spread their ideas. In the 1920s, the reach of the KKK spread far into the North and Midwest, and members controlled a number of state governments. Its membership and power began to decline during the Great Depression, but experienced a major resurgence later.

American Civil Liberties Union

The American Civil Liberties Union (ACLU), founded in 1920, grew from the American Union Against Militarism. This former organization helped conscientious objectors avoid going to war during WWI, and also helped those being prosecuted under the Espionage Act (1917) and the Sedition Act (1918), many of whom were immigrants. Their major goals were to protect immigrants and other citizens who were threatened with prosecution for their political beliefs, and to support labor unions, which were also under threat by the government during the Red Scare.

Anti-Defamation League

In 1913, the Anti-Defamation League was formed to prevent anti-Semitic behavior and practices. Its actions also worked to prevent all forms of racism, and to prevent individuals from being discriminated against for any reason involving their race. They spoke against the Ku Klux Klan, as well as other racist or anti-Semitic organizations. This organization still exists, and still works to fight discrimination against minorities of all kinds.

Great Depression

The Great Depression, which began in 1929 with the Stock Market Crash, grew out of several factors that had developed over the previous years including:
- Growing economic disparity between the rich and middle-class, with the rich amassing wealth much more quickly than the lower classes
- Disparity in economic distribution in industries
- Growing use of credit, leading to an inflated demand for some goods
- Government support of new industries rather than providing additional support for agriculture
- Risky stock market investments, leading to the stock market crash

Additional factors contributing to the Depression also included the Labor Day Hurricane in the Florida Keys (1935) and the Great Hurricane of 1938, in Long Island, along with the Dust Bowl in the Great Plains, which destroyed crops and resulted in the displacement of as many as 2.5 million people.

> ➢ **Review Video: The Great Depression**
> *Visit mometrix.com/academy and enter Code: 635912*

Franklin D. Roosevelt's "New Deal"

Franklin D. Roosevelt was elected president in 1932 with his promise of a "New Deal" for Americans. His goals were to provide government work programs to provide jobs, wages and relief to numerous workers throughout the beleaguered US. Congress gave Roosevelt almost free rein to produce relief legislation.

The goals of this legislation were:
- Relief: Accomplished largely by creating jobs
- Recovery: Stimulate the economy through the National Recovery Administration
- Reform: Pass legislation to prevent future similar economic crashes

The Roosevelt Administration also passed legislation regarding ecological issues, including the Soil Conservation Service, aimed at preventing another Dust Bowl.

The administration passed several laws and established several institutions to initiate the "reform" portion of the New Deal, including:
- Glass-Steagall Act—separated investment from the business of banking
- Securities Exchange Commission (SEC)—helped regulate Wall Street investment practices, making them less dangerous to the overall economy
- Wagner Act—provided worker and union rights to improve relations between employees and employers. This act was later amended by the Taft-Hartley Act of 1947 and the Landrum Griffin Act of 1959, which further clarified certain elements.
- Social Security Act of 1935—provided pensions as well as unemployment insurance
- Davis-Bacon Act (1931)—provided fair compensation for contractors and subcontractors.
- Walsh-Healey Act (1936)—established a minimum wage, child labor laws, safety standards, and overtime pay.

Other actions focused on insuring bank deposits and adjusting the value of American currency. Most of these regulatory agencies and government policies and programs still exist today.

Roosevelt's "alphabet organizations"

So-called alphabet organizations set up during Roosevelt's administration included:
- Civilian Conservation Corps (CCC)—provided jobs in the forestry service
- Agricultural Adjustment Administration (AAA)—increased agricultural income by adjusting both production and prices.
- Tennessee Valley Authority (TVA)—organized projects to build dams in the Tennessee River for flood control and production of electricity, resulting in increased productivity for industries in the area, and easier navigation of the Tennessee River
- Public Works Administration (PWA) and Civil Works Administration (CWA)—initiated over 34,000 projects, providing employment
- Works Progress Administration (WPA)—helped unemployed persons to secure employment on government work projects or elsewhere

Interventionist and Isolationist approaches in World War II

When war broke out in Europe in 1939, President Roosevelt stated that the US would remain neutral. However, his overall approach was considered "interventionist," as he was willing to provide any necessary aid to the Allies short of actually entering the conflict. Thus the US supplied a wide variety of war materials to the Allied nations.

Isolationists believed the US should not provide any aid to the Allies, including supplies. They felt Roosevelt, by assisting the Allies, was leading the US into a war for which it was not prepared. Led by Charles A. Lindbergh, the Isolationists believed any involvement in the European conflict endangered the US by weakening its national defense.

US entrance into WWII

In 1937, Japan invaded China, prompting the US to halt all exports to Japan. Roosevelt also did not allow Japanese interests to withdraw money held in US banks. In 1941, General Tojo rose to power as the Japanese Premier. Recognizing America's ability to bring a halt to Japan's expansion, he authorized the bombing of Pearl Harbor on December 7, of that year. The US responded by declaring war on Japan. Because of the Tipartite Pact among the Axis Powers, Germany and Italy then declared war on the US, followed by Bulgaria and Hungary.

Surrender of Germany

In 1941, Hitler violated the non-aggression pact he had signed with Stalin in 1939 by invading the USSR. Stalin then joined the Allies. Stalin, Roosevelt and Winston Churchill planned to defeat Germany first, then Japan, bringing the war to an end.

Starting in 1942 through 1943, the Allies drove Axis forces out of Africa. In addition, the Germans were soundly defeated at Stalingrad.

Between July 1943 and May 1945, Allied troops liberated Italy. June 6, 1944, known as D-Day, the Allies invaded France at Normandy. Soviet troops moved on the eastern front at the same time, driving German forces back. April 25, 1945, Berlin was surrounded by Soviet troops. On May 7, Germany surrendered.

Surrender of Japan

War continued with Japan after Germany's surrender. Japanese forces had taken a large portion of Southeast Asia and the Western Pacific, all the way to the Aleutian Islands in Alaska. General Doolittle bombed several Japanese cities while American troops scored a victory at Midway. Additional fighting in the Battle of the Coral Sea further weakened Japan's position. As a final blow, the US dropped two atomic bombs, one on Hiroshima and the other on Nagasaki, Japan. This was the first time atomic bombs had ever been used in warfare, and the devastation was horrific and demoralizing. Japan surrendered on September 2, 1945.

Yalta Conference and the Potsdam Conference

In February 1945, Joseph Stalin, Franklin D. Roosevelt and Winston Churchill met in Yalta to discuss the post-war treatment of Europe, particularly Germany. Though Germany had not yet surrendered, its defeat was imminent. After Germany's official surrender, Clement Attlee, Harry Truman and Joseph Stalin met to formalize those plans. This meeting was called the Potsdam Conference.

Basic provisions of these agreements included:
- Dividing Germany and Berlin into four zones of occupation
- Demilitarization of Germany
- Poland remaining under Soviet control
- Outlawing the Nazi Party
- Trials for Nazi leaders
- Relocation of numerous German citizens
- The USSR joined the United Nations, established in 1945
- Establishment of the United Nations Security Council, consisting of the US, the UK, the USSR, China and France

Agreements made with post-war Japan

General Douglas MacArthur directed the American military occupation of Japan after the country surrendered. The goals the US occupation included removing Japan's military and making the country a democracy. A 1947 constitution removed power from the emperor and gave it to the people, as well as granting voting rights to women. Japan was no longer allowed to declare war, and a group of 25 government officials were tried for war crimes. In 1951, the US finally signed a peace treaty with Japan. This treaty allowed Japan to rearm itself for purposes of self-defense, but stripped the country of the empire it had built overseas.

Changes in US treatment of immigrants during and after World War II

In 1940, the US passed the Alien Registration Act, which required all aliens older than fourteen to be fingerprinted and registered. They were also required to report changes of address within five days.

Tension between whites and Japanese immigrants in California, which had been building since the beginning of the century, came to a head with the bombing of Pearl Harbor in 1941. Believing that even those Japanese living in the US were likely to be loyal to their native country, the president ordered numerous Japanese to be arrested on suspicion of subversive action isolated in exclusion zones known as War Relocation Camps. Over 120,000 Japanese Americans, two thirds of them citizens of the US, were sent to these camps during the war.

442nd Regimental Combat Team, the Tuskegee Airmen, and the Navajo Code Talkers

The 442nd Regimental Combat Team consisted of Japanese Americans fighting in Europe for the US. The most highly decorated unit per member in US history, they suffered a 93 percent casualty rate during the war.

The Tuskegee Airmen were African American aviators, the first black Americans allowed to fly for the military. In spite of not being eligible to become official navy pilots, they flew over 15,000 missions and were highly decorated.

The Navajo Code Talkers were native Navajo who used their traditional language to transmit information among Allied forces. Because Navajo is a language and not simply a code, the Axis powers were never able to translate it. Use of Navajo Code Talkers to transmit information was instrumental in the taking of Iwo Jima and other major victories of the war.

Circumstances and opportunities for women during World War II

Women served widely in the military during WWII, working in numerous positions, including the Flight Nurses Corps. Women also moved into the workforce while men were overseas, leading to over 19 million women in the US workforce by 1944. Rosie the Riveter stood as a symbol of these women and a means of recruiting others to take needed positions. Women, as well as their families left behind during wartime, also grew Victory Gardens to help provide food.

Atomic bomb

The atomic bomb, developed during WWII, was the most powerful bomb ever invented. A single bomb, carried by a single plane, held enough power to destroy an entire city. This devastating effect was demonstrated with the bombing of Hiroshima and Nagasaki in 1945 in what later became a

- 150 -

controversial move, but ended the war. The bombings resulted in as many as 200,000 immediate deaths and many more as time passed after the bombings, mostly due to radiation poisoning.

Whatever the arguments against the use of "The Bomb", the post WWII era saw many countries develop similar weapons to match the newly expanded military power of the US. The impact of those developments and use of nuclear weapons continues to haunt international relations today.

State of the US after World War II

Following WWII, the US became the strongest political power in the world, becoming a major player in world affairs and foreign policies. The US determined to stop the spread of Communism, naming itself the "arsenal of democracy."

In addition, America had emerged with a greater sense of itself as a single, integrated nation, with many regional and economic differences diminished. The government worked for greater equality and the growth of communications increased contact among different areas of the country.

Both the aftermath of the Great Depression and the necessities of WWII had given the government greater control over various institutions as well as the economy. This also meant the American government took on greater responsibility for the well being of its citizens, both in the domestic arena, such as providing basic needs, and in protecting them from foreign threats. This increased role of providing basic necessities for all Americans has been criticized by some as "the welfare state."

> **Review Video: <u>World War II</u>**
> *Visit **mometrix.com/academy** and enter **Code: 759402***

Harry S. Truman

Harry S. Truman took over the presidency from Franklin D. Roosevelt near the end of WW II. He made the final decision to drop atomic bombs on Japan, and he played a major role in the final decisions regarding treatment of post-war Germany.

On the domestic front, Truman initiated a 21-point plan known as the Fair Deal. This plan expanded Social Security, provided public housing, and made the Fair Employment Practices Act permanent. Truman helped support Greece and Turkey, under threat from the USSR, supported South Korea against communist North Korea, and helped with recovery in Western Europe. He also participated in the formation of NATO, the North Atlantic Treaty Organization.

Korean War

The Korean War began in 1950 and ended in 1953. For the first time in history, a world organization—the United Nations—played a military role in a war. North Korea sent Communist troops into South Korea, seeking to bring the entire country under Communist control. The UN sent out a call to member nations, asking them to support South Korea. Truman sent troops, as did many other UN member nations. The war ended three years later with a truce rather than a peace treaty, and Korea remains divided at 38 degrees North Latitude, with Communist rule remaining in the North and a democratic government ruling the South.

Dwight D. Eisenhower

Eisenhower carried out a middle-of-the-road foreign policy and brought about several steps forward in equal rights. He worked to minimize tensions during the Cold War, and negotiated a peace treaty with Russia after the death of Stalin. He enforced desegregation by sending troops to Little Rock, Arkansas when the schools there were desegregated, and also ordered the desegregation of the military. Organizations formed during his administration included the Department of Health, Education and Welfare, and the National Aeronautics and Space Administration (NASA).

John F. Kennedy

Although cut short by his assassination, during his term JFK instituted economic programs that led to a period of continuous expansion in the US unmatched since before WW II. He formed the Alliance for Progress and the Peace Corps, organizations intended to help developing nations. He also oversaw the passage of new civil rights legislation, and drafted plans to attack poverty and its causes, along with support of the arts. Kennedy's presidency ended when he was assassinated by Lee Harvey Oswald in 1963.

Cuban Missile Crisis

The Cuban Missile Crisis occurred in 1962, during John F. Kennedy's presidency. Russian Premier Nikita Khrushchev decided to place nuclear missiles in Cuba to protect the island from invasion by the US. American U-2 planes flying over the island photographed the missile bases as they were being built. Tensions rose, with the US concerned about nuclear missiles so close to its shores, and the USSR concerned about American missiles that had been placed in Turkey. Eventually, the missile sites were removed, and a US naval blockade turned back Soviet ships carrying missiles to Cuba. During negotiations, the US agreed to remove their missiles from Turkey and agreed to sell surplus wheat to the USSR. A telephone hot line between Moscow and Washington was set up to allow instant communication between the two heads of state to prevent similar incidents in the future.

Lyndon B. Johnson

Kennedy's Vice President, Lyndon Johnson, assumed the presidency after Kennedy's assassination. He supported civil rights bills, tax cuts, and other wide-reaching legislation that Kennedy had also supported. Johnson saw America as a "Great Society," and enacted legislation to fight disease and poverty, renew urban areas, support education and environmental conservation. Medicare was instituted under his administration. He continued Kennedy's supported of space exploration, and he is also known, although less positively, for his handling of the Vietnam War.

Civil Rights Movement

In the 1950s, post-war America was experiencing a rapid growth in prosperity. However, African Americans found themselves left behind. Following the lead of Mahatma Gandhi, who lead similar class struggles in India; African Americans began to demand equal rights. Major figures in this struggle included: Rosa Parks—often called the "mother of the Civil Rights Movement," her refusal to give up her seat on the bus to a white man served as a seed from which the movement grew. Martin Luther King, Jr.—the best-known leader of the movement, King drew on Gandhi's beliefs and encouraged non-violent opposition. He led a march on Washington in 1963, received the Nobel

Peace Prize in 1968, and was assassinated in 1968. Malcolm X—espousing less peaceful means of change, Malcolm X became a Black Muslim, and supported black nationalism. Stokely Carmichael—Carmichael invented the term "Black Power" and served as head of the Student Nonviolent Coordinating Committee. He believed in black pride and black culture, and felt separate political and social institutions should be developed for blacks. Adam Clayton Powell—chairman of the Coordinating Committee for Employment, he led rent strikes and other actions, as well as a bus boycott, to increase the hiring of blacks. Jesse Jackson—Jackson was selected to head the Chicago Operation Breadbasket in 1966 by Martin Luther King, Jr., and went on to organize boycotts and other actions. He also had an unsuccessful run for President.

Montgomery Bus Boycott—in 1955, Rosa Parks refused to give her seat on the bus to a white man. As a result, she was tried and convicted of disorderly conduct and of violating local ordinances. A 381-day boycott ensued, protesting segregation on public buses.

Desegregation of Little Rock—In 1957, after the Supreme Court decision on Brown vs. Board of Education, which declared "separate but equal" unconstitutional, the Arkansas school board voted to desegregate their schools. Even though Arkansas was considered progressive, its governor brought in the National Guard to prevent nine black students from entering Central High School in Little Rock. President Eisenhower responded by federalizing the National Guard and ordering them to stand down.

Birmingham Campaign—Protestors organized a variety of actions such as sit-ins and an organized march to launch a voting campaign. When the City of Birmingham declared the protests illegal, the protestors, including Martin Luther King, Jr., persisted and were arrested and jailed.

Legislation passed as a result of the Civil Rights movement

1. Brown vs. Board of Education (1954)—the Supreme Court declared that "separate but equal" accommodations and services were unconstitutional.
2. Civil Rights Act of 1964—declared discrimination illegal in employment, education, or public accommodation.
3. Voting Rights Act of 1965—ended various activities practiced, mostly in the South, to bar blacks from exercising their voting rights. These included poll taxes and literacy tests.

Vietnam War

After World War II, the US pledged, as part of its foreign policy, to come to the assistance of any country threatened by Communism. When Vietnam was divided into a Communist North and democratic South, much like Korea before it, the eventual attempts by the North to unify the country under Communist rule led to intervention by the US.

On the home front, the Vietnam War became more and more unpopular politically, with Americans growing increasingly discontent with the inability of the US to achieve the goals it had set for the Asian country. When President Richard Nixon took office in 1969, his escalation of the war led to protests at Kent State in Ohio, during which several students were killed by National Guard troops.

Protests continued, eventually resulting in the end of the compulsory draft in 1973. In that same year, the US departed Vietnam. In 1975, the south surrendered, and Vietnam became a unified country under Communist rule.

- 153 -

US Cold War foreign policy acts

Marshall Plan—sent aid to war-torn Europe after WW II, largely focusing on preventing the spread of communism.

Containment—proposed by George F. Kennan, Containment focused on containing the spread of Soviet communism.

Truman Doctrine—Harry S. Truman stated that the US would provide both economic and military support to any country threatened by Soviet takeover.

National Security Act—passed in 1947, this act created the Department of Defense, the Central Intelligence Agency, and the National Security Council.

The combination of these acts led to the cold war, with Soviet communists attempting to spread their influence and the US and other countries trying to contain or stop this spread.

NATO, the Warsaw Pact, and the significance of the Berlin Wall

NATO, the North Atlantic Treaty Organization, came into being in 1949. It essentially amounted to an agreement among the US and Western European countries that an attack on any one of these countries was to be considered an attack against the entire group.

Under the influence of the Soviet Union, the Eastern European countries of USSR, Bulgaria, East Germany, Poland, Romania, Albania, Poland and Czechoslovakia responded with the Warsaw Pact, which created a similar agreement among those nations.

In 1961, a wall was built to separate Communist East Berlin from democratic West Berlin. A similar, though metaphorical, wall lay between east and west, as well, and was referred to as the Iron Curtain.

Arms race

After the war, major nations, particularly the US and USSR, rushed to develop the atomic bomb, and later the hydrogen bomb, as well as many other highly advanced weapons systems. These countries seemed determined to outpace each other with the development of numerous, deadly weapons. These weapons were expensive and extremely dangerous, and it is possible that the war between US and Soviet interests remained "cold" due to the fear that one side or the other would use these terrifyingly powerful weapons.

End of the cold war and the dissolution of the Soviet Union

In the late 1980s, Mikhail Gorbachev ruled the Soviet Union. He introduced a series of reform programs. Also during this period, the Berlin Wall came down, ending the separation of East and West Germany. The Soviet Union relinquished its power over the various republics in Eastern Europe, and they became independent nations with their own individual governments. With the end of the USSR, the cold war also came to an end.

> ➤ **Review Video: <u>Resolution of the Cold War</u>**
> *Visit **mometrix.com/academy** and enter **Code: 278032***

Technological advances that occurred after the Second World War

Numerous technological advances after the Second World War led to more effective treatment of diseases, more efficient communication and transportation, and new means of generating power. Advances in medicine increased the lifespan of people in developed countries, and near-instantaneous communication began to make the world a much smaller place.
- Discovery of penicillin (1928)
- Supersonic air travel (1947)
- First commercial airline flight (1948)
- Nuclear power (1951)
- Orbital leading to manned space flight (Sputnik—1957)
- First man on the moon (1969)

US policy toward immigrants after World War II

Prior to WW II, the US had been limiting immigration for several decades. After WW II, policy shifted slightly to accommodate political refugees from Europe and elsewhere. So many people were displaced by the war that in 1946, The UN formed the International Refugee Organization to deal with the problem.

In 1948, the US Congress passed the Displaced Persons Act, which allowed over 400,000 European refugees to enter the US, most of them concentration camp survivors and refugees from Eastern Europe. In 1952, the President's Escapee Program allowed refugees from Communist Europe to enter the US, as did the Refugee Relief Act, passed in 1953.

At the same time, however, the Internal Security Act of 1950 allowed deportation of declared Communists, and Asians were subjected to a quota based on race, rather than country of origin. Later changes included:
- 1962—Migration and Refugee Assistance Act—helped assist refugees in need.
- 1965—Immigration Act—ended quotas based on nation of origin.
- 1986—Immigration Reform and Control Act—prohibited the hiring of illegal immigrants, but also granted amnesty to about three million illegals already in the country.

Richard Nixon's presidency

Richard Nixon is best known for illegal activities during his presidency, but other important events marked his tenure as president, including:
- Vietnam War comes to an end
- Improved diplomatic relations between the US and China, and the US and the USSR
- National Environmental Policy Act passed, providing for environmental protection
- Compulsory draft ended
- Supreme Court legalizes abortion in Roe v Wade
- Watergate

The Watergate scandal of 1972 ended Nixon's presidency, when he resigned rather than face impeachment and removal from office.

Gerald Ford's presidency

Gerald Ford was appointed to the vice presidency after Nixon's vice president Spiro Agnew resigned under charges of tax evasion. With Nixon's resignation, Ford became president.

Ford's presidency saw negotiations with Russia to limit nuclear arms, as well as struggles to deal with inflation, economic downturn, and energy shortages. Ford's policies sought to reduce governmental control of various businesses and reduce the role of government overall. He also worked to prevent escalation of conflicts in the Middle East.

Carter administration

Jimmy Carter was elected president in 1976. Faced with a budget deficit, high unemployment, and continued inflation, Carter also dealt with numerous matters of international diplomacy including:
- Panama Canal Treaties
- Camp David Accords—negotiations between Anwar el-Sadat, the president of Egypt, and Menachem Begin, the Israeli Prime Minister, leading to a peace treaty between the two nations.
- Strategic Arms Limitation Talks (SALT) and resulting agreements and treaties
- Iran Hostage Crisis—when the Shah of Iran was deposed, an Islamic cleric, the Ayatollah Ruholla Khomeini, came into power. Fifty-three American hostages were taken and held for 444 days in the US Embassy.

Ronald Reagan's presidency

Ronald Reagan, at 69, became the oldest American president. The two terms of his administration included notable events such as:
- Reaganomics, also known as supply-side or trickle-down economics, involving major tax cuts in the upper income brackets
- Economic Recovery Tax Act of 1981
- First female justice appointed to the Supreme Court, Sandra Day O'Connor
- Massive increase in the national debt—increased from $600 billion to $3 trillion
- Reduction of nuclear weapons via negotiations with Mikhail Gorbachev
- Loss of the space shuttle Challenger
- Iran-Contra scandal—cover-up of US involvement in revolutions in El Salvador and Nicaragua
- Deregulation of savings and loan industry

George Herbert Walker Bush

Reagan's presidency was followed by a term under his former Vice President, George H. W. Bush. His run for president included the famous "thousand points of light" speech, which was instrumental in increasing his standing in the election polls.

During Bush's presidency, numerous major international events took place, including:
- Fall of the Berlin wall and Germany's unification
- Panamanian dictator Manuel Noriega captured and tried on drug and racketeering charges
- Dissolution of the Soviet Union
- Gulf War, or Operation Desert Storm, triggered by Iraq's invasion of Kuwait

- Tiananmen Square Massacre in Beijing, China
- Ruby Ridge
- The arrival of the World Wide Web

William Clinton's presidency

William Jefferson Clinton was the second president in US history to be impeached, but he was not convicted, and maintained high approval ratings in spite of the impeachment. Major events during his presidency included:
- Family and Medical Leave Act
- Don't Ask Don't Tell, a compromise position regarding homosexuals serving in the military
- North American Free Trade Agreement, or NAFTA
- Defense of Marriage Act
- Oslo Accords
- Siege at Waco, Texas, involving the Branch Davidians led by David Koresh
- Bombing of the Murrah Federal Building in Oklahoma City, Oklahoma
- Troops sent to Haiti, Bosnia and Somalia to assist with domestic problems in those areas

George W. Bush

Amidst controversy, George W. Bush, son of George Herbert Walker Bush, became president after William Clinton. The election was tightly contested, and though he did not win the popular vote, he won the electoral vote. In the end a Supreme Court ruling was necessary to resolve the issue. His second term was also tightly contested. However, in the election for his second term, Bush won both the popular and the electoral vote.

On 9/11/2001, during his first year in office, Bush's presidency was challenged by the first terrorist attack on American soil when al-Qaeda terrorists flew planes into the World Trade Center, destroying it, and into the Pentagon, causing major damage. This event led to major changes in security in the US, especially regarding airline travel. It also led to US troops being deployed in Afghanistan.

Later, Bush initiated war in Iraq with the claim that the country held weapons of mass destruction. On March 20, 2003, the US, along with troops from more than 20 other countries, invaded Iraq.

The last months of Bush's administration saw a serious economic meltdown in the US and worldwide. Dramatic increases in oil prices resulted in extreme increases of gasoline prices. This, along with the meltdown of the mortgage industry, created serious and overwhelming economic issues for the Bush administration.

Obama Presidency to date

In 2008, Barack Obama, a Senator from Illinois, became the first African-American US president. His administration has focused on improving the lot of a country suffering from a major recession. His major initiatives have included:
- Economic bailout packages
- Improvements in women's rights
- Moves to broaden gay rights
- Health care reform legislation
- Reinforcement of the war in Afghanistan

World History and Geography

Geographic realm of Europe

The geographic realm of Europe is made up of five geographic regions (Western Europe, the British Isles, Northern Europe, Southern [Mediterranean] Europe, and Eastern Europe). It is home to one of the largest population clusters in the world. Despite the relatively small size of its territory, Europe's people and their actions have affected (and continue to affect) all the world's realms. Technological innovations, political revolutions, and vast empires have influenced the behaviors of people on each continent. European colonial endeavors have established communities and impacted the formation of ideologies the world over. Europe's natural and human resources have helped the realm to survive and grow throughout the years. For approximately the last 50 years, Europe has been engaged in a unification program known as the European Union. Currently, 25 of the realm's 48 nation-states are members of the Union.

Economic geography of Europe

The economy of Europe is dominated by the European Union, which, if considered as a whole, has the largest economy in the world. Though the functional region of Western Europe has historically been the hub of economic activity in the realm, this situation is changing with the development of other core regions, productive complementarities, and interregional/international trade markets. Levels of economic development tend to decline as one moves from west to east across the realm; this too is changing with the growth of the economies of former member countries of the Soviet Union, and their increasing interactions with other regions and realms. Europe's agricultural and fishing sectors are highly developed, and still center on Western Europe. Europe's manufacturing sector is also quite developed. While many of the realm's industries are concentrated in Western Europe, deindustrialization in the region has resulted in the outsourcing of labor to areas such as Eastern Europe and China. Financial activity in the realm is concentrated in several cities, with London as the largest.

Geographic realm of Russia

Russia, the largest territorial state on Earth, is an example of a geographic realm which has undergone tremendous amounts of change throughout its existence. Tsars conquered and dominated Russian territory, which was subsequently inhabited by Soviets, who then shaped the domain and its peoples into the Soviet Union. Though World War II tested the empire, it also validated the U.S.S.R.'s status as a global superpower, which it retained until the late 1980's. Internal factors (such as mismanagement of a communist government) and external factors (including the Second World War, pressure from anti-communist leaders, and the global decline of colonialism) eventually led to the dissolution of the Soviet Union in 1991. Consequent cultural, economic, and social diversity have given rise to the establishment of four geographical regions (each of which contains subregions): the Russian Core, the Eastern Frontier, Siberia, and the Far East.

Economic geography of Russia

The economic geography of Russia is highly varied, and characterized by discrete core and peripheral regions of economic activity. Despite the presence of substantial natural resources (such as gas and oil) and a well-educated labor force, the effects of the transition from a failed centrally-planned economy during the Soviet Era to a free market continue to hinder the development of the economies in certain regions. In the agricultural sector, production has decreased drastically with attempts at the privatization of collective farms and restructuring of the economy. Also, the harsh climate in the realm has had an effect on agricultural production. The levels of meat, milk, vegetables, and grains have decreased yearly since 1989. This has had negative ramifications in a country that is largely dependent on its own food production. The inefficiencies and inadequacies held over from the Soviet Union continue to disturb Russia's industrial sector, particularly in the extraction of raw materials and the distribution of goods. Still, Russia is the most industrialized of all the former Soviet republics.

Geographic realm of North America

The geographic realm of North America is home to two countries, Canada and the United States (which is currently considered a global superpower). This realm is characterized by pluralistic (diverse) societies which, unfortunately, are often plagued by social inequalities. It is also a postindustrial realm, which means that the economies of Canada and the United States each experienced increases in the amount of available information technology and rapid expansions of the tertiary (service) sector of industry after the industrialization processes in those countries. The eight regions of North America (many of which stretch across the U.S.-Canada boundary) are largely differentiated by differences in the various economic activities practiced in different areas. These regions include the Continental Core, the South, the Southwest, the West Coast, the Agricultural Heartland, French Canada, the New England/Maritime Provinces, and the Marginal Interior.

Note: "North America" can also be used to refer to the whole continent, which also includes the region of Central America as well as Greenland.

Economic geography of the United States

As a current superpower, the United States has one of the most advanced economies in the world. Like Canada, the United States contains many deposits of natural resources. For instance, the North American realm has more coal reserves than any other. The spatial organization of regional agricultural production in the United States exists within the framework of a modified Von Thunen model, with the "megalopolis" of New England at its center, and belts of specialized activity extending westward. Though the manufacturing sector is less important in a postindustrial economy, this type of activity is still practiced in the United States, and tends to cluster around several urban-industrial nodes, especially within the Manufacturing Belt (located in the Northeast United States). Increased mechanization and advancements in technology have eliminated many "blue-collar" jobs in this region. Most laborers in the U.S. workforce are employed in quaternary economic activity. States offering noneconomic amenities (such as weather and proximity to urban centers and universities) have experienced higher levels of growth than other regions.

Economic geography of Canada

As one of the world's wealthiest nations, Canada has a largely postindustrial economy, with employment concentrated in the service sector (particularly retail). However, unlike many developed countries, primary economic activities (specifically logging and oil production) are important aspects of the country's economy. Canada has a large and varied (though regionally variable) supply of natural resources, such as oil, nickel, and lead. Canadian agricultural products (especially wheat and grains) are exported in high levels to the United States, Europe, and East Asia.

Another unusual aspect of Canada's economy (as compared to those of other highly-developed nations) is the historical secondary status of the manufacturing sector of industry. Though it is certainly not unimportant, manufacturing has never been as vital to the nation's economy as primary or tertiary activities. Many of Canada's industrial firms are branches of U.S. companies. Regional disparities in wealth and economy strength have increased regionalism throughout the region.

Geographic realm of Central America

The geographic realm of Central America, which is sometimes referred to as Middle America, covers the territory between southern North America and the boundary between Panama and Colombia. The exact demarcations of the realm vary from source to source; however, the economic subregion recognized by the United Nations includes all mainland states of North America south of the U.S.-Mexico border in the realm. Basically, this definition counts Mexico and Belize as members of the Central America realm, while other definitions assign these countries to the North American realm. Due to the influence of Spanish and Portuguese colonialism in Central America, this realm and South America are often jointly referred to as Latin America. Central America is divided into four regions: Mexico, the seven states of Central America (Belize, Costa Rica, El Salvador, Guatemala, Honduras, Nicaragua, and Panama), the larger islands of the Caribbean (the Greater Antilles), and the smaller islands of the Caribbean (the Lesser Antilles).

Economic geography of Central America

The economic geography of Central America includes the least developed territories in the Americas, with the exception of Mexico. Under the Mainland-Rimland framework, Central America is divided into a Euro-Amerindian Mainland (made up of mainland Middle America from Mexico to Panama, excluding parts of the Caribbean coast) and a Euro-African rimland (consisting of the coastal zone and the Caribbean islands). Economic activity on the Mainland has historically been oriented around haciendas (privately-owned estates maintained more for prestige and self-sufficiency than maximum production), and is therefore less dependent on trade with other nations. Governmental and social pressures have led to the forced specialization of productive activity in or the parceling out of haciendas in this area. The Rimland's economy has traditionally focused on plantation production, characterized by efficient production of one crop specifically for export and the importation of labor. The Rimland's economy is thus more dependent on the fluctuating global market. Plantation systems, like hacienda systems, continue to metamorphose under internal and external pressures; still, their effects remain visible in the region.

Geographic realm of South America

The geographic realm of South America is made up of four regions: Brazil, the Northeastern countries, the West, and the Southern Cone.

South America and Central America are often collectively referred to as Latin America, due to the enduring cultural and social influences of former Spanish and Portuguese colonial presences in these areas. These influences are most visible in the languages, architecture, music, and visual arts of the peoples of South America. Roman Catholicism and traditional systems relating to land ownership, also transmitted from European countries, continue to be major factors in the evolution of South American societies. In addition, the cultural practices and beliefs of Native Americans have been and continue to be vital shaping forces in the realm.

Economic geography of South America

The economic geography of South America is characterized by high levels of regional disparity. In many of the realm's countries (such as Brazil, Bolivia, and Venezuela), the richest 20% of the population may control over 60% of the nation's wealth, while the poorest 20% may own less than 5% of that wealth. Although several South American nations have become involved in the mining of oil, coal, and valuable minerals in high amounts, the realm's main economic focus is agriculture. The South American realm is unusual, because subsistence farming and commercial farming exist side by side; generally, a geographic realm is dominated by one or the other. Commercial farmers in this area tend to be involved in cattle ranching, wheat farming, grain farming (in a "Corn Belt" zone similar to that in the United States), or plantation-type agriculture. Commercial agricultural endeavors tend to be located near the coasts of the South American continent, with small pockets of activity in the interior. Subsistence-level farming takes place on all other arable land.

Geographic realm of North Africa/Southwest Asia

The size and geographic diversity of the geographic realm of North Africa/Southwest Asia have spawned a number of different labels for the region, none of which are completely satisfactory. These labels include the Islamic realm, the Arab World, the dry world, Africa, and Asia. Though Islam and aridity do dominate the religious and climatic aspects of the realm, which domination is not complete, and the heterogeneity within these groups alone makes a difficulty with the notion of referring to the realm by a single characteristic. The use of relative location is seen as less divisive. The North Africa realm is composed of three regions (Egypt, North Africa, and the Southwest), and Southwest Asia is composed of four (the Middle East [this label is also disputed, due to what some see as the pejorative connotations of the term], the Arabian Peninsula, the North, and the East).

Economic geography of North Africa/Southwest Asia

The economic geography of the realm of North Africa/Southwest Asia is primarily agricultural. Through much of the fertile farmland associated with Mesopotamia and the Fertile Crescent (another ancient culture hearth characterized by its advanced agricultural activity) has dried up, many residents of this realm continue to produce resilient crops (particularly cereals), mostly at subsistence levels. Another important aspect of the economic geography of this realm is the vast oil reserves located on the southern Arabian Peninsula, in North Africa, and near the Caspian Sea. While oil is considered one of the most important natural resources on our planet, its presence in North Africa/Southwest Asia has improved the quality of life for only a small portion of the population. This realm exhibits a large gap between the rich and the poor.

Geographic realm of Sub-Saharan Africa

The geographic realm of Sub-Saharan Africa is composed of the territory between the southern border of the Sahara Desert and the southernmost coast of the country of South Africa. The boundary between the North Africa realm and the Sub-Saharan realm is a prime example of a transition zone; several states straddle this hypothetical divide. This area of the globe constitutes a fairly distinctive cultural realm, due to a fusion of traditional African beliefs and cultures with the influences of European colonialism.

Many countries in this realm exhibit export-oriented transport systems and European concepts of political geography while retaining their traditional languages, religions, and social practices. The realm of Sub-Saharan Africa is the least developed realm in the world, and the majority of its

- 161 -

residents engage in agricultural production. This realm is made up of four regions: West Africa, East Africa, Equatorial Africa, and Southern Africa.

Economic geography of Sub-Saharan Africa

The economic geography of the realm of Sub-Saharan Africa is primarily agricultural. Though many raw materials useful to industrialized countries (such as oil and diamonds) are located within this realm, most residents of Sub-Saharan Africa have little or no access to the technology needed to extract these resources, or to the world economy. Agriculturalists in this realm generally produce at the subsistence level (partially due to the harsh physical conditions—hot, dry weather—of the realm). Grain crops are produced more easily in drier areas, while root crops are grown in relatively wetter areas. Peoples in Sub-Saharan Africa also depend on pastoralism (especially the raising of goats, cattle, and chicken) and fishing for their livelihoods. Though this realm is the least developed in the world, farmers are attempting to better their situations by introducing cash crops to their land. Still, many in the area (which has the highest rate of population growth in the world) remain malnourished.

Geographic realm of South Asia

The geographic realm of South Asia, which is one of the world's largest population agglomerations, has India at its center. This realm is delineated by natural boundaries: the Himalayan Mountains to the north and east, and the Arabian Sea and the Bay of Bengal to the south. India was once the cornerstone of civilization, and later a key part of the British colonial empire. Violent conflicts over the control of territory within South Asia have culminated in the creation of six states. This realm, with its many languages and variety of religious affiliations, contains deep cultural divisions. It contains five regions: the Ganges Plain, Pakistan, the mountainous North, Bangladesh, and the Dravidian South (including the island of Sri Lanka).

Economic geography of South Asia

The economic geography of South Asia is low-income, as the area continues to experience the effects of former British colonization. When they came to South Asia, European powers changed trade patterns in the realm; Europe replaced India as the provider of manufactured goods for the realm. This caused a decrease in South Asian industry. Colonialists also exploited raw materials in the realm. Today, each of the states in South Asia has a low-income economy, due largely to the fact that these economies tend to center on inefficient and relatively less productive agricultural methods. Most residents of this region live in villages and survive directly on their parcels of land (often measuring less than an acre). Low-technology production methods keep crop yields (both per acre and per worker) at the subsistence level. Also, local traditions of inheritance often subdivide already undersized plots, preventing the organization of progressive measures, such as cooperative farming and shared irrigation in many states. The lack of a strong official agricultural development policy at the state and federal levels also inhibits the maturation of agricultural production.

Geographic realm of East Asia

The geographic realm of East Asia has China at its center; this realm houses the largest concentration of human population in the world. Culturally, the 1.3 billion Chinese people dominate this realm, while the Japanese dominate economically. In fact, the economic activity and success of Japan have recently led to the tentative identification of the Pacific Rim region, a functional region with Japan as its anchor. The conceptualization of this region, as well as its practical development in the real world, continue to affect several realms and regions facing the Pacific Ocean. East Asia contains five regions: China Proper (eastern and northeastern China), which includes (somewhat precariously) North Korea, the mountains and plateaus of Xizang (the former Tibet), the deserts of Xinjiang, Mongolia, and the Pacific Rim (including Japan, Taiwan, South Korea, Thailand, and sometimes Malaysia), most of which was formerly referred to as the Jakota Triangle.

Economic geography of East Asia

The economic geography of East Asia is highly variable: Japan is one of the most developed countries on the globe, while Mongolia is one of the least developed. The wide inter- and intraregional variations in this realm's development level, therefore, demonstrate that it is inappropriate to label entire realms as "developed" or "underdeveloped." Agriculturalists in the realm tend to inhabit the fertile basins of the great rivers of the east, and produce grains such as wheat. East Asia is also home to large deposits of raw materials such as coal and natural gas. Economic development in the nations of the Jakota Triangle (Japan, South Korea, and Taiwan) is thought to presage the future growth and modernization of the other political entities in the region. Japan, in particular, has experienced rapid growth in all industrial sectors, and possesses long-established trading relationships with nations across the globe. China, the other giant of the realm, has developed a mixed-market economy that displays both capitalistic and communistic characteristics.

Geographic realm of Southeast Asia

The geographic realm of Southeast Asia contains ethnic and linguistic groups that are particularly diverse. The high occurrence of conflicts for territory and/or power in this realm throughout history has led some to refer to the realm as "the Eastern Europe of Asia." Some use the term Indochina synonymously with Southeast Asia, which is appropriate because it conveys the identities of the two major cultural contributors to the realm. The ethnic affinities of those in this realm tend to lie with China, while cultural influences (specifically religious) arrived in the region from India. The two major regions of Southeast Asia are differentiated by their spatial separation. Indochina is the eastern, mainland part of the region; the archipelagoes of the Philippines and Indonesia make up the other region.

Economic geography of Southeast Asia

The economic geography of Southeast Asia resembles that of East Asia. It is a study in economic contrasts; like Eastern Europe, this realm is a shatter belt. Singapore, for example, has the second-busiest port in the world, and is a major banking and financial center. Indonesia, Thailand, and the Philippines have grown from foreign direct investments (a manner of transferring capital across political boundaries, in which the investor exercises control over the acquired asset) in local industries. Also, the islands of Southeast Asia contain large petroleum reserves. Countries such as Vietnam and Cambodia, on the other hand, are some of the least developed countries in the world. This is partially due to the effects of the transition from a planned economy to a market economy. Levels of unemployment tend to be high in both urban and rural areas, as masses of people leave their farmlands (typically rice and/or grains) for crowded cities with limited job opportunities. The lack of a cohesive infrastructure, coupled with political instability, continue to cause issues with economic growth in these countries.

Geographic realm of Australia

The geographic realm of Australia is formed by the regions of Australia and New Zealand. This realm is distinguished from other areas of the world by its continental isolation and the strong influence of Western culture among its peoples, who are demographically unique. Today, the furthest northwestern points of Australia may be considered part of the Pacific Rim region of East Asia. Australia is anomalous alongside Southeast Asia and the regions of the Pacific, due to its relatively high level of economic development. Still, some of the peoples of New Zealand remain traditional societies. The realm of Australia is made up of four regions. Australia the state is divided into an urbanized core and an arid interior, and New Zealand is made up of two large islands that are physically and culturally distinct.

Economic geography of Australia

The economic geography of Australia, as well as New Zealand, relies principally on the exportation of livestock products; Australia also participates in farming (especially wheat) and mining activities. Dependence on a constantly fluctuating world market places this realm's economy in a precarious position. Despite the plethora of advantages enjoyed by residents of the realm (plentiful farmlands, diverse mineral deposits, access to waterways, and underground water resources, as well as political stability), the Australian economy's growth has declined. Though it is considered one of the most developed realms in the world, Australia must now compete with the emerging Pacific Rim for trade opportunities. Australia has attempted to integrate itself into the Pacific Rim by exporting raw materials to countries in that region. Agriculturalists in this realm produce grains, rice, and certain fruits, while pastoralists produce wool and meat raising sheep. Manufacturing in Australia remains oriented to local domestic markets, partially due to the high costs of shipping and transportation to and from the relatively isolated realm.

Geographic realm of the Pacific

The geographic realm of the Pacific is made up of the thousands of islands (large and small) that are situated in the Pacific Ocean, between Asia and Australia to the west and the Americas to the east. This geographic realm is more fragmented than any other; it is also culturally heterogeneous. The Pacific Realm is traditionally subdivided into three regions: Melanesia (the most populous Pacific region), which is associated with New Guinea; Micronesia (so named for the small sizes of this region's constituent islands), which is located to the north; and Polynesia, which extends from the Hawaiian archipelago southward to Easter Island and southwestward to New Zealand. The regions of Melanesia and Polynesia meet in New Zealand (the residents of which are descended from Polynesian peoples) and Australia (whose indigenous population is Melanesian).

Economic geography of the Pacific Realm

The economic geography of the Pacific Realm is based on tourism. Though this realm covers a larger total area than any other, it possesses the least land area. Coral atolls, ancient volcanoes, open sea, and tropical vegetation offer travelers one spectacular view after another. The region of Melanesia produces valuable export items such as palm oil, coffee, and cocoa, in addition to the subsistence-level production of root crops and bananas. Melanesia also houses large mineral deposits. Micronesia is also involved in agriculture; fertile soils in this region help to diversify crop production. Polynesia, the region that includes the Hawaiian Islands, has a highly developed tourism economy. Most states in the Pacific Realm have high or upper-middle income economies.

Prehistory

Prehistory is the period of human history before writing was developed. The three major periods of prehistory are:
- Lower Paleolithic—Humans used crude tools.
- Upper Paleolithic—Humans began to develop a wider variety of tools. These tools were better made and more specialized. They also began to wear clothes, organize in groups with definite social structures, and to practice art. Most lived in caves during this time period.
- Neolithic—Social structures became even more complex, including growth of a sense of family and the ideas of religion and government. Humans learned to domesticate animals and produce crops, build houses, start fires with friction tools, and to knit, spin and weave.

Anthropology

Anthropology is the study of human culture. Anthropologists study groups of humans, how they relate to each other, and the similarities and differences between these different groups and cultures. Anthropological research takes two approaches: cross-cultural research and comparative research. Most anthropologists work by living among different cultures and participating in those cultures in order to learn about them.

There are three major divisions within anthropology:
- Biological and cultural anthropology
- Archaeology
- Linguistics

Archeology studies past human cultures by evaluating what they leave behind. This can include bones, buildings, art, tools, pottery, graves, and even trash. Archeologists maintain detailed notes and records of their findings and use special tools to evaluate what they find. Photographs, notes, maps, artifacts, and surveys of the area can all contribute to evaluation of an archeological site.

By studying all these elements of numerous archeological sites, scientists have been able to theorize that humans or near-humans have existed for about 600,000 years. Before that, more primitive humans are believed to have appeared about one million years ago. These humans eventually developed into Cro-Magnon man, and then Homo sapiens, or modern man.

Civilization

Civilizations are defined as having the following characteristics:
- Use of metal to make weapons and tools
- Written language
- A defined territorial state
- A calendar

The earliest civilizations developed in river valleys where reliable, fertile land was easily found, including:
- Nile River valley in Egypt
- Mesopotamia
- Indus River
- Hwang Ho in China

The very earliest civilizations developed in the Tigris-Euphrates valley in Mesopotamia, which is now part of Iraq, and in Egypt's Nile valley. These civilizations arose between 4,000 and 3,000 BCE. The area where these civilizations grew is known as the Fertile Crescent. There, geography and the availability of water made large-scale human habitation possible.

The earliest civilizations are also referred to as fluvial civilizations because they were founded near rivers. Rivers and the water they provide were vital to these early groupings, offering:
- Water for drinking and cultivating crops
- A gathering place for wild animals that could be hunted
- Easily available water for domesticated animals
- Rich soil deposits as a result of regular flooding

Irrigation techniques helped direct water where it was most needed, to sustain herds of domestic animals and to nourish crops of increasing size and quality.

Human development from the Lower Paleolithic to the Iron Age

Human development has been divided into several phases:
- Lower Paleolithic or Old Stone Age, about one million years ago—early humans used tools like needles, hatchets, awls, and cutting tools.
- Upper Paleolithic or New Stone Age, 6,000-8,000 BCE—also known as the Neolithic, textiles and pottery are developed. Humans of this era discovered the wheel, began to practice agriculture, made polished tools, and had some domesticated animals.
- Bronze Age, 3,000 BCE—metals are discovered and the first civilizations emerge as humans become more technologically advanced.
- Iron Age, 1,200-1,000 BCE—metal tools replace stone tools as humans develop knowledge of smelting.

Fertile Crescent

James Breasted, an archeologist from the University of Chicago, coined the term Fertile Crescent to describe the area in the Near East where the earliest civilizations arose. The region includes modern day Iraq, Syria, Lebanon, Israel/Palestine and Jordan. It is bordered on the south by the Arabian Desert, the west by the Mediterranean Sea, and to the north and east by the Taurus and Zagros Mountains respectively. This area not only provided the raw materials for the development of increasingly advanced civilizations, but also saw waves of migration and invasion, leading to the earliest wars and genocides as groups conquered and absorbed each other's cultures and inhabitants.

Egyptian, Sumerian, Babylonian and Assyrian cultures

The Egyptians were one of the most advanced ancient cultures, having developed construction methods to build the great pyramids, as well as a form of writing known as hieroglyphics. Their religion was highly developed and complex, and included advanced techniques for the preservation of bodies after death. They also made paper by processing papyrus, a plant commonly found along the Nile, invented the decimal system, devised a solar calendar, and advanced overall knowledge of arithmetic and geometry.

> ➤ **Review Video:** Egyptians
> Visit *mometrix.com/academy* and enter *Code:* **398041**

The Sumerians were the first to invent the wheel, and also brought irrigation systems into use. Their cuneiform writing was simpler than Egyptian hieroglyphs, and they developed the timekeeping system we still use today.

> ➤ **Review Video:** <u>Early Mesopotamia: The Sumerians</u>
> Visit **mometrix.com/academy** and enter **Code: 939880**

The Babylonians are best known for the Code of Hammurabi, an advanced law code.

> ➤ **Review Video:** <u>Early Mesopotamia: The Babylonians</u>
> Visit **mometrix.com/academy** and enter **Code: 686617**

The Assyrians developed horse-drawn chariots and an organized military.

Hebrew, Persian, Minoan, and Mycenaean cultures

The Hebrew or ancient Israelite culture developed the monotheistic religion that eventually developed into modern Judaism, Christianity, and Islam.

> ➤ **Review Video:** <u>Early Mesopotamia: The Jews</u>
> Visit **mometrix.com/academy** and enter **Code: 899354**

The Persians were conquerors, but those they conquered were allowed to keep their own laws, customs, and religious traditions rather than being forced to accept those of their conquerors. They also developed an alphabet and practicing Zoroastrianism, Mithraism and Gnosticism, religions that have influenced modern religious practice.

The Minoans used a syllabic writing system and built large, colorful palaces. These ornate buildings included sewage systems, running water, bathtubs, and even flush toilets. Their script, known as Linear Script A, has yet to be deciphered.

The Mycenaeans practiced a religion that grew into the Greek pantheon, worshipping Zeus and other Olympian gods. They developed Linear Script B, a writing system used to write an ancient form of classical Greek.

Phoenicians as well as early culture in India and ancient China

Skilled seafarers and navigators, the Phoenicians used the stars to navigate their ships at night. They developed a purple dye that was in great demand in the ancient world, and worked with glass and metals. They also devised their own phonetic alphabet, using symbols to represent individual sounds rather than whole words or syllables.

In the Indus Valley, an urban civilization arose in what is now India. These ancient humans developed the concept of zero in mathematics, practiced an early form of the Hindu religion, and developed a caste system which is still prevalent in India today. Archeologists are still uncovering information about this highly developed ancient civilization.

In ancient China, human civilization developed along the Yangtze River, starting as long as 500,000 years ago. These people produced silk, grew millet, and made pottery, including Longshan black pottery.

Civilizations of Mesopotamia

The major civilizations of Mesopotamia, in what is now called the Middle East, were:
- Sumerians
- Amorites
- Hittites
- Assyrians
- Chaldeans
- Persians

These cultures controlled different areas of Mesopotamia during various time periods, but were similar in that they were autocratic. This meant a single ruler served as the head of the government and often, the main religious ruler, as well. These, often tyrannical, militaristic leaders, controlled all aspects of life, including law, trade, and religious activity. Portions of the legacies of these civilizations remain in cultures today. These include mythologies, religious systems, mathematical innovations and even elements of various languages.

Sumer

Sumer, located in the southern part of Mesopotamia, consisted of a dozen city-states. Each city-state had its own gods, and the leader of each city-state also served as the high priest. Cultural legacies of Sumer include:
- The invention of writing
- Invention of the wheel
- The first library—established in Assyria by Ashurbanipal
- The Hanging Gardens of Babylon—one of the Seven Wonders of the Ancient World
- First written laws—Ur-Nammu's Codes and the Codes of Hammurabi
- The *Epic of Gilgamesh*—the first epic story in history

Kushite culture

Kush, or Cush, was located south of ancient Egypt, and the earliest existing records of this civilization were found in Egyptian texts. At one time, Kush was the largest empire on the Nile River, surpassing even Egypt.

In Neolithic times, Kushites lived in villages, with buildings made of mud bricks. They were settled rather than nomadic, and practiced hunting and fishing, cultivated grain, and also herded cattle. Kerma, the capitol, was a major center of trade.

Kush determined leadership through matrilineal descent of their kings, as did Egypt. Their heads of state, the Kandake or Kentake, were female. Their polytheistic religion included the primary Egyptian gods as well as regional gods, including a lion god, which is commonly found in African cultures.

Archeological evidence indicates the Kushites were a mix of Mediterranean and Negroid peoples. Kush was conquered by Nubia in 800 BCE.

Minoan civilization

The Minoans lived on the island of Crete, just off the coast of Greece. This civilization reigned from 2700 to 1450 BCE. The Minoans developed writing systems known to linguists as Linear A and Linear B. Linear A has not yet been translated; Linear B evolved into classical Greek script. "Minoans" is not the name they used for themselves, but is instead a variation on the name of King Minos, a king in Greek mythology believed by some to have been a denizen of Crete.

The Minoan civilization subsisted on trade, and their way of life was often disrupted by earthquakes and volcanoes. Much is still unknown about the Minoans, and archeologists continue to study their architecture and archeological remains. The Minoan culture eventually fell to Greek invaders and was supplanted by the Mycenaean civilization.

Elements of ancient Indian civilization that affect today's world

The civilizations of ancient India gave rise to both Hinduism and Buddhism, major world religions that have found their way to countries far away from their place of origin. Practices such as yoga, increasingly popular in the West, can trace their roots to these earliest Indian civilizations. Literature from ancient India includes the *Mahabharata* containing the *Bhagavad Gita,* the *Ramayana*, *Arthashastra*, and the *Vedas*, a collection of sacred texts.

Indo-European languages, including English, find their beginnings in these ancient cultures. Ancient Indo-Aryan languages such as Sanskrit are still used in some formal Hindu practices. Yoga poses are still formally referred to by Sanskrit names.

Earliest civilizations in China

Many historians believe Chinese civilization is the oldest uninterrupted civilization in the world. The Neolithic age in China goes back 10,000 years, with agriculture in China beginning as early as 7,000 years ago. Their system of writing dates to 1,500 BCE.

The Yellow River served as the center for the earliest Chinese settlements. In Ningxia, in northwest China, there are carvings on cliffs that date back to the Paleolithic Period, at least 6,000 years ago, indicating the extreme antiquity of Chinese culture. Literature from ancient China includes works by Confucius, *Analects*, the *Tao Te Ching*, and a variety of poetry.

Ancient cultures of the Americas

Less is known of ancient American civilizations since less was left behind. Those we know something of include:
- The Norte Chico civilization in Peru, an agricultural society of 20 individual communities, that existed over 5,000 years ago. This culture is also known as Caral-Supe, and is the oldest known civilization in the Americas.
- The Anasazi, or Ancient Pueblo People, in what is now the southwestern United States. Emerging about 1200 BCE, the Anasazi built complex adobe dwellings, and were the forerunners of later Pueblo Indian cultures.
- The Maya emerged in southern Mexico and northern Central America as early as 2,600 BCE. They developed a written language and a complex calendar.

Mycenaean civilization

The Mycenaean civilization was the first major civilization in Europe. In contrast to the Minoans, whom they displaced, the Mycenaeans relied more on conquest than on trade. Mycenaean states included Sparta, Metropolis and Corinth. The history of this civilization, including the Trojan War, was recorded by the Greek poet, Homer. His work was largely considered mythical until archeologists discovered evidence of the city of Troy in Hisarlik, Turkey.

Archeologists continue to add to the body of information about this ancient culture, translating documents written in Linear B, a script derived from the Minoan Linear A. It is theorized that the Mycenaean civilization was eventually destroyed in either a Dorian invasion or an attack by Greek invaders from the north. This theory has not been proven, nor is it certain who the invaders might have been.

Dorian invasion

A Dorian invasion does not refer to an invasion by a particular group of people, but rather is a hypothetical theory to explain the end of the Mycenaean civilization and the growth of classical Greece. Ancient tradition refers to these events as "the return of the Heracleidae," or the sons (descendents) of Hercules. Archeologists and historians still do not know exactly who conquered the Mycenaean, but it is believed to have occurred around 1200 BCE, contemporaneous with the destruction of the Hittite civilization in what is now modern Turkey. The Hittites speak of an attack by people of the Aegean Sea, or the "Sea People." Only Athens was left intact.

Spartans and the Athenians

Both powerful city-states, the Spartans and the Athenians nurtured contrasting cultures.

The Spartans, located in Peloponnesus, were ruled by an oligarchic military state. They practiced farming, disallowed trade for Spartan citizens, and valued military arts and strict discipline. They emerged as the strongest military force in the area, and maintained this status for many years. In one memorable encounter, a small group of Spartans held off a huge army of Persians at Thermopylae.

The Athenians were centered in Attica, where there was little land available for farming. Like the Spartans, they descended from invaders who spoke Greek. Their government was very different from Sparta's; it was in Athens that democracy was created by Cleisthenes of Athens in 510 BCE. Athenians excelled in art, theater, architecture, and philosophy.

Athens and Sparta fought each other in the Peloponnesian War, 431-404 BCE.

Impact of Ancient Greece on modern society

Ancient Greece made numerous major contributions to cultural development, including:
- Theater—Aristophanes and other Greek playwrights laid the groundwork for modern theatrical performance.
- Alphabet—the Greek alphabet, derived from the Phoenician alphabet, developed into the Roman alphabet, and then into our modern-day alphabet.
- Geometry—Pythagoras and Euclid pioneered much of the system of geometry still taught today. Archimedes made various mathematical discoveries, including the value of pi.

- Historical writing—much of ancient history doubles as mythology or religious texts. Herodotus and Thucydides made use of research and interpretation to record historical events.
- Philosophy—Socrates, Plato, and Aristotle served as the fathers of Western philosophy. Their work is still required reading for philosophy students.

> ➤ **Review Video: <u>Ancient Greece</u>**
> *Visit **mometrix.com/academy** and enter **Code: 800829***

Alexander the Great

Born to Philip II of Macedon and tutored by Aristotle, Alexander the Great is considered one of the greatest conquerors in history. He conquered Egypt, the Achaemenid/Persian Empire, a powerful empire founded by Cyrus the Great that spanned three continents, and he traveled as far as India and the Iberian Peninsula. Though Alexander died at the early age of 32, his conquering efforts spread Greek culture into the east. This cultural diffusion left a greater mark on history than did his empire, which fell apart due to internal conflict not long after his death. Trade between the East and West increased, as did an exchange of ideas and beliefs that influenced both regions greatly. The Hellenistic traditions his conquest spread were prevalent in Byzantine culture until as late as the 15th century.

Hittite Empire

The Hittites were centered in what is now Turkey, but their empire extended into Palestine and Syria. They conquered the Babylonian civilization, but adopted their religion and their system of laws. Overall, the Hittites tended to tolerate other religions, unlike many other contemporary cultures, and absorbed foreign gods into their own belief systems rather than forcing their religion onto peoples they conquered. The Hittite Empire reached its peak in 1600-1200 BCE. After a war with Egypt, which weakened them severely, they were eventually conquered by the Assyrians in 700 BCE.

Persian Wars

The Persian Empire, ruled by Cyrus the Great, encompassed an area from the Black Sea to Afghanistan, and beyond into Central Asia. After the death of Cyrus, Darius became king in 522 BCE. The empire reached its zenith during his reign.

From 499-448 BCE, the Greeks and Persians fought in the Persian Wars. Battles of the Persian Wars included:
- The Battle of Marathon, in which heavily outnumbered Greek forces managed to achieve victory.
- The Battle of Thermopylae, in which a small band of Spartans held off a throng of Persian troops for several days.
- The Battle of Salamis, a naval battle that again saw outnumbered Greeks achieving victory.
- The Battle of Plataea, another Greek victory, but one in which they outnumbered the Persians.

The Persian Wars did not see the end of the Persian Empire, but discouraged additional attempts to invade Greece.

Maurya Empire

The Maurya Empire was a large, powerful empire established in India. It was one of the largest ever to rule in the Indian subcontinent, and existed from 322 to 185 BCE, ruled by Chandragupta after the withdrawal from India of Alexander the Great. The Maurya Empire was highly developed, including a standardized economic system, waterworks, and private corporations. Trade to the Greeks and others became common, with goods including silk, exotic foods, and spices. Religious development included the rise of Buddhism and Jainism. The laws of the Maurya Empire protected not only civil and social rights of the citizens, but also protected animals, establishing protected zones for economically important creatures such as elephants, lions and tigers.

This period of time in Indian history was largely peaceful due to the strong Buddhist beliefs of many of its leaders. The empire finally fell after a succession of weak leaders, and was taken over by Demetrius, a Greco-Bactrian king who took advantage of this lapse in leadership to conquer southern Afghanistan and Pakistan around 180 BCE.

Development and growth of the Chinese empires

In China, history was divided into a series of dynasties. The most famous of these, the Han Dynasty, existed from 206 BCE to 220 CE. Accomplishments of the Chinese Empires included:
- Building the Great Wall of China
- Numerous inventions, including paper, paper money, printing, and gunpowder
- High level of artistic development
- Silk production

The Chinese Empires were comparable to Rome as far as their artistic and intellectual accomplishments, as well as the size and scope of their influence.

Roman Empire and Republic

Rome began humbly, in a single town that grew out of Etruscan settlements and traditions, founded, according to legend, by twin brothers Romulus and Remus, who were raised by wolves. Romulus killed Remus, and from his legacy grew Rome.

A thousand years later, the Roman Empire covered a significant portion of the known world, from what is now Scotland, across Europe, and into the Middle East. Hellenization, or the spread of Greek culture throughout the world, served as an inspiration and a model for the spread of Roman culture. Rome brought in belief systems of conquered peoples as well as their technological and scientific accomplishments, melding the disparate parts into a Roman core.

Rome's overall government was autocratic, but local officials came from the provinces where they lived. This limited administrative system was probably a major factor in the long life of the empire.

> ➤ **Review Video: Roman Republic: Part I**
> Visit *mometrix.com/academy* and enter *Code:* **360192**

> ➤ **Review Video: Roman Republic: Part II**
> Visit *mometrix.com/academy* and enter *Code:* **881514**

Byzantine Empire

In the early fourth century, the Roman Empire split, with the eastern portion becoming the Eastern Empire, or the Byzantine Empire. In 330 CE, Constantine founded the city of Constantinople, which became the center of the Byzantine Empire. Its major influences came from Mesopotamia and Persia, in contrast to the Western Empire, which maintained traditions more closely linked to Greece and Carthage.

Byzantium's position gave it an advantage over invaders from the west and the east, as well as control over trade from both regions. It protected the Western empire from invasion from the Persians and the Ottomans, and practiced a more centralized rule than in the West. The Byzantines were famous for lavish art and architecture, as well as the Code of Justinian, which collected Roman law into a clear system.

Nicene Creed

The Byzantine Empire was Christian-based but incorporated Greek language, philosophy and literature and drew its law and government policies from Rome. However, there was as yet no unified doctrine of Christianity, as it was a relatively new religion that had spread rapidly and without a great deal of organization.

In 325, the First Council of Nicaea addressed this issue. From this conference came the Nicene Creed, addressing the Trinity and other basic Christian beliefs. The Council of Chalcedon in 451 stated that any rejection of the Trinity was blasphemy.

Fall of the Western Roman Empire

Germanic tribes, including the Visigoths, Ostrogoths, Vandals, Saxons and Franks, controlled most of Europe. The Roman Empire faced major opposition on that front. The increasing size of the empire also made it harder to manage, leading to dissatisfaction throughout the empire as Roman government became less efficient.

Germanic tribes refused to adhere to the Nicene Creed, instead following Arianism, which led the Roman Catholic Church to declare them heretics. The Franks proved a powerful military force in their defeat of the Muslims in 732. In 768, Charlemagne became king of the Franks. These tribes waged several wars against Rome, including the invasion of Britannia by the Angles and Saxons. Far-flung Rome lost control over this area of its Empire, and eventually Rome itself was invaded.

Differences between Roman Catholic and Eastern Orthodox churches

Emperor Leo III ordered the destruction of all icons throughout the Byzantine Empire. Images of Jesus were replaced with a cross, and images of Jesus, Mary or other religious figures were considered blasphemy on grounds of idolatry.

The current Pope, Gregory II, called a synod to discuss the issue. The synod declared that destroying these images was heretical, and that strong disciplinary measures would result for anyone who took this step. Leo's response was an attempt to kidnap Pope Gregory, but this plan ended in failure when his ships were destroyed by a storm.

Viking invasions

Vikings invaded Northern France in the tenth century, eventually becoming the Normans. Originating in Scandinavia, the Vikings were accomplished seafarers with advanced knowledge of trade routes. With overpopulation plaguing their native lands, they began to travel. From the eighth to the eleventh centuries, they spread throughout Europe, conquering and colonizing. Vikings invaded and colonized England through several waves, including the Anglo-Saxon invasions that displaced Roman control. Their influence remained significant in England, affecting everything from the language of the country to place names and even the government and social structure.

By 900, Vikings had settled in Iceland. They proceeded then to Greenland and eventually to North America, arriving in the New World even before the Spanish and British who claimed the lands several centuries later. They also traded with the Byzantine Empire until the eleventh century when their significant level of activity came to an end.

Tenth century events in the West and the East

In Europe, the tenth century is largely known as the Dark Ages, as numerous Viking invasions disrupted societies that had been more settled under Roman rule. Vikings settled in Northern France, eventually becoming the Normans. By the eleventh century, Europe would rise again into the High Middle Ages with the beginning of the Crusades.

In China, wars also raged. This led the Chinese to make use of gunpowder for the first time in warfare.

In the Americas, the Mayan Empire was winding down while the Toltec became more prominent. Pueblo Indian culture was also at its zenith.

In the East, the Muslims and the Byzantine Empire were experiencing a significant period of growth and development.

Feudalism

A major element of the social and economic life of Europe, feudalism developed as a way to ensure European rulers would have the wherewithal to quickly raise an army when necessary. Vassals swore loyalty and promised to provide military service for lords, who in return offered a fief, or a parcel of land, for them to use to generate their livelihood. Vassals could work the land themselves, have it worked by peasants or serfs—workers who had few rights and were little more than slaves—or grant the fief to someone else. The king legally owned all the land, but in return promised to protect the vassals from invasion and war. Vassals returned a certain percentage of their income to the lords, who in turn passed a portion of their income on to the king.

A similar practice was manorialism, in which the feudal system was applied to a self-contained manor. These manors were often owned by the lords who ran them, but were usually included in the same system of loyalty and promises of military service that drove feudalism.

> ➤ **Review Video:** <u>Feudalism</u>
> *Visit* **mometrix.com/academy** *and enter* *Code:* **165907**

Influence of the Roman Catholic Church over medieval society

The Roman Catholic Church extended significant influence both politically and economically throughout medieval society. The church supplied education, as there were no established schools or universities. To a large extent, the church had filled a power void left by various invasions throughout the former Roman Empire, leading it to exercise a role that was far more political than religious. Kings were heavily influenced by the Pope and other church officials, and churches controlled large amounts of land throughout Europe.

Black Death

The Black Death, believed to be bubonic plague, came to Europe probably brought by fleas carried on rats that were regular passengers on sailing vessels. It killed in excess of a third of the entire population of Europe and effectively ended feudalism as a political system. Many who had formerly served as peasants or serfs found different work, as a demand for skilled labor grew. Nation-states grew in power, and in the face of the pandemic, many began to turn away from faith in God and toward the ideals of ancient Greece and Rome for government and other beliefs.

Crusades

The Crusades began in the eleventh century and progressed well into the twelfth. The major goal of these various military ventures was to slow the progression of Muslim forces into Europe and to expel them from the Holy Land, where they had taken control of Jerusalem and Palestine.

Alexius I, the Eastern emperor, called for helped from Pope Urban II when Palestine was taken. In 1095, the Pope, hoping to reunite Eastern and Western Christian influences, encouraged all Christians to help the cause. Amidst great bloodshed, this Crusade recaptured Jerusalem, but over the next centuries, Jerusalem and other areas of the Holy Land changed hands numerous times.

The Second Crusade, in 1145, consisted of an unsuccessful attempt to retake Damascus. The Third Crusade, under Pope Gregory VIII, attempted to recapture Jerusalem, but failed. The Fourth Crusade, under Pope Innocent III, attempted to come into the Holy Land via Egypt.

The Crusades led to greater power for the Pope and the Catholic Church in general and also opened numerous trading and cultural routes between Europe and the East.

Political developments in India through the eleventh century

After the Mauryan dynasty, the Guptas ruled India, maintaining a long period of peace and prosperity in the area. During this time, the Indian people invented the decimal system as well as the concept of zero. They produced cotton and calico, as well as other products in high demand in Europe and Asia, and developed a complex system of medicine.

The Gupta Dynasty ended in the eleventh century with a Muslim invasion of the region. These sultans ruled for several centuries. Tamerlane, one of the most famous, expanded India's borders and founded the Mogul Dynasty. His grandson Akbar promoted freedom of religion and built a wide-spread number of mosques, forts, and other buildings throughout the country.

Chinese and Japanese governments and their development through the eleventh century

After the Mongols, led by Genghis Khan and his grandson Kublai Khan, unified the Mongol Empire, China was led by the Ming and Manchu Dynasties. Both these Dynasties were isolationist, ending China's interaction with other countries until the eighteenth century. The Ming Dynasty was known for its porcelain, while the Manchus focused on farming and road construction as the population grew.

Japan developed independent of China, but borrowed the Buddhist religion, the Chinese writing system, and other elements of Chinese society. Ruled by the divine emperor, Japan basically functioned on a feudal system led by Daimyos, or lords, and soldiers known as samurai. Japan remained isolationist, not interacting significantly with the rest of the world until the 1800s.

Developments in Africa through the eleventh century

Only a few areas of Africa were amenable to habitation, due to the large amount of desert and other inhospitable terrain. Egypt remained important, though most of the northern coast became Muslim as their armies spread through the area. Ghana rose as a trade center in the ninth century, lasting into the twelfth century, primarily trading in gold, which it exchange for Saharan salt. Mali rose somewhat later, with the trade center Timbuktu becoming an important exporter of goods such as iron, leather and tin. Mali also dealt in agricultural trade, becoming one of the most significant trading centers in West Africa. The Muslim religion dominated, and technological advancement was sparse.

African culture was largely defined through migration, as Arab merchants and others settled on the continent, particularly along the east coast. Scholars from the Muslim nations gravitated to Timbuktu, which in addition to its importance in trade, had also become a magnet for those seeking knowledge and education.

Islam

Born in 570 CE, Mohammed became prominent in 610, leading his followers in a new religion called Islam, which means submission to God's will. Before this time, the Arabian Peninsula was inhabited largely by Bedouins, nomads who battled amongst each other and lived in tribal organizations. But by the time Mohammed died in 632, most of Arabia had become Muslim to some extent.

Mohammed conquered Mecca, where a temple called the Kaaba had long served as a center of the nomadic religions. He declared this temple the most sacred of Islam, and Mecca as the holy city. His writings became the Koran, or Qur'an, divine revelations he said had been delivered to him by the angel Gabriel.

> ➤ **Review Video: Islam**
> Visit *mometrix.com/academy* and enter *Code:* **359164**

Mohammed's teachings gave the formerly tribal Arabian people a sense of unity that had not existed in the area before. After his death, the converted Muslims of Arabia conquered a vast territory, creating an empire and bringing advances in literature, technology, science and art just as Europe was declining under the scourge of the Black Death. Literature from this period includes the *Arabian Nights* and the *Rubaiyat* of Omar Khayyam.

Later in its development, Islam split into two factions, the Shiite and the Sunni Muslims. Conflict continues today between these groups.

Ottoman Empire

By 1400, the Ottomans had grown in power in Anatolia and had begun attempts to take Constantinople. In 1453 they finally conquered the Byzantine capital and renamed it Istanbul. The Ottoman Empire's major strength, much like Rome before it, lay in its ability to unite widely disparate people through religious tolerance. This tolerance grew from the Islamic belief that Muslims, Christians and Jews were fundamentally related as "People of the Book," and enabled the Ottomans to develop a widely varied culture. They also believed in just laws and just government, with government centered in a monarch, known as the sultan.

Renaissance

Renaissance literally means "rebirth." After the darkness of the Dark Ages and the Black Plague, interest rose again in the beliefs and politics of ancient Greece and Rome. Art, literature, music, science, and philosophy all burgeoned during the Renaissance.

Many of the ideas of the Renaissance began in Florence, Italy, spurred by the Medici family. Education for the upper classes expanded to include law, math, reading, writing, and classical Greek and Roman works. As the Renaissance progressed, the world was presented through art and literature in a realistic way that had never been explored before. This realism drove culture to new heights.

Artists of the Renaissance included Leonardo da Vinci, also an inventor, Michelangelo, also an architect, and others who focused on realism in their work. In literature, major contributions came from the humanist, authors like Petrarch, Erasmus, Sir Thomas More, and Boccaccio, who believed man should focus on reality rather than on the ethereal. Shakespeare, Cervantes and Dante followed in their footsteps, and their works found a wide audience thanks to Gutenberg's development of the printing press.

Scientific developments of the Renaissance included the work of Copernicus, Galileo and Kepler, who challenged the geocentric philosophies of the church by proving the earth was not the center of the solar system.

> **Review Video: Renaissance**
> Visit **mometrix.com/academy** and enter **Code: 123100**

Reformation period

The Reformation consisted of the Protestant Revolution and the Catholic Reformation. The Protestant Revolution rose in Germany when Martin Luther protested abuses of the Catholic Church. John Calvin led the movement in Switzerland, while in England King Henry VIII made use of the Revolution's ideas to further his own political goals.

> **Review Video: Martin Luther**
> Visit **mometrix.com/academy** and enter **Code: 691828**

The Catholic Reformation occurred in response to the Protestant Revolution, leading to various changes in the Catholic Church. Some provided wider tolerance of different religious viewpoints, but others actually increased the persecution of those deemed to be heretics.

> ➢ **Review Video: The Counter Reformation**
> *Visit mometrix.com/academy and enter Code:* **950498**

From a religious standpoint, the Reformation occurred due to abuses by the Catholic Church such as indulgences and dispensations, religious offices being offered up for sale, and an increasingly dissolute clergy.

Politically, the Reformation was driven by increased power of various ruling monarchs, who wished to take all power to themselves rather than allowing power to remain with the church. They also had begun to chafe at papal taxes and the church's increasing wealth. The ideas of the Protestant Revolution removed power from the Catholic Church and the Pope himself, playing nicely into the hands of those monarchs, such as Henry VIII, who wanted out from under the church's control.

> ➢ **Review Video: The Protestants**
> *Visit mometrix.com/academy and enter Code:* **583582**

Scientific Revolution

In addition to holding power in the political realm, church doctrine also governed scientific belief. During the Scientific Revolution, astronomers and other scientists began to amass evidence that challenged the church's scientific doctrines. Major figures of the Scientific Revolution included:

- Nicolaus Copernicus—wrote *Revolutions of the Celestial Spheres*, arguing that the Earth revolved around the sun.
- Tycho Brahe—catalogued astronomical observations.
- Johannes Kepler—developed Laws of Planetary Motions.
- Galileo Galilei—defended the heliocentric theories of Copernicus and Kepler, discovered four moons of Jupiter, and died under house arrest by the Church, charged with heresy.
- Isaac Newton—discovered gravity, studied optics, calculus and physics, and believed the workings of nature could be observed, studied, and proven through observation.

> ➢ **Review Video: The Scientific Revolution**
> *Visit mometrix.com/academy and enter Code:* **974600**

Enlightenment

During the Enlightenment, philosophers and scientists began to rely more and more on observation to support their ideas, rather than building on past beliefs, particularly those held by the church. A focus on ethics and logic drove their work.

Major philosophers of the Enlightenment included:

- Rene Descartes—"I think, therefore I am." He believed strongly in logic and rules of observation.
- David Hume—pioneered empiricism and skepticism, believing that truth could only be found through direct experience, and that what others said to be true was always suspect.
- Immanuel Kant—believed in self-examination and observation, and that the root of morality lay within human beings.

- Jean-Jacques Rousseau—developed the idea of the social contract, that government existed by the agreement of the people, and that the government was obligated to protect the people and their basic rights. His ideas influenced John Locke and Thomas Jefferson.

> ➤ **Review Video:** <u>Age of Enlightenment</u>
> *Visit **mometrix.com/academy** and enter **Code: 143022***

American Revolution and the French Revolution

Both the American and French Revolution came about as a protest against the excesses and overly controlling nature of their respective monarchs. In America, the British colonies had been left mostly self-governing until the British monarchs began to increase control, leading the colonies to revolt. In France, the nobility's excesses had led to increasingly difficult economic conditions, with inflation, heavy taxation and food shortages creating horrible burdens on the people. Both revolutions led to the development of republics to replace the monarchies that were displaced. However, the French Revolution eventually led to the rise of the dictator Napoleon Bonaparte, while the American Revolution produced a working republic from the beginning.

> ➤ **Review Video:** <u>American Revolutionary War</u>
> *Visit **mometrix.com/academy** and enter **Code: 935282***

Events and figures of the French Revolution

In 1789, King Louis XVI, faced with a huge national debt, convened parliament. The Third Estate, or Commons, a division of the French parliament, then claimed power, and the king's resistance led to the storming of the Bastille, the royal prison.

> ➤ **Review Video:** <u>The French Revolution: The Estates General</u>
> *Visit **mometrix.com/academy** and enter **Code: 805480***

> ➤ **Review Video:** <u>The French Revolution: The National Assembly</u>
> *Visit **mometrix.com/academy** and enter **Code: 338451***

The people established a constitutional monarchy. When King Louis XVI and Marie Antoinette attempted to leave the country, they were executed on the guillotine. From 1793 to 1794, Robespierre and extreme radicals, the Jacobins, instituted a Reign of Terror, executing thousands of nobles as well as anyone considered an enemy of the Revolution. Robespierre was then executed, as well, and the Directory came into power.

> ➤ **Review Video:** <u>The French Revolution: Robespierre</u>
> *Visit **mometrix.com/academy** and enter **Code: 363792***

This governing body proved incompetent and corrupt, allowing Napoleon Bonaparte to come to power in 1799, first as a dictator, then as emperor. While the French Revolution threw off the power of a corrupt monarchy, its immediate results were likely not what the original perpetrators of the revolt had intended.

> ➤ **Review Video:** <u>The French Revolution: Napoleon Bonaparte</u>
> *Visit **mometrix.com/academy** and enter **Code: 263709***

Russian Revolution of 1905

In Russia, rule lay in the hands of the Czars, and the overall structure was feudalistic. Beneath the Czars was a group of rich nobles, landowners whose lands were worked by peasants and serfs. The Russo-Japanese War (1904-1905) made conditions much worse for the lower classes. When peasants demonstrated outside the Czar's Winter Palace, the palace guard fired upon the crowd. The demonstration had been organized by a trade union leader, and after the violent response, many unions as well as political parties blossomed and began to lead numerous strikes. When the economy ground to a halt, Czar Nicholas II signed a document known as the October Manifesto, which established a constitutional monarchy and gave legislative power to parliament. However, he violated the Manifesto shortly thereafter, disbanding parliament and ignoring the civil liberties granted by the Manifesto. This eventually led to the Bolshevik Revolution of 1917.

Bolshevik Revolution of 1917

Throughout its modern history, Russia had lagged behind other countries in development. The continued existence of a feudal system, combined with harsh conditions and the overall size of the country, led to massive food shortages and increasingly harsh conditions for the majority of the population. The tyrannical rule favored by the Czars only made this worse, as did repeated losses in various military conflicts. Increasing poverty, decreasing supplies, and the Czar's violation of the October Manifesto which had given some political power and civil rights to the people finally came to a head with the Bolshevik Revolution.

A workers' strike in Petrograd in 1917 set the revolutionary wheels in motion when the army sided with the workers. While parliament set up a provisional government made up of nobles, the workers and military joined to form their own governmental system known as soviets, which consisted of local councils elected by the people.

The ensuing chaos opened the doors for formerly exiled leaders Vladimir Lenin, Joseph Stalin and Leon Trotsky to move in and gain popular support as well as the support of the Red Guard. Overthrowing parliament, they took power, creating a communist state in Russia. This development led to the spread of Communism throughout Eastern Europe and elsewhere, greatly affecting diplomatic policies throughout the world for several decades.

Industrial Revolution

The Industrial Revolution began in Great Britain, bringing coal- and steam-powered machinery into widespread use. Industry began a period of rapid growth with these developments. Goods that had previously been produced in small workshops or even in homes were produced more efficiently and in much larger quantities in factories. Where society had been largely agrarian based, the focus swiftly shifted to an industrial outlook.

As electricity and internal combustion engines replaced coal and steam as energy sources, even more drastic and rapid changes occurred. Western European countries in particular turned to colonialism, taking control of portions of Africa and Asia to assure access to the raw materials needed to produce factory goods. Specialized labor became very much in demand, and businesses grew rapidly, creating monopolies, increasing world trade, and creating large urban centers. Even agriculture changed fundamentally as the Industrial Revolution led to a second Agricultural Revolution as the addition of the new technologies advanced agricultural production.

The first phase of the Industrial Revolution took place from roughly 1750 to 1830. The textile industry experienced major changes as more and more elements of the process became mechanized. Mining benefited from the steam engine. Transportation became easier and more widely available as waterways were improved and the railroad came into prominence.

In the second phase, from 1830 to 1910, industries further improved in efficiency and new industries were introduced as photography, various chemical processes, and electricity became more widely available to produce new goods or new, improved versions of old goods. Petroleum and hydroelectric became major sources of power. During this time, the industrial revolution spread out of Western Europe and into the US and Japan.

The Industrial Revolution led to widespread education, a wider franchise, and the development of mass communication in the political arena.

Economically, conflicts arose between companies and their employees, as struggles for fair treatment and fair wages increased. Unions gained power and became more active. Government regulation over industries increased, but at the same time, growing businesses fought for the right to free enterprise.

In the social sphere, populations increased and began to concentrate around centers of industry. Cities became larger and more densely populated. Scientific advancements led to more efficient agriculture, greater supply of goods, and increased knowledge of medicine and sanitation, leading to better overall health.

> **Review Video: <u>The Industrial Revolution</u>**
> *Visit **mometrix.com/academy** and enter **Code: 372796***

Nationalism

Nationalism, put simply, is a strong belief in, identification with, and allegiance to a particular nation and people. Nationalistic belief unified various areas that had previously seen themselves as fragmented which led to patriotism and, in some cases, imperialism. As nationalism grew, individual nations sought to grow, bringing in other, smaller states that shared similar characteristics such as language and cultural beliefs. Unfortunately, a major side effect of these growing nationalistic beliefs was often conflict and outright war.

In Europe, imperialism led countries to spread their influence into Africa and Asia. Africa was eventually divided among several European countries that needed the raw materials to be found there. Asia also came under European control, with the exception of China, Japan and Siam (now Thailand). In the US, Manifest Destiny became the rallying cry as the country expanded west. Italy and Germany formed larger nations from a variety of smaller states.

> **Review Video: <u>Nationalism</u>**
> *Visit **mometrix.com/academy** and enter **Code: 865693***

World War I in the European theater

WW I began in 1914 with the assassination of Archduke Franz Ferdinand, heir to the throne of Austria-Hungary, by a Serbian national. This led to a conflict between Austria-Hungary and Serbia that quickly escalated into the First World War. Europe split into the Allies—Britain, France and Russia, and later Italy, Japan and the US, against the Central Powers—Austria-Hungary, Germany and Turkey. As the war spread, countries beyond Europe became involved.

The war left Europe deeply in debt, and particularly devastated the German economy. The ensuing Great Depression made matters worse, and economic devastation opened the door for Communist, Fascist and Socialist governments to gain power.

Trench warfare

Fighting during WW I took place largely in a series of trenches built along the Eastern and Western Fronts. These trenches added up to about 24,000 miles, each side having dug at least 12,000 miles' worth during the course of the war. This produced fronts that stretched nearly 400 miles, from the coast of Belgium to the border of Switzerland.

The Allies made use of straightforward open-air trenches with a front line, supporting lines, and communications lines. By contrast, the German trenches sometimes included well-equipped underground living quarters.

Communism and Socialism

At their roots, socialism and communism both focus on public ownership and distribution of goods and services. However, communism works toward revolution by drawing on what it sees to be inevitable class antagonism, eventually overthrowing the upper classes and the systems of capitalism. Socialism makes use of democratic procedures, building on the existing order. This was particularly true of the Utopian-Socialists, who saw industrial capitalism as oppressive, not allowing workers to prosper.

While socialism struggled between the World Wars, communism took hold, especially in Eastern Europe. After WW II, democratic socialism became more common. Later, capitalism took a stronger hold again, and today most industrialized countries in the world function under an economy that mixes elements of capitalism and socialism.

> ➤ **Review Video:** <u>Socialism</u>
> *Visit **mometrix.com/academy** and enter **Code: 917677***

Rise of the Nazi party in Germany

The Great Depression had a particularly devastating effect on Germany's economy, especially after the US was no longer able to supply reconstruction loans to help the country regain its footing. With unemployment rising rapidly, dissatisfaction with the government grew. Fascist and Communist parties rose, promising change and improvement.

Led by Adolf Hitler, the Fascist, Nazi Party eventually gained power in Parliament based on these promises and the votes of desperate German workers. When Hitler became Chancellor, he launched numerous expansionist policies, violating the peace treaties that had ended WW I. His military buildup and conquering of neighboring countries sparked the aggression that soon led to WW II.

Blitzkrieg

The blitzkrieg, or "lightning war," consisted of fast, powerful surprise attacks that disrupted communications, made it difficult if not impossible for the victims to retaliate, and demoralized Germany's foes. The "blitz," or the aerial bombing of England in 1940, was one example, with bombings occurring in London and other cities 57 nights in a row. The Battle of Britain, from 1940 to 1941, also brought intense raids by Germany's air force, the Luftwaffe, mostly targeting ports and British air force bases. Eventually, Britain's Royal Air Force blocked the Luftwaffe, ending Germany's hopes for conquering Britain.

Battle of the Bulge

Following the D-Day Invasion, Allied forces gained considerable ground, and began a major campaign to push through Europe. In December of 1944, Hitler launched a counteroffensive, attempting to retake Antwerp, an important port. The ensuing battle became the largest land battle on the war's Western Front, and was known as the Battle of the Ardennes, or the Battle of the Bulge.

The battle lasted from December 16, 1944 to January 28, 1945. The Germans pushed forward, making inroads into Allied lines, but in the end the Allies brought the advance to a halt. The Germans were pushed back, with massive losses on both sides. However, those losses proved crippling to the German army.

Holocaust

As Germany sank deeper and deeper into dire economic straits, the tendency was to look for a person or group of people to blame for the problems of the country. With distrust of the Jewish people already ingrained, it was easy for German authorities to set up the Jews as scapegoats for Germany's problems.

Under the rule of Hitler and the Nazi party, the "Final Solution" for the supposed Jewish problem was devised. Millions of Jews, as well as Gypsies, homosexuals, Communists, Catholics, the mentally ill and others, simply named as criminals, were transported to concentration camps during the course of the war. At least six million were slaughtered in death camps such as Auschwitz, where horrible conditions and torture of prisoners were commonplace.

The Allies were aware of rumors of mass slaughter throughout the war, but many discounted the reports. Only when troops went in to liberate the prisoners was the true horror of the concentration camps brought to light.

The Holocaust resulted in massive loss of human life, but also in the loss and destruction of cultures. Because the genocide focused on specific ethnic groups, many traditions, histories, knowledge, and other cultural elements were lost, particularly among the Jewish and Gypsy populations.

After World War II, the United Nations recognized genocide as a "crime against humanity." The UN passed the Universal Declaration of Human Rights in order to further specify what rights the organization protected. Nazi war criminals faced justice during the Nuremberg Trials. There individuals, rather than their governments, were held accountable for war crimes.

> ➢ **Review Video:** <u>The Holocaust</u>
> *Visit **mometrix.com/academy** and enter **Code: 350695***

Major occurrences of genocide in modern history

Armenian genocide—occurred in the 1900s when the Young Turks, heirs to the Ottoman Empire, slaughtered over a million Armenians between 1915 and 1917. This constituted nearly half the Armenian population at the time.

Russian purges under Stalin—Scholars have attributed deaths between 3 and 60 million, both directly and indirectly, to the policies and edicts of Joseph Stalin's regime. The deaths took place from 1921 to 1953, when Stalin died. In recent years, many scholars have settled on a number of deaths near 20 million but this is still disputed today.

Rwandan Genocide—in 1994, hundreds of thousands of Tutsi and Hutu sympathizers were slaughtered during the Rwandan Civil War. The UN did not act or authorize intervention during these atrocities.

World War II and the Cold War

With millions of military and civilian deaths and over 12 million persons displaced, WW II left large regions of Europe and Asia in disarray. Communist governments moved in with promises of renewed prosperity and economic stability. The Soviet Union backed Communist regimes in much of Eastern Europe. In China, Mao Zedong led communist forces in the overthrow of the Chinese Nationalist Party and instituted a Communist government in 1949.

While the new Communist governments restored a measure of stability to much of Eastern Europe, it brought its own problems, with dictatorial governments and an oppressive police force. The spread of Communism also led to several years of tension between Communist countries and the democratic west, as the west fought to slow the spread of oppressive regimes throughout the world. With both sides in possession of nuclear weapons, tensions rose. Each side feared the other would resort to nuclear attack. This standoff lasted until 1989, when the Berlin Wall fell. The Soviet Union was dissolved two years later.

United Nations

The United Nations (UN) came into being toward the end of World War II. A successor to the less-than-successful League of Nations, formed after World War I, the UN built and improved on those ideas. Since its inception, the UN has worked to bring the countries of the world together for diplomatic solutions to international problems, including sanctions and other restrictions. It has also initiated military action, calling for peacekeeping troops from member countries to move against countries violating UN policies.

One example of UN involvement in an international conflict is the Korean War, the first war in which an international alliance of this kind was actively involved.

Decolonization

A rise of nationalism among European colonies led to many of them declaring independence. India and Pakistan became independent of Britain at this time, and numerous African and Asian colonies declared independence, as well. This period of decolonization lasted into the 1960s.

Some colonies moved successfully into independence but many, especially in Africa and Asia, struggled to create stable governments and economies, and suffered from ethnic and religious conflicts. Some of those countries still struggle today.

Korean War

In 1910, Japan took control of Korea, and maintained this control until 1945, when Soviet and US troops occupied the country. The Soviet Union controlled North Korea, while the US controlled South Korea. In 1947, the UN ordered elections in Korea to unify the country but the Soviet Union refused to allow them to take place, instead setting up a communist government in North Korea. In 1950, the US withdrew troops, and the North Korean troops moved to invade South Korea.

The Korean War was the first war in which the UN—or any international organization—played a major role. The US, Australia, Canada, France, Netherlands, Great Britain, Turkey, China, USSR and other countries sent troops at various times, for both sides, throughout the war. In 1953, the war ended in a truce, but no peace agreement was ever achieved, and Korea remains divided.

Vietnam War

Vietnam had previously been part of a French colony called French Indochina.

The Vietnam War began with the French Indochina War from 1946-1954, in which France battled with the Democratic Republic of Vietnam, ruled by Ho Chi Minh.

In 1954, a siege at Dien Bien Phu ended in a Vietnamese victory. Vietnam was then divided into North and South, much like Korea. Communist forces controlled the North and the South was controlled by South Vietnamese forces, supported by the US. Conflict ensued, leading to a war. US troops eventually lead the fight, in support of South Vietnam. The war became a major political issue in the US, with many citizens protesting American involvement.

In 1976, South Vietnam surrendered, and Vietnam became the Socialist Republic of Vietnam.

Role of the Middle East in international relations and economics

Its location on the globe, with ease of access to Europe and Asia, and its preponderance of oil deposits, makes the middle eastern countries a crucial factor in many international issues both diplomatic and economic. Because of its central location, the Middle East has been a hotbed for violence since before the beginning of recorded history. Conflicts over land, resources, religious and political power continue in the area today, spurred by conflict over control of the area's vast oil fields as well as over territories that have been disputed for literally hundreds—and even thousands—of years.

Globalism

In the modern era, globalism has emerged as a popular political ideology. Globalism is based in the idea that all people and all nations are interdependent. Each nation is dependent on one or more other nations for production of and markets for goods, and for income generation. Today's ease of international travel and communication, including technological advances such as the airplane, has heightened this sense of interdependence.

The global economy, and the general idea of globalism, has shaped many economic and political choices since the beginning of the twentieth century. Many of today's issues, including environmental awareness, economic struggles, and continued warfare, often require the cooperation of many countries if they are to be dealt with effectively.

With countries worldwide often seeking the same resources, some, particularly nonrenewable resources, have experienced high demand. At times this has resulted in wild price fluctuations. One major example is the demand for petroleum products such as oil and natural gas.

Increased travel and communication make it possible to deal with diseases in remote locations; however, it also allows diseases to be spread via travelers, as well.

A major factor contributing to increased globalization over the past few decades has been the Internet. By allowing instantaneous communication with anyone nearly anywhere on the globe, the Internet has led to interaction between far-flung individuals and countries, and an ever increasing awareness of happenings all over the world.

Practice Test

Job Knowledge

1. What is the *most efficient* way to send another person a copy of an e-mail without letting the intended recipient know?
   a. Add a cc.
   b. Forward it.
   c. Add a bcc.
   d. Send it through postal mail.

2. An instructor lists all student grades on a particular test. The most popular grade is an 86, attained by 13 of the 22 students. What is 86 considered?
   a. The mean
   b. The average
   c. The range
   d. The mode

3. Where is the U.S. banking system regulated?
   a. On the local level
   b. On the state level
   c. On the federal level
   d. On both the state and the federal level

4. During which president's administration was Medicare and Medicaid started?
   a. Lyndon Johnson
   b. Franklin Roosevelt
   c. Herbert Hoover
   d. Theodore Roosevelt

5. What is the main way the U.S. government controls our money supply?
   a. Changes in interest rates
   b. Raising taxes
   c. Striving for high economic growth
   d. Regulating inflation

6. The economic systems of the United States and Russia are both most closely tied to:
   a. the government
   b. their geography
   c. historical events
   d. technology

7. What is the title of the leader of North Korea?
   a. President
   b. Prime minister
   c. Premier
   d. Chancellor

8. How is a database best defined?
   a. A tool for collecting and organizing information
   b. An accounting program for keeping track of revenue and expenses
   c. An index describing a company's departments
   d. A listing of computer software

9. What is a true statement about motivating people?
   a. People have to be self-motivated.
   b. People are always motivated by money.
   c. Fear of losing a job is a good long-term motivator.
   d. All people are motivated by the same things.

10. An employer makes a rule that employees speak only English on the job. What law is this most likely to violate?
   a. Immigration Reform and Control Act
   b. Title VII
   c. Civil Rights Act of 1991
   d. Anti-Discrimination Act

11. Which is a true statement about noncitizens living in the United States?
   a. They are illegally residing here.
   b. They can receive Social Security benefits.
   c. They are not eligible for food stamps.
   d. They do not contribute to the U.S. economy.

12. Which word most accurately describes *perestroika*?
   a. Construction
   b. Administration
   c. Openness
   d. Revolution

13. Who led Poland as president from 1990 to 1995?
   a. Vaclav Havel
   b. Nicolae Ceausescu
   c. Lech Walesa
   d. Helmut Kohl

14, Which group was responsible for a large part of the terrorism in Northern Ireland throughout most of the last half of the 20th century?
   a. Al-Qaeda
   b. Independent Muslims
   c. Sinn Fein
   d. Catholics

15. An effort to destroy an ethnic group, a particular race, or a religious or national group is called:
    a. terrorism
    b. globalization
    c. stabilization
    d. genocide

16. Which 1992 treaty established the euro as the single currency for Europe?
    a. General Agreement on Trade and Tariffs
    b. European Union Treaty
    c. Maastricht Treaty
    d. World Trade Organization Agreement

17. Whose ideas led to the theory of relativity, that time and space are not absolute?
    a. Albert Einstein
    b. Niels Bohr
    c. Max Planck
    d. James Watson

18. Which country put the first satellite in space, in 1957?
    a. Russia
    b. United States
    c. Germany
    d. Korea

19. In the 1980s, some Latin American countries took up *neoliberalism*. What was the main idea of this economic model?
    a. Government dependence and monopolization
    b. Free markets and privatization
    c. Denationalization and taxation
    d. Industrialization and regulation

20. Which word is best defined as the unlimited power to govern?
    a. Oligarchy
    b. Communism
    c. Absolutism
    d. Patriarchy

21. How many Federal Reserve banks are in the United States?
    a. 1
    b. 2
    c. 12
    d. 27

22. Which phrase, coined during the Cold War, best describes a First World country?
    a. A stateless nation
    b. An impoverished and unstable country
    c. An industrialized but not democratic country
    d. An industrial democracy

23. In 2002, President George W. Bush cited certain countries as being part of an "axis of evil." Which country was *not* part of that description?
   a. Iran
   b. Iraq
   c. North Korea
   d. Afghanistan

24. What was the Patriot Act created to confront and work against?
   a. Terrorism
   b. Weapons of mass destruction
   c. Free trade
   d. Global warming

25. Which freedom is *not* covered by the First Amendment to the Constitution?
   a. Freedom of the press
   b. Freedom from cruel and unusual punishment
   c. Freedom of assembly
   d. Freedom to petition the government

26. Which amendment guarantees a speedy trial in the United States?
   a. Fourth Amendment
   b. Sixth Amendment
   c. Eighth Amendment
   d. Fourteenth Amendment

27. What does "suffrage" most nearly mean?
   a. Women's right to vote
   b. Minority right to vote
   c. Reforming the right to vote
   d. Right to vote

28. What is the clearest way to describe a candidate who currently holds a political office?
   a. Incumbent
   b. Delegate
   c. Legislator
   d. Lame duck

29. How long is the elected term for a member of the Senate?
   a. 3 years
   b. 4 years
   c. 5 years
   d. 6 years

30. How long must a candidate for president have resided in the United States?
   a. 7 years
   b. 10 years
   c. 14 years
   d. From birth

31. Which is *not* a constitutional responsibility of the president of the United States?
    a. Negotiating treaties with Senate approval
    b. Recommending legislation
    c. Choosing chairpersons for standing committees of Congress
    d. Seeking counsel of cabinet secretaries

32. Which government body has the *least* influence on foreign policy?
    a. Congress
    b. State Department
    c. Defense Department
    d. National Security Council

33. Which factor is *least* likely to be considered to affect a country's gross domestic product (GDP)?
    a. The size of its workforce
    b. The amount of its capital
    c. Technology in place
    d. Education of its workforce

34. What does the Index of Coincident Indicators mainly measure?
    a. The condition of the economy
    b. Housing starts
    c. Gross domestic product
    d. Changes in the business cycle

35. What does "underemployment" most nearly mean?
    a. A company is not producing at its optimal level.
    b. A worker is doing a job he is overqualified for.
    c. All available workers are not being utilized.
    d. Workers in one area are not paid what workers in another area are for the same job.

36. What is the most likely result when the minimum wage is raised?
    a. A decrease in saving
    b. A decrease in inflation
    c. An increase in saving
    d. An increase in inflation

37. What is the most important component to a successful market economy?
    a. Price
    b. Government
    c. Banks
    d. Demand

38. An athlete will buy the same amount of spinach each week regardless of its price. What can be said of spinach and the athlete?
    a. The athlete's purchases are dependent on her income's elasticity.
    b. The athlete considers spinach a low utility purchase.
    c. The athlete has an inelastic demand for spinach.
    d. The athlete has an unlimited demand for spinach.

39. Two drivers set out for a destination 150 miles away. Car A travels at an average speed of 75 miles per hour. Car B travels at an average speed of 60 miles per hour. How soon *after* Car A arrives at the destination will Car B show up?
    a. 15 minutes
    b. 30 minutes
    c. 45 minutes
    d. 60 minutes

40. A book retails for $35.00. A book store marks it 15% off, today only. Those with frequent buyer cards get an additional 10% off when they show their card at the register. What will the book cost a frequent buyer today?
    a. $26.25
    b. $26.78
    c. $29.75
    d. $31.50

41. Six people step onto an elevator with a weight limit of 1,500 pounds. One person weighs 325 pounds. What would the average weight of each of the other people need to be to be within the limit?
    a. 195 pounds
    b. 235 pounds
    c. 250 pounds
    d. 300 pounds

42. The check for a $10,000 lottery win has 32% deducted for taxes. What is the amount of the check?
    a. $3,200
    b. $6,800
    c. $9,680
    d. $9.968

43. A man makes a $25,000 loan at 6% interest to a friend. The man repays $5,000. How much is still owed?
    a. $20,000
    b. $21,500
    c. $23,800
    d. $26,410

44. A man spends one-fourth of his day at school, one-twelfth of his day eating and doing errands, and one-half of his day working at his family business. How much of his day is left for sleeping?
    a. 4 hours
    b. 5 hours
    c. 6 hours
    d. 8 hours

45. What is a true statement about the subject line in an email?
    a. Most people do not bother reading it.
    b. It should be just one or two words.
    c. It is not necessary on most business emails.
    d. It should convey what the message is about.

46. When speaking to a heterogeneous audience of adults, to whom should planned remarks be targeted?
    a. To the middle part of the group
    b. To the most educated of the group
    c. To the least educated of the group
    d. To the least educated for the first half, to the most educated for the remainder

47. What does the Lindbergh Law primarily address?
    a. Aviation
    b. Kidnapping
    c. Food preparation
    d. Convicted criminals

48. Which leader was *not* part of the Allied Big Three who met for the Yalta Conference during World War II?
    a. Winston Churchill
    b. Franklin D. Roosevelt
    c. Douglas MacArthur
    d. Joseph Stalin

49. Which word describes a way to separate a computer network from viruses and outside networks?
    a. Bug
    b. Filter
    c. Firewall
    d. Encryption

50. In what year did the first human set foot on the moon?
    a. 1960
    b. 1962
    c. 1967
    d. 1969

51. Which part of a computer is considered to be its brain?
    a. Central processing unit (CPU)
    b. Random access memory (RAM)
    c. Operating system (OS)
    d. Universal resource locator (URL)

52. In order to add the fractions 5/7 and 3/8, what must first be found?
    a. Lowest common denominator
    b. The greatest common factor
    c. A multiple of 5
    d. The lowest factored numerator

53. Which 20th century American painter chose flowers and desert scenes as her most often painted subjects?
    a. Grandma Moses
    b. M. C. Escher
    c. Georgia O'Keeffe
    d. Mary Cassatt

54. Who wrote *The Catcher in the Rye*?
    a. George Orwell
    b. Holden Caulfield
    c. Joseph Heller
    d. J. D. Salinger

55. What is a true statement about individual employees' goals?
    a. They should be difficult for the employee to attain.
    b. They should be aligned with the organization's goals.
    c. They should be set up by a manager.
    d. There should be consequences for not attaining them.

56. The Immigration Reform and Control Act (IRCA) of 1986 required employers to:
    a. permit employees to speak their native language
    b. give hiring preference to people born in the United States
    c. verify that all employees can legally work in the United States
    d. give hiring preference to individuals born outside the United States

57. Who was the first woman secretary of state?
    a. Condoleezza Rice
    b. Hillary Clinton
    c. Sandra Day O'Connor
    d. Madeleine Albright

58. What is Three Mile Island in Pennsylvania mainly known for?
    a. Water pollution
    b. A nuclear power accident
    c. An oil spill
    d. A UFO sighting

59. Which is a phrase used to describe irresponsible and inflammatory reporting by the press?
    a. Propaganda
    b. Penny press
    c. Free speech
    d. Yellow journalism

60. What is a term used for a person who flees a nation for political freedom?
    a. Prisoner of war
    b. Nonresident alien
    c. Immigrant
    d. Refugee

English Expression

DIRECTIONS: In the four passages that follow, words and phrases are underlined and numbered. Read the alternate suggestions for each underlined part and choose the one that seems to work best with the style and tone of the article and is grammatically correct. The original response is always listed as the first option. Read each passage through before reviewing the questions and responses.

Passage 1

Questions 1 and 2 pertain to the following excerpt:

About fifty years ago, most of the public schools in the United States (1) <u>were segregated, that is, the schools were racially unbalanced</u>. This situation was apparent throughout the country but was especially prevalent in the South. There, neighborhoods were dotted with "black" schools and "white" schools. It would have been (2) <u>practically</u> unusual to find a white student in a "black" school, and the reverse was true too.

1. a. were segregated, that is; the schools were racially unbalanced
   b. were segregated that is, the schools were racially unbalanced
   c. were segregated, that is the schools were racially unbalanced
   d. were segregated that is the schools were racially unbalanced

2. a. practically
   b. pragmatically
   c. peculiarly
   d. particularly

Questions 3 and 4 pertain to the following excerpt:

In the period after World War II, clusters of people moved to where the work was—often from the South to the West, where shipyards were especially eager to get workers. These jobs were often filled by minority (3) <u>worker,</u> causing those areas of the country to become segregated. Economic factors had caused segregation in the North (4) <u>too</u> the North was where some people had found jobs and homes and had happily settled.

3. a. worker
   b. worker's
   c. workers'
   d. workers

4. a. too
   b. too;
   c. too,
   d. too:

- 195 -

Questions 5 and 6 pertain to the following excerpt:

This happened (5) <u>on account of</u> the interpretation of the 1896 Supreme Court decision in the *Plessey v. Ferguson* case. The consensus then was that black and white people were (6) <u>"separate but equal.".</u> It was inferred that since both the "black" schools and the "white" schools had comparable facilities, were staffed by trained teachers, and had grade-level-appropriate curricula, both schools provided the same type of education.

5. a. on account of
    b. because of
    c. cause of
    d. by way of

6. a. "separate but equal.".
    b. "separate but equal".
    c. "separate but equal,".
    d. "separate but equal."

Questions 7 to 9 pertain to the following excerpt:

The 1954 *Brown v. Board of Education of Topeka* Supreme Court ruling said that segregating students by race was unconstitutional. In short, segregation was illegal. (7) <u>Chief justice</u> Earl Warren (8) <u>"said that when black students are segregated, it causes harm."</u> He advocated a mixture of black and white students in schools around the country. Warren said that learning for both racial groups would improve (9) <u>when there were</u> both black and white students in the same school.

7. a. Chief justice
    b. The chief justice
    c. The chief Justice
    d. Chief Justice

8. a. "said that when black students are segregated, it causes harm."
    b. said that when black students are segregated, it causes harm.
    c. said "that when black students are segregated, it causes harm."
    d. said that "when black students are segregated," it causes harm.

9. a. when there were
    b. when there was
    c. when, there were
    d. when, there was

Questions 10 to 12 pertain to the following excerpt:

To achieve this goal, the Supreme Court ordered students to be bused from their school to another one—sometimes very far away—as the school districts (10) <u>attempted to create the racial balance</u> in all of their schools. Students often drove by a school right in (11) <u>his own neighborhood</u> to one in the next county. If school districts had not abided by the Supreme Court decision, (12) <u>they would of lost</u> their government funding.

10. a. attempted to create the racial balance
    b. attempt creating the racial balance
    c. attempted to create a racial balance
    d. attempt creating a racial balance

11. a. his own neighborhood
    b. her own neighborhood
    c. its own neighborhood
    d. their own neighborhood

12. a. they would of lost
    b. they would not of lost
    c. they would have lost
    d. they would not have lost

Passage 2

Questions 13 to 16 pertain to the following excerpt:

Most journalists would agree that print newspapers today are in survival mode. The past decade has been an unsettled one for national and local papers, as online technology has provided (13) <u>enhanced opportunity's"</u> for readers to get news that is usually (14) <u>free, extensive, and available</u> at any time of the day or night. Add our (15) <u>countries'</u> current poor economic conditions to the equation and publishers of most large national newspapers don't need to read quarterly figures. They know that the (16) <u>circulation figures for print newspapers continue</u> to fall.

13. a. "enhanced opportunity's"
    b. enhanced opportunity's
    c. "enhanced opportunities"
    d. enhanced opportunities

14. a. free, extensive, and available
    b. free extensive and available
    c. free, extensive, and available,
    d. free extensive, and available

15. a. countries'
    b. country's
    c. countries
    d. countrys'

- 197 -

16. a. circulation figures for print newspapers continue
    b. circulation figures for print newspapers continues
    c. circulation figure for print newspapers continue
    d. circulation figure for print newspapers continues

Questions 17 to 20 pertain to the following excerpt:

> Since they employ so many people in a variety of capacities, newspaper publishers have a dilemma that is (17) <u>not only going to get more worse</u> with time. They know that their reading audience is moving to online content. Although most of (18) <u>there</u> older readers are still loyal to the print edition of the newspaper, the number of new, younger readers is in decline. These tech-savvy readers get almost all of their news through the electronic (20) <u>media their computers cell phones and handheld devices</u>. News executives, many of them not completely comfortable with technology themselves, must figure out a way to be successful in this easily accessible electronic world.

17. a. not only going to get more worse
    b. not only going to get more worse
    c. only going to get more worse
    d. only going to get worse

18. a. there
    b. their
    c. theyre
    d. they're

19. The writer wants to add this sentence to the paragraph:

    They must solve their problem before their company is no longer viable.

The best place to put this sentence would be after the sentence ending with:
    a. . . . moving to online content.
    b. . . . younger readers is in decline.
    c. . . . cell phones, and handheld devices.
    d. . . . in this easily accessible electronic world.

20. a. media their computers cell phones and handheld devices
    b. media, their computers, cell phones, and handheld devices
    c. media: their computers, cell phones, and handheld devices
    d. media: their computers, cell, phones and handheld devices

- 198 -

Questions 21 to 25 pertain to the following excerpt:

> Advertising online may not have the impact a print advertisement can have. Think of (22) <u>a full page advertisement</u> in (23) *The New York Times* or *USA Today*. A well-placed print ad is often difficult for readers (24) <u>to ignore it.</u> The opposite tends to be true with online advertising—savvy readers can click past an ad in a second. Advertisers are still gauging the effectiveness of placing their ads on online (25) <u>newscites.</u>

21. Which of the following sentences would provide the best introduction to paragraph 3?
    a. Many newspapers contain advertisements of different sizes.
    b. A logical place to gain revenue is advertising.
    c. Advertising is big business.
    d. Don't count out advertising.

22. a. a full page advertisement
    b. a full, page advertisement
    c. a full-page-advertisement
    d. a full-page advertisement

23. a. The New York Times
    b. The New York Times:
    c. The New York Times,
    d. The New York Times—

24. a. to ignore it
    b. to ignore them
    c. to be ignored
    d. to ignore

25. a. newscites
    b. news sites
    c. news sights
    d. newsites

Questions 26 to 30 pertain to the following excerpt:

> Some newspapers have experimented with charging a (26) <u>fee for access to their</u> online news sites. Successful (27) <u>subscription, based</u> online newspapers have content that is (28) <u>both unique or valuable</u>. Since many reputable websites offer their news at no charge and update it constantly, it is difficult for most newspapers to compete online. (29) <u>Subscribers'</u> seem to have no reason to pay for (30) <u>his</u> newspaper's content.

26. a. fee for access to their
    b. fee for accessing to their
    c. fees for assess to their
    d. fee assessing to their

- 199 -

27. a. subscription, based
    b. subscription based
    c. subscription-based
    d. subscription based,

28. a. both unique or valuable
    b. both unique, or valuable
    c. both unique, and valuable
    d. both unique and valuable

29. a. Subscribers'
    b. Subscriber's
    c. Subscribers
    d. Subscriber

30. a. his
    b. her
    c. their
    d. its

Questions 31 to 36 pertain to the following excerpt:

> News is big business. Publishers and owners of print newspapers must figure out ways to (33) <u>keep their readers loyal, produce revenue, and</u> stay viable in (34) <u>todays' changing world</u>. Most newspaper executives know that the window of time (35) <u>to adopted</u> to the changing market narrows each week.

31. What is the best place to put this additional sentence?

That's why the next year will be crucial to this market.
    a. Before Sentence 1
    b. After Sentence 1
    c. After Sentence 2
    d. After Sentence 3

32. Who is the most likely audience for this passage?
    a. The general reading public
    b. Newspaper executives
    c. Newspaper readers
    d. Newspaper advertisers

33. a. keep their readers loyal, produce revenue, and
    b. keep their readers loyal produce revenue and
    c. keep their readers loyal, produce, revenue, and
    d. keep their readers, loyal produce, revenue and

34. a. today's changing world
    b. todays changing world
    c. today's changing world
    d. to-day's changing world

- 200 -

35. a. to adopted
    b. to adapted
    c. to adapt
    d. to adopt

36. Which sentence works to summarize the passage?
    a. Newspapers won't be around much longer.
    b. The industry's very livelihood is at stake.
    c. Many people wonder what will happen next.
    d. Many people get their news today on the Internet.

Passage 3

Questions 37 to 41 pertain to the following excerpt:

Cronyism (37) <u>was</u> best (38) <u>described like</u> when a person in (39) <u>an authoritarian position</u> gives a job to a loyal friend or social contact simply because of (40) <u>their relationship to each other.</u> Many times the person hired or appointed is not particularly qualified to perform the job and learns the duties once in (41) <u>place</u>—on-the-job-training.

37. a. was
    b. were
    c. is
    d. are

38. a. described like
    b. described as
    c. described when
    d. described if

39. a. an authoritative position
    b. a position of authority
    c. a position
    d. the know

40. a. their relationship to each other.
    b. each's relationship to the other.
    c. ones' relationship with the other.
    d. the relationship one has with the other.

41. a. place—on
    b. place. On
    c. place; on
    d. place on

Questions 42 to 44 pertain to the following excerpt:

> Cronyism is a problem for business and government because the most qualified (or even a marginally qualified) person is (42) <u>overlooked with regard to a position</u> in favor of an administrator's or (43) <u>managers'</u> buddy with zero experience in that line of work. This friend, or crony, usually won't perform the duties of the job with any efficiency or skill and (44) <u>the company, business, or organization</u> can suffer as money and time is wasted and the job is not being done as well as it could be.

42. a. overlooked with regard to a position
    b. overlooked with a position
    c. overlooked during a position
    d. overlooked for a position

43. a. managers'
    b. managers
    c. manager
    d. manager's

44. a. the company, business, or organization
    b. the company business, or organization
    c. the company—business—or organization
    d. the company; business; or organization;

Questions 45 to 47 pertain to the following excerpt:

> Some of those in political office (45) <u>felt compelled</u> to surround themselves with the friends and supporters who have often provided the financial backing to help them win the election. Indeed, the term "cronyism" often refers to jobs and appointments given by those in political office (46) <u>significantly to financial support</u>. Sometimes the elected official's cabinet is made up almost entirely of longstanding buddies who may or may not know what they are doing. The political appointment may be an expected outcome for a successful election. This is a particular problem, since public money is used to pay these government workers. It is to be (47) <u>expected, then,</u> that all eligible candidates are considered for all open appointments.

45. a. felt compelled
    b. felt compelling
    c. feel compelled
    d. feel compelling

46. a. significantly to financial support
    b. to significant financial supporters
    c. to significantly support finances
    d. to supporters who are significant

47. a. expected, then,
    b. expected then,
    c. expected, then
    d. expected then

Questions 48 to 50 pertain to the following excerpt:

Some historians (48) <u>cite</u> President John Kennedy's appointment of his longtime friend Robert McNamara as (49) <u>secretary of defense</u> as a classic case of cronyism. McNamara had no experience at all in foreign affairs or defense strategies, yet was given this highly influential and important appointment by his friend. Robert McNamara is often mentioned as the person directly responsible for getting the United States involved in the war in Vietnam—(50)

48. a. cite
    b. site
    c. sight
    d. sighed

49. a. secretary of defense
    b. Secretary of defense
    c. Secretary Of Defense
    d. Secretary of Defense

50. Which ending to this sentence provides the best conclusion to the passage?
    a. a war that is said to be a disastrous event in our country's history.
    b. a war that was fought for many years.
    c. a war that many people today may not understand.
    d. a war that has cronyism to thank for its inception.

Passage 4

Questions 51 to 53 pertain to the following excerpt:

A nuclear nonproliferation treaty was signed in 1968 to attempt to stop the spread of nuclear technology. The United Nations was instrumental in (51) <u>ensuring</u> that the text of the treaty conveyed what it meant to—that the United States and other so-called nuclear states (France, United Kingdom, the then–Soviet Union, (52) <u>Peoples Republic Of China</u>) could not provide nuclear weapons to nonnuclear states—those states that did not have them. The treaty was signed by over sixty countries, but some refused. (53) Israel, Pakistan, India, and North Korea have admitted having nuclear weapons but won't agree to abide by the treaty.

51. a. ensuring
    b. assuring
    c. insuring
    d. reassuring

52. a. Peoples Republic Of China
    b. People's Republic of China
    c. Peoples Republic of China
    d. People's Republic Of China

- 203 -

53. Which sentence best joins the previous sentence with the one following?
    a. Here are the names of the countries.
    b. All of these countries cite the same reasons.
    c. There are a variety of reasons.
    d. They won't sign the treaty.

Questions 54 to 56 pertain to the following excerpt:

(54) The first pillar ensures safety with all nuclear weaponry presently in possession of countries in the treaty. Those countries that have signed the treaty agree that they will not receive, create, or otherwise get or use another country's help to acquire nuclear weapons. They vow that they won't use those nuclear weapons they may already have (55) <u>excepting</u> to protect (56) <u>their self.</u>

54. Which sentence best introduces this paragraph?
    a. The nuclear nonproliferation treaty comprises three parts, or pillars.
    b. The nuclear nonproliferation treaty is made up of pillars.
    c. The nuclear nonproliferation treaty is multi-faceted.
    d. The nuclear nonproliferation treaty is three-tiered.

55. a. excepting
    b. accepting
    c. except
    d. accept

56. a. their self.
    b. their selves.
    c. them self.
    d. themselves.

Questions 57 to 60 pertain to the following excerpt:

The second pillar of the treaty says that those (57) <u>nuclear weapons' countries</u> should work toward disarmament, meaning (58) <u>therefore, that</u> they are to eliminate those weapons that they may already have. This part of the treaty may be difficult to enforce and (59) <u>implying</u> international trust that all countries will eventually work toward that end. Since the treaty asks countries to negotiate this pillar in (60) <u>Good Faith</u>, it may make enforcement procedures difficult as the treaty is presently written. Still, countries signing the treaty have agreed that disarmament is an ultimate goal.

57. a. nuclear weapons' countries
    b. nuclear weapons countries
    c. countries with nuclear weapons
    d. countries with nuclear weapons'

58. a. therefore, that
    b. therefore that
    c. that
    d. OMIT phrase

- 204 -

59. a. implying
    b. implies
    c. applying
    d. applies

60. a. Good Faith
    b. good faith
    c. "Good Faith"
    d. "good faith"

Questions 61 to 65 pertain to the following excerpt:

> The third pillar of the treaty allows for <u>peacetime</u> use of nuclear energy. Compliance (62) <u>about</u> this part of the (63) <u>treaty; means</u> that countries are still able to use the nuclear energy they presently have, but not as part of nuclear weaponry. Nuclear materials (64) <u>that are</u> generally considered to be ingredients for nuclear weapons (e.g., uranium, plutonium) should be carefully overseen.

61. a. peacetime
    b. peaceable
    c. peacelike
    d. peaceful

62. a. about
    b. among
    c. with
    d. over

63. a. treaty; means
    b. treaty, means
    c. treaty. Means
    d. treaty means

64. a. that are
    b. which are
    c. are
    d. OMIT the underlined portion

65. Which sentence could best be used as a final sentence of this passage?
    a. The three pillars of the treaty combine for a strong program among those who have signed.
    b. The treaty is ultimately meaningless, since not all nuclear materials are being overseen in this way.
    c. The three pillars contain essentially the same information and should be combined into one.
    d. The three pillars of the treaty ensure that there are no nuclear problems in our world.

Use the following directions to answer questions 66 – 68:

In the following sentence, certain words and phrases are underlined and numbered. Each sentence is followed by alternatives for each underlined part. Choose the alternative that best expresses the idea in standard written English. If you think the original version is best, choose option A—the same as the original version.

Central American (66) <u>countrys</u> are (67) <u>numerously</u> mentioned in (68) <u>News</u>, mainly on account of the political problems in this part of the world.

66. a. countrys
    b. country's
    c. countries'
    d. countries

67. a. numerously
    b. often
    c. hardly
    d. continuously

68. a. News
    b. news
    c. the news
    d. the News

Question 69 pertains to the following excerpt:

The North Korean security forces are notorious for interfering with the decisions of the court. Most of the time, the end result of court cases can easily be concluded before the judiciary have even started discussions.

69. Which of the following would be the best opening sentence for this paragraph?
    a. The North Korean court system is known for its widespread corruption.
    b. Most court systems in the world are conducted differently from the United States.
    c. North Korea's citizens must endure inequities throughout the court system.
    d. Judges in North Korea are not equitable with their decisions.

Question 70 pertains to the following excerpt:

The United States Border Patrol works hard to ensure that our country's borders are safe. The job formerly consisted of mainly halting entry of illegal aliens and contraband across our borders. The job has become much more than that. (70)

70. If the writer wants to add a sentence here to explain how the job has become "more than that," which of the following sentences best accomplishes that goal?
    a. Border patrol agents now must protect against terrorists and illegal weapons crossing the border.
    b. Border patrol agents work constantly to protect our country's citizens.
    c. Border patrol agents must know how to recognize all sorts of ways illegal aliens may be able to sneak into the country.
    d. Border patrol agents must recognize that they have a dangerous job.

Written Essay

You will have 30 minutes to write an essay on an assigned topic. Sample topics are provided below. Choose one.

As you create your essay, you should present and support your point of view. Your writing will be evaluated on the quality of the writing and not on your opinion. A good essay will have an organized structure, clear thesis, and logical supporting details. Ensure that you are presenting your topic in a way that appeals to your target audience. Use clear and appropriate word choice throughout. Ensure that grammar, punctuation, and spelling are correct. Your response can be of any length.

1. Sudan's borders were drawn during British colonial times. The Sudanese north comprises Muslim Arabs, while Africans of various faiths are mainly in the south. The people living in Sudan's south have experienced slave raids since Islamic law was imposed there in 1983. Describe how and why the conflict in Sudan has become even more serious since 1989.

2. Conservative and liberal thinkers have vastly differing views about fundamental components of our society, our government, our rights, and life in general. Identify at least three key issues and the differences of viewpoints held by those thinkers coming from the left as contrasted with those coming from the right.

Answers and Explanations

Job Knowledge

1. C: "Bcc" means "blind carbon copy." When an email is sent this way, the original recipient does not know who else may be getting it. Sending a cc means that all recipients know who is getting a copy. Forwarding an email is a way to send it to someone else without letting the intended recipient know, but it is not the most efficient way.

2. D: The mode is the value that occurs most often in a listing.

3. D: The U.S. banking system is one of the most regulated banking systems in the world, with regulations within each state and the federal government.

4. A: Although many programs were introduced under Franklin Roosevelt's New Deal, the Medicaid and Medicare programs were started by Johnson.

5. A: The Federal Reserve System raises and lowers the prime rate to regulate the nation's money supply.

6. B: The waterways of the United States are closely tied to its ability to transport the goods that are able to be grown year-round within the country. This greatly affects the economy. The U.S. government has a laissez-faire policy as it applies to the economy. Russia's geography means that there is a short growing season. The country has a very small coastline and waterways that do not connect. Their economy is defined by their geography.

7. C: The premier is the head of the cabinet in North Korea's government.

8. A: Among the choices listed, a database is best defined as a tool that is used for collecting and organizing information. The other choices are all potential uses for a database, but choice A is the best general definition.

9. A: Good managers will set up an environment where people will be motivated to work.

10. B: Title VII prohibits intentional discrimination and practices with the effect of discriminating against individuals because of their race, color, national origin, religion, or gender.

11. B: Noncitizens are able to receive Medicaid, food stamps, and Social Security benefits. They contribute to the economy by working, paying taxes, and buying products.

12. D: *Perestroika* was an economic restructuring in Soviet society.

13. C: Lech Walesa was the president during this time. Helmut Kohl was the German chancellor. Ceausescu was a Communist dictator. Havel was elected president of the Czech Republic in 1989.

14. C: Sinn Fein is a party that wants Northern Ireland's independence from Britain. Al-Qaeda is a Muslim terrorist group.

15. D: "Globalization" means to be adopted on a global scale; "stabilization" means to make a situation or thing stable.

16. C: The Maastricht Treaty was signed in the Netherlands and created both the European Union and the euro as its currency.

17. A: Max Planck was a German physicist who studied radiation. Niels Bohr studied properties of the atom. James Watson worked with Crick to identify the model for DNA.

18. A: Germany developed rocket technology and the United States put a man on the moon in 1969.

19. B: Neoliberalism is an economic model encouraged by the United States which encourages free markets and private ownership of businesses.

20. C: In absolutism, the ruler is sovereign. Kings often said that they were governed by divine right and were responsible to only God. Patriarchy is a social organization where descent follows the male line. An oligarchy is a small group of people who control a government. Communism is where a communist party holds power alone.

21. C: There are Federal Reserve banks in (1) Atlanta; (2) Boston; (3) Chicago; (4) Cleveland; (5) Dallas; (6) Kansas City, Missouri; (7) Minneapolis; (8) New York; (9) Philadelphia; (10) Richmond; (11) St. Louis; (12) San Francisco.

22. D: A stateless nation is one that wants statehood but does not have it (Kurds in the Middle East). An industrialized but not democratic country is how a Second World country is usually described. An impoverished and unstable country is a description of a Third World country.

23. D: In 2002, the United States was involved with nation building in Afghanistan.

24. A: The Patriot Act was specifically formed to combat terrorism.

25. B: The First Amendment covers freedom of the press, petitioning the government, and assembling peacefully. "Cruel and unusual punishment" is covered in the Eighth Amendment.

26. B: The Fourth Amendment outlaws unreasonable search and seizure. The Eighth Amendment protects against excessive bail. The Fourteenth Amendment states the rights of citizenship.

27. D: *Suffrage* can encompass many groups, but the word means "the right to vote."

28. A: A delegate is a person chosen to serve on a particular committee or group. A legislator is a lawmaker. A lame duck is a person who is holding an office but will not retain it.

29. D: Senators are elected for a term of 6 years.

30. C: A candidate must have resided in the United States for at least 14 years.

31. C: Chairpersons for standing committees of Congress are chosen by leaders of the majority party.

32. A: Although Congress must agree to pay for foreign policy dictated by the president, it does not decide foreign policy.

33. D: The education of the workforce generally does not affect GDP. The size of the workforce implies that there are people who are ready and willing to work. The amount of capital means that there is a sufficient number of factories and assets available to create goods and services. Technology includes the skills and knowledge people have to direct and enable the workforce.

34. A: The Index has four different indicators to assess the country's economic growth.

35. B: Underemployment means that workers are doing jobs they are somehow overqualified to do.

36. D: Raising the minimum wage ultimately causes a rise in the rate of inflation, since employers' labor costs are raised. Employers pass this increase on as higher prices for their goods and services.

37. A: Price determines what goods will be produced, who will be producing them, and how they will be produced. Banks and demand are both affected by price. Government is not a big part of a market economy and is more a part of a command economy.

38. C: An inelastic demand is not very sensitive to changes in price. "Utility" means satisfaction or usefulness, which is not affected if the athlete buys the same amount of spinach every week.

39. B: Car A would arrive in 2 hours (150 miles/75 mph = 2). Car B would arrive in 2 hours and 30 minutes. In 2 hours at 60 mph, the car would go 120 miles, with 30 miles left to travel.

40. B: To find the correct price, first subtract 15% from the price of the book ($35.00 – 5.25 = $29.75). Then subtract 10% from the discounted price ($29.75 – $2.97 = $26.78). Choice A is incorrect because the 2 percent figures cannot be added together. Choice C is just 15% off the original price. Choice D is just 10% off the original price.

41. B: Subtract 325 from 1500, and then divide by the 5 people left. Choice A is incorrect because the resulting figure after subtracting 325 is divided by 6, and not 5. Choice C is incorrect because it is the total (1500) divided by 6. Choice D is incorrect because it is the total divided by 5.

42. B: Multiply $10,000 by .32 = $3,200. Subtract this amount from the total winnings: $10,000 – $3,200 = $6,800.

43. B: Multiply $25,000 by .06 = $1,500. Add the interest to the principal: $25,000 + $1,500 = $26,500. Subtract the $5,000 payment: $26,500 – $5,000 = $21,500.

44. A: In a 24-hour day, one-fourth = 6 hours. Subtract this from 24 to get 18 hours. One-twelfth of his day = 2 hours. Subtract this from 18 to get 16 hours. One-half of his day = 12 hours. Subtract this from 16 to get 4 hours.

45. D: A subject line is an important part of an email and should contain a strong clue about what the message is about.

46. A: The group will be made up of people with varying education levels, attitudes, prior knowledge, and interests.

47. B: The law was created as a result of the 1932 kidnapping and murder of Charles Lindbergh's baby son.

48. C: Douglas MacArthur was Roosevelt's general who advised him during this time but was not one of the Big Three. Winston Churchill was the British prime minister, Roosevelt was the ailing U.S. president, and Joseph Stalin was the head of the Soviet Union.

49. C: A firewall protects a computer from other computers and viruses. Encryption is a way to send something so that it can be read by only the recipient. A filter screens incoming messages. A bug is a problem with a computer.

50. D: The first man walked on the moon on July 20, 1969.

51. A: The CPU is the most important part of the computer. RAM is the type of memory a computer uses. A URL is part of a web address. The OS is software used by the computer.

52. A: The denominator is the number on the bottom of a fraction. The denominator must be the same to add fractions, so before adding, the least common denominator must be found.

53. C: Grandma Moses painted scenes of farm life. Escher was Dutch and was known for his lithographs and woodcuts. Mary Cassatt painted portraits of mothers and children.

54. D: George Orwell wrote *1984.* Holden Caulfield is the main character in *The Catcher in the Rye.* Joseph Heller wrote *Catch-22.*

55. B: Goals should closely align with what the company or organization is trying to do. Although employees are usually rewarded for reaching their goals, they are not typically penalized for not reaching them. They should be set by the employee and should be attainable—but not necessarily difficult.

56. C: The law requires employers to ensure that those they hire are legally permitted to work in the United States.

57. D: Madeleine Albright was chosen as secretary of state in 1997 by President Clinton. Condoleezza Rice was secretary of state under George W. Bush, Hillary Clinton was secretary of state under Barack Obama. Sandra Day O'Connor was a U.S. Supreme Court judge.

58. B: It was the site of a nuclear power accident in 1979.

59. D: Free speech means that people can generally say what they want to. Propaganda is misinformation and half-truths about something. "Penny press" is the phrase used to describe the early newspapers published in the United States.

60. D: Although an immigrant or a nonresident alien can be a refugee, the term for people who flee for political reasons is "refugee."

English Expression

1. A: The phrase "that is" continues with the same thought as what precedes it, so it belongs in the same sentence, but it begins a new independent clause, which requires a semicolon rather than a comma.

2. D: Both B and C mean "logically."

3. D: The plural form of "worker" is needed to make the sentence complete.

4. B: The semicolon is often used to join two closely related simple sentences.

5. B: The reasoning is "because of" the decision.

6. D: There is only one period and it is enclosed in the quotation mark. This is considered the end-of-sentence punctuation.

7. D: The words "Chief Justice" refer to Earl Warren's title and both should be capitalized.

8. B: The words mentioned here are not presented as a quote, so quotation marks should not be used.

9. A: The plural noun "students" means that "were" is used here. There is no need for a comma after "when."

10. C: The phrase aligns with the way the sentence is written. Since there is no particular racial balance referred to in the passage, "a" is used and not "the" when referring to that balance.

11. D: The plural "students" is the subject of the sentence. The plural "their" must be used to describe whose neighborhood it is.

12. C: The sentence mentions that school districts had to abide by the decision or lose funding. "Would of" is improper grammar. "Would have" is correct here.

13. D: There is no indication that the phrase is a quote, so quotation marks should not be used here. The plural of "opportunity" is "opportunities."

14. A: The words "free" and "extensive" should be separated by a comma, and so should "extensive" and "and." There should not be a comma after "available," since it is not part of the list.

15. B: The passage is referring to one country (the United States), and the noun "country" is in the possessive form here—apostrophe *s*.

16. A: Since "figures" is the subject of the sentence (it must be "figures" and not "figure," since it refers to more than one newspaper), "continue" must align with that word. "The figures continue" is correct but not "The figures continues."

17. D: "More worse" is considered to be bad grammar. Using "not only" implies that there will be a "but" to complete the thought, which is not the case here.

18. B: The word refers to the newspaper's older readers—the possessive form. "There" means "in that place." "Theyre" is not a word. "They're" is the contracted form of "they are."

19. D: The sentence ties up the paragraph and is best used to conclude it.

20. C: The colon after "media" indicates that the words that follow will further explain it. These items are listed, so there should be a comma after each one.

21. B: The sentence provides an overview of the solution to the problem. Sentence A provides a fact about print advertising, which is not really what the paragraph is about. Sentence C provides a statement that does not address the main idea of the paragraph—that advertising may not work as well online as it does in a print paper. Sentence D infers that advertising may work well online, which contradicts what the paragraph seems to state.

22. D: The words "full-page" are hyphenated to form an adjective phrase describing "advertisement."

23. A: There are only two newspapers listed and they are separated by "or." They do not have to be additionally separated by a comma or any other punctuation mark.

24. D: The word "it" is not needed here, since it is clear from the sentence that "ignore" is referring to "ads." Adding "it" or "them" is incorrect grammatically. "To be ignored" implies that the readers will be ignored, changing the meaning of the sentence.

25. B: "News sites" is short for "news websites." This is the only acceptable spelling.

26. A: The fee is charged for readers to gain access to the site. "Assess" means to evaluate or review something. The -*ing* form of either word is not grammatically correct here.

27. C: The words "subscription based" describe "online newspapers." The words must be joined with a hyphen to form an adjective phrase that is read together. The commas are not necessary.

28. D: The word "both" means that the words following will go together. The conjunction "or" can't be used here, as it means "either." There is no need for a comma, since there are only two adjectives listed to describe the content.

29. C: The plural form of "subscriber" is used with "seem." There is no apostrophe, since the word is not in the possessive form.

30. C: The subject of the sentence is plural: subscribers. The pronoun "their" is plural.

31. D: The sentence provides a summary and conclusion to the passage, so should appear at the end of the piece.

32. A: The passage provides information that it is likely all newspaper executives and advertisers already know. The newspaper reader is one segment of the audience of general readers, to whom this piece is most likely directed.

33. A: The phrases "keep their readers loyal" and "produce revenue" are part of a list of ways newspaper owners will try to save their business. The listed phrases must each be separated by a comma.

34. C: The noun "today's" is in the singular possessive form, with "changing world" further describing "today."

35. C: "Adapt" refers to what the news executives have to do. "Adopt" is not used correctly here. The present tense is used in the sentence, so the verb "adapt" should correctly be used in the present tense.

36. B: This sentence discusses the entire newspaper industry, which has been the subject of the article. Answer A provides an opinion that may or may not be correct. Answer C does not summarize the article but just provides a thought about newspapers. Answer D restates a fact that readers will already be aware of.

37. C: The sentence is written in the present tense, and the noun "cronyism" is written in the singular form.

38. B: The words following this phrase provide a definition of the phrase.

39. B: An authoritarian position is a strict position. The person appointing another to a job must be in a position of authority—one that will allow him or her to make such appointments or hires.

40. A: This response provides the most succinct way to make this point.

41. A: The dash is used here to add words, almost as an afterthought. A semicolon is used to join two simple sentences. The words appearing after "place" cannot stand alone, so cannot be considered a simple sentence.

42. D: The person is not noticed for a particular position—he or she is overlooked for it. Other responses indicate complicated or confusing ways to say this.

43. D: The singular form of "manager" is used in this sentence, and this is made possessive by adding an apostrophe *s*.

44. A: Each item on the list is separated by a comma.

45. C: The sentence and the paragraph are both written in the present tense. "Compelled" means "obligated," which is the form of "compel" that is needed here.

46. B: The jobs are given to those who provide a good, or significant, amount of financial support to the person seeking office.

47. D: No commas are needed to set off the word "then" in this sentence.

48. A: "Cite" means to quote, or mention. This is the meaning needed for this sentence.

49. D: This political office is a title and as such, the first and last words must be capitalized.

50. A: The end of this sentence provides a reason why McNamara's decision to enter the war may not have been one an experienced official may have made. It provides a conclusion to the article by giving an example of how cronyism can backfire.

51. A: The word "ensuring" means "making certain," and it is used correctly in this sentence.

52. B: "Of" is not capitalized in this country's official name (nor would it be in a title), and "People" is in its possessive form.

53. B: The sentence that follows implies that each of these non-signing countries provides the same reason for not signing.

54. A: The sentence provides a meaning for the word "pillar," which is introduced at the beginning of the next sentence and used within the rest of the passage.

55. C: "Except" means "but" or "only in this instance.

56. D: This sentence is talking about the countries involved with the treaty, so "themselves" is used.

57. C: "Nuclear weapons' countries" is awkward phrasing and should not be used here. There is no possessive form when the phrase is converted to "countries with nuclear weapons."

58. D: This phrase can be omitted without changing the meaning of the sentence.

59. B: The sentence is written in the present tense. "Applies" means "pertains to" or "relates to." This is not the meaning conveyed in this sentence.

60. B: "Good faith" is a phrase meaning "with fairness and trust." It is not presented in quotes or capitalized, since it is an accepted English-language phrase.

61. D: The sentence infers that nuclear energy should be used only for good.

62. C: Countries comply "with" an agreement or treaty—meaning that they will uphold what they have signed.

63. D: This part of the sentence does not need a semicolon, comma, or period, since it is not a clause or phrase.

64. D: The phrase can be omitted and the sentence does not lose its meaning.

65. A: The pillars are only as effective as those who have signed them.

66. D: The word is written in the plural form and an apostrophe is not needed, since there is no possession here.

67. B: The word "numerously" implies that there is a number associated with the amount of times it is mentioned, which is not the case. "Continuously" means that it does not stop. "Hardly" infers that they are not mentioned much, which is in contrast with the rest of the sentence.

68. C: "News" is not a proper noun, so should not be capitalized. It is preceded by "the" when used as a collective noun, as it is here.

69. A: The sentence provides a general introduction to what comes next in the short paragraph.

70. A: This sentence provides details to explain the statement made in the sentence above it.

Secret Key #1 - Time is Your Greatest Enemy

Pace Yourself

Wear a watch. At the beginning of the test, check the time (or start a chronometer on your watch to count the minutes), and check the time after every few questions to make sure you are "on schedule."

If you are forced to speed up, do it efficiently. Usually one or more answer choices can be eliminated without too much difficulty. Above all, don't panic. Don't speed up and just begin guessing at random choices. By pacing yourself, and continually monitoring your progress against your watch, you will always know exactly how far ahead or behind you are with your available time. If you find that you are one minute behind on the test, don't skip one question without spending any time on it, just to catch back up. Take 15 fewer seconds on the next four questions, and after four questions you'll have caught back up. Once you catch back up, you can continue working each problem at your normal pace.

Furthermore, don't dwell on the problems that you were rushed on. If a problem was taking up too much time and you made a hurried guess, it must be difficult. The difficult questions are the ones you are most likely to miss anyway, so it isn't a big loss. It is better to end with more time than you need than to run out of time.

Lastly, sometimes it is beneficial to slow down if you are constantly getting ahead of time. You are always more likely to catch a careless mistake by working more slowly than quickly, and among very high-scoring test takers (those who are likely to have lots of time left over), careless errors affect the score more than mastery of material.

Secret Key #2 - Guessing is not Guesswork

You probably know that guessing is a good idea. Unlike other standardized tests, there is no penalty for getting a wrong answer. Even if you have no idea about a question, you still have a 20-25% chance of getting it right.

Most test takers do not understand the impact that proper guessing can have on their score. Unless you score extremely high, guessing will significantly contribute to your final score.

Monkeys Take the Test

What most test takers don't realize is that to insure that 20-25% chance, you have to guess randomly. If you put 20 monkeys in a room to take this test, assuming they answered once per question and behaved themselves, on average they would get 20-25% of the questions correct.

Put 20 test takers in the room, and the average will be much lower among guessed questions. Why?

1. The test writers intentionally write deceptive answer choices that "look" right. A test taker has no idea about a question, so he picks the "best looking" answer, which is often wrong. The monkey has no idea what looks good and what doesn't, so it will consistently be right about 20-25% of the time.
2. Test takers will eliminate answer choices from the guessing pool based on a hunch or intuition. Simple but correct answers often get excluded, leaving a 0% chance of being correct. The monkey has no clue, and often gets lucky with the best choice.

This is why the process of elimination endorsed by most test courses is flawed and detrimental to your performance. Test takers don't guess; they make an ignorant stab in the dark that is usually worse than random.

$5 Challenge

Let me introduce one of the most valuable ideas of this course—the $5 challenge:

You only mark your "best guess" if you are willing to bet $5 on it.
You only eliminate choices from guessing if you are willing to bet $5 on it.

Why $5? Five dollars is an amount of money that is small yet not insignificant, and can really add up fast (20 questions could cost you $100). Likewise, each answer choice on one question of the test will have a small impact on your overall score, but it can really add up to a lot of points in the end.

The process of elimination IS valuable. The following shows your chance of guessing it right:

If you eliminate wrong answer choices until only this many remain:	Chance of getting it correct:
1	100%
2	50%
3	33%

However, if you accidentally eliminate the right answer or go on a hunch for an incorrect answer, your chances drop dramatically—to 0%. By guessing among all the answer choices, you are GUARANTEED to have a shot at the right answer.

That's why the $5 test is so valuable. If you give up the advantage and safety of a pure guess, it had better be worth the risk.

What we still haven't covered is how to be sure that whatever guess you make is truly random. Here's the easiest way:

Always pick the first answer choice among those remaining.

Such a technique means that you have decided, **before you see a single test question**, exactly how you are going to guess, and since the order of choices tells you nothing about which one is correct, this guessing technique is perfectly random.

This section is not meant to scare you away from making educated guesses or eliminating choices; you just need to define when a choice is worth eliminating. The $5 test, along with a pre-defined random guessing strategy, is the best way to make sure you reap all of the benefits of guessing.

Secret Key #3 - Practice Smarter, Not Harder

Many test takers delay the test preparation process because they dread the awful amounts of practice time they think necessary to succeed on the test. We have refined an effective method that will take you only a fraction of the time.

There are a number of "obstacles" in the path to success. Among these are answering questions, finishing in time, and mastering test-taking strategies. All must be executed on the day of the test at peak performance, or your score will suffer. The test is a mental marathon that has a large impact on your future.

Just like a marathon runner, it is important to work your way up to the full challenge. So first you just worry about questions, and then time, and finally strategy:

Success Strategy

1. Find a good source for practice tests.
2. If you are willing to make a larger time investment, consider using more than one study guide. Often the different approaches of multiple authors will help you "get" difficult concepts.
3. Take a practice test with no time constraints, with all study helps, "open book." Take your time with questions and focus on applying strategies.
4. Take a practice test with time constraints, with all guides, "open book."
5. Take a final practice test without open material and with time limits.

If you have time to take more practice tests, just repeat step 5. By gradually exposing yourself to the full rigors of the test environment, you will condition your mind to the stress of test day and maximize your success.

Secret Key #4 - Prepare, Don't Procrastinate

Let me state an obvious fact: if you take the test three times, you will probably get three different scores. This is due to the way you feel on test day, the level of preparedness you have, and the version of the test you see. Despite the test writers' claims to the contrary, some versions of the test WILL be easier for you than others.

Since your future depends so much on your score, you should maximize your chances of success. In order to maximize the likelihood of success, you've got to prepare in advance. This means taking practice tests and spending time learning the information and test taking strategies you will need to succeed.

Never go take the actual test as a "practice" test, expecting that you can just take it again if you need to. Take all the practice tests you can on your own, but when you go to take the official test, be prepared, be focused, and do your best the first time!

Secret Key #5 - Test Yourself

Everyone knows that time is money. There is no need to spend too much of your time or too little of your time preparing for the test. You should only spend as much of your precious time preparing as is necessary for you to get the score you need.

Once you have taken a practice test under real conditions of time constraints, then you will know if you are ready for the test or not.

If you have scored extremely high the first time that you take the practice test, then there is not much point in spending countless hours studying. You are already there.

Benchmark your abilities by retaking practice tests and seeing how much you have improved. Once you consistently score high enough to guarantee success, then you are ready.

If you have scored well below where you need, then knuckle down and begin studying in earnest. Check your improvement regularly through the use of practice tests under real conditions. Above all, don't worry, panic, or give up. The key is perseverance!

Then, when you go to take the test, remain confident and remember how well you did on the practice tests. If you can score high enough on a practice test, then you can do the same on the real thing.

General Strategies

The most important thing you can do is to ignore your fears and jump into the test immediately. Do not be overwhelmed by any strange-sounding terms. You have to jump into the test like jumping into a pool—all at once is the easiest way.

Make Predictions

As you read and understand the question, try to guess what the answer will be. Remember that several of the answer choices are wrong, and once you begin reading them, your mind will immediately become cluttered with answer choices designed to throw you off. Your mind is typically the most focused immediately after you have read the question and digested its contents. If you can, try to predict what the correct answer will be. You may be surprised at what you can predict.

Quickly scan the choices and see if your prediction is in the listed answer choices. If it is, then you can be quite confident that you have the right answer. It still won't hurt to check the other answer choices, but most of the time, you've got it!

Answer the Question

It may seem obvious to only pick answer choices that answer the question, but the test writers can create some excellent answer choices that are wrong. Don't pick an answer just because it sounds right, or you believe it to be true. It MUST answer the question. Once you've made your selection, always go back and check it against the question and make sure that you didn't misread the question and that the answer choice does answer the question posed.

Benchmark

After you read the first answer choice, decide if you think it sounds correct or not. If it doesn't, move on to the next answer choice. If it does, mentally mark that answer choice. This doesn't mean that you've definitely selected it as your answer choice, it just means that it's the best you've seen thus far. Go ahead and read the next choice. If the next choice is worse than the one you've already selected, keep going to the next answer choice. If the next choice is better than the choice you've already selected, mentally mark the new answer choice as your best guess.

The first answer choice that you select becomes your standard. Every other answer choice must be benchmarked against that standard. That choice is correct until proven otherwise by another answer choice beating it out. Once you've decided that no other answer choice seems as good, do one final check to ensure that your answer choice answers the question posed.

Valid Information

Don't discount any of the information provided in the question. Every piece of information may be necessary to determine the correct answer. None of the information in the question is there to throw you off (while the answer choices will certainly have information to throw you off). If two seemingly unrelated topics are discussed, don't ignore either. You can be confident there is a relationship, or it wouldn't be included in the question, and you are probably going to have to determine what is that relationship to find the answer.

Avoid "Fact Traps"

Don't get distracted by a choice that is factually true. Your search is for the answer that answers the question. Stay focused and don't fall for an answer that is true but irrelevant. Always go back to the question and make sure you're choosing an answer that actually answers the question and is not just a true statement. An answer can be factually correct, but it MUST answer the question asked. Additionally, two answers can both be seemingly correct, so be sure to read all of the answer choices, and make sure that you get the one that BEST answers the question.

Milk the Question

Some of the questions may throw you completely off. They might deal with a subject you have not been exposed to, or one that you haven't reviewed in years. While your lack of knowledge about the subject will be a hindrance, the question itself can give you many clues that will help you find the correct answer. Read the question carefully and look for clues. Watch particularly for adjectives and nouns describing difficult terms or words that you don't recognize. Regardless of whether you completely understand a word or not, replacing it with a synonym, either provided or one you more familiar with, may help you to understand what the questions are asking. Rather than wracking your mind about specific detailed information concerning a difficult term or word, try to use mental substitutes that are easier to understand.

The Trap of Familiarity

Don't just choose a word because you recognize it. On difficult questions, you may not recognize a number of words in the answer choices. The test writers don't put "make-believe" words on the test, so don't think that just because you only recognize all the words in one answer choice that that answer choice must be correct. If you only recognize words in one answer choice, then focus on that one. Is it correct? Try your best to determine if it is correct. If it is, that's great. If not, eliminate it. Each word and answer choice you eliminate increases your chances of getting the question correct, even if you then have to guess among the unfamiliar choices.

Eliminate Answers

Eliminate choices as soon as you realize they are wrong. But be careful! Make sure you consider all of the possible answer choices. Just because one appears right, doesn't mean that the next one won't be even better! The test writers will usually put more than one good answer choice for every question, so read all of them. Don't worry if you are stuck between two that seem right. By getting down to just two remaining possible choices, your odds are now 50/50. Rather than wasting too much time, play the odds. You are guessing, but guessing wisely because you've been able to knock out some of the answer choices that you know are wrong. If you are eliminating choices and realize that the last answer choice you are left with is also obviously wrong, don't panic. Start over and consider each choice again. There may easily be something that you missed the first time and will realize on the second pass.

Tough Questions

If you are stumped on a problem or it appears too hard or too difficult, don't waste time. Move on! Remember though, if you can quickly check for obviously incorrect answer choices, your chances of guessing correctly are greatly improved. Before you completely give up, at least try to knock out a couple of possible answers. Eliminate what you can and then guess at the remaining answer choices before moving on.

Brainstorm

If you get stuck on a difficult question, spend a few seconds quickly brainstorming. Run through the complete list of possible answer choices. Look at each choice and ask yourself, "Could this answer the question satisfactorily?" Go through each answer choice and consider it independently of the others. By systematically going through all possibilities, you may find something that you would otherwise overlook. Remember though that when you get stuck, it's important to try to keep moving.

Read Carefully

Understand the problem. Read the question and answer choices carefully. Don't miss the question because you misread the terms. You have plenty of time to read each question thoroughly and make sure you understand what is being asked. Yet a happy medium must be attained, so don't waste too much time. You must read carefully, but efficiently.

Face Value

When in doubt, use common sense. Always accept the situation in the problem at face value. Don't read too much into it. These problems will not require you to make huge leaps of logic. The test writers aren't trying to throw you off with a cheap trick. If you have to go beyond creativity and make a leap of logic in order to have an answer choice answer the question, then you should look at the other answer choices. Don't overcomplicate the problem by creating theoretical relationships or explanations that will warp time or space. These are normal problems rooted in reality. It's just that the applicable relationship or explanation may not be readily apparent and you have to figure things out. Use your common sense to interpret anything that isn't clear.

Prefixes

If you're having trouble with a word in the question or answer choices, try dissecting it. Take advantage of every clue that the word might include. Prefixes and suffixes can be a huge help. Usually they allow you to determine a basic meaning. Pre- means before, post- means after, pro - is positive, de- is negative. From these prefixes and suffixes, you can get an idea of the general meaning of the word and try to put it into context. Beware though of any traps. Just because con- is the opposite of pro-, doesn't necessarily mean congress is the opposite of progress!

Hedge Phrases

Watch out for critical hedge phrases, led off with words such as "likely," "may," "can," "sometimes," "often," "almost," "mostly," "usually," "generally," "rarely," and "sometimes." Question writers insert these hedge phrases to cover every possibility. Often an answer choice will be wrong simply because it leaves no room for exception. Unless the situation calls for them, avoid answer choices that have definitive words like "exactly," and "always."

Switchback Words

Stay alert for "switchbacks." These are the words and phrases frequently used to alert you to shifts in thought. The most common switchback word is "but." Others include "although," "however," "nevertheless," "on the other hand," "even though," "while," "in spite of," "despite," and "regardless of."

New Information

Correct answer choices will rarely have completely new information included. Answer choices typically are straightforward reflections of the material asked about and will directly relate to the question. If a new piece of information is included in an answer choice that doesn't even seem to relate to the topic being asked about, then that answer choice is likely incorrect. All of the information needed to answer the question is usually provided for you in the question. You should not have to make guesses that are unsupported or choose answer choices that require unknown information that cannot be reasoned from what is given.

Time Management

On technical questions, don't get lost on the technical terms. Don't spend too much time on any one question. If you don't know what a term means, then odds are you aren't going to get much further since you don't have a dictionary. You should be able to immediately recognize whether or not you know a term. If you don't, work with the other clues that you have—the other answer choices and terms provided—but don't waste too much time trying to figure out a difficult term that you don't know.

Contextual Clues

Look for contextual clues. An answer can be right but not the correct answer. The contextual clues will help you find the answer that is most right and is correct. Understand the context in which a phrase or statement is made. This will help you make important distinctions.

Don't Panic

Panicking will not answer any questions for you; therefore, it isn't helpful. When you first see the question, if your mind goes blank, take a deep breath. Force yourself to mechanically go through the steps of solving the problem using the strategies you've learned.

Pace Yourself

Don't get clock fever. It's easy to be overwhelmed when you're looking at a page full of questions, your mind is full of random thoughts and feeling confused, and the clock is ticking down faster than you would like. Calm down and maintain the pace that you have set for yourself. As long as you are on track by monitoring your pace, you are guaranteed to have enough time for yourself. When you get to the last few minutes of the test, it may seem like you won't have enough time left, but if you only have as many questions as you should have left at that point, then you're right on track!

Answer Selection

The best way to pick an answer choice is to eliminate all of those that are wrong, until only one is left and confirm that is the correct answer. Sometimes though, an answer choice may immediately look right. Be careful! Take a second to make sure that the other choices are not equally obvious. Don't make a hasty mistake. There are only two times that you should stop before checking other answers. First is when you are positive that the answer choice you have selected is correct. Second is when time is almost out and you have to make a quick guess!

Check Your Work

Since you will probably not know every term listed and the answer to every question, it is important that you get credit for the ones that you do know. Don't miss any questions through careless mistakes. If at all possible, try to take a second to look back over your answer selection and make sure you've selected the correct answer choice and haven't made a costly careless mistake (such as marking an answer choice that you didn't mean to mark). The time it takes for this quick double check should more than pay for itself in caught mistakes.

Beware of Directly Quoted Answers

Sometimes an answer choice will repeat word for word a portion of the question or reference section. However, beware of such exact duplication. It may be a trap! More than likely, the correct choice will paraphrase or summarize a point, rather than being exactly the same wording.

Slang

Scientific sounding answers are better than slang ones. An answer choice that begins "To compare the outcomes…" is much more likely to be correct than one that begins "Because some people insisted…"

Extreme Statements

Avoid wild answers that throw out highly controversial ideas that are proclaimed as established fact. An answer choice that states the "process should used in certain situations, if…" is much more likely to be correct than one that states the "process should be discontinued completely." The first is a calm rational statement and doesn't even make a definitive, uncompromising stance, using a hedge word "if" to provide wiggle room, whereas the second choice is a radical idea and far more extreme.

Answer Choice Families

When you have two or more answer choices that are direct opposites or parallels, one of them is usually the correct answer. For instance, if one answer choice states "x increases" and another answer choice states "x decreases" or "y increases," then those two or three answer choices are very similar in construction and fall into the same family of answer choices. A family of answer choices consists of two or three answer choices, very similar in construction, but often with directly opposite meanings. Usually the correct answer choice will be in that family of answer choices. The "odd man out" or answer choice that doesn't seem to fit the parallel construction of the other answer choices is more likely to be incorrect.

Special Report: How to Overcome Test Anxiety

The very nature of tests caters to some level of anxiety, nervousness, or tension, just as we feel for any important event that occurs in our lives. A little bit of anxiety or nervousness can be a good thing. It helps us with motivation, and makes achievement just that much sweeter. However, too much anxiety can be a problem, especially if it hinders our ability to function and perform.

"Test anxiety," is the term that refers to the emotional reactions that some test-takers experience when faced with a test or exam. Having a fear of testing and exams is based upon a rational fear, since the test-taker's performance can shape the course of an academic career. Nevertheless, experiencing excessive fear of examinations will only interfere with the test-taker's ability to perform and chance to be successful.

There are a large variety of causes that can contribute to the development and sensation of test anxiety. These include, but are not limited to, lack of preparation and worrying about issues surrounding the test.

Lack of Preparation

Lack of preparation can be identified by the following behaviors or situations:

- Not scheduling enough time to study, and therefore cramming the night before the test or exam
- Managing time poorly, to create the sensation that there is not enough time to do everything
- Failing to organize the text information in advance, so that the study material consists of the entire text and not simply the pertinent information
- Poor overall studying habits

Worrying, on the other hand, can be related to both the test taker, or many other factors around him/her that will be affected by the results of the test. These include worrying about:

- Previous performances on similar exams, or exams in general
- How friends and other students are achieving
- The negative consequences that will result from a poor grade or failure

There are three primary elements to test anxiety. Physical components, which involve the same typical bodily reactions as those to acute anxiety (to be discussed below). Emotional factors have to do with fear or panic. Mental or cognitive issues concerning attention spans and memory abilities.

Physical Signals

There are many different symptoms of test anxiety, and these are not limited to mental and emotional strain. Frequently there are a range of physical signals that will let a test taker know that he/she is suffering from test anxiety. These bodily changes can include the following:

- Perspiring
- Sweaty palms
- Wet, trembling hands
- Nausea
- Dry mouth
- A knot in the stomach
- Headache
- Faintness
- Muscle tension
- Aching shoulders, back and neck
- Rapid heart beat
- Feeling too hot/cold

To recognize the sensation of test anxiety, a test-taker should monitor him/herself for the following sensations:

- The physical distress symptoms as listed above
- Emotional sensitivity, expressing emotional feelings such as the need to cry or laugh too much, or a sensation of anger or helplessness
- A decreased ability to think, causing the test-taker to blank out or have racing thoughts that are hard to organize or control.

Though most students will feel some level of anxiety when faced with a test or exam, the majority can cope with that anxiety and maintain it at a manageable level. However, those who cannot are faced with a very real and very serious condition, which can and should be controlled for the immeasurable benefit of this sufferer.

Naturally, these sensations lead to negative results for the testing experience. The most common effects of test anxiety have to do with nervousness and mental blocking.

Nervousness

Nervousness can appear in several different levels:

- The test-taker's difficulty, or even inability to read and understand the questions on the test
- The difficulty or inability to organize thoughts to a coherent form
- The difficulty or inability to recall key words and concepts relating to the testing questions (especially essays)
- The receipt of poor grades on a test, though the test material was well known by the test taker

Conversely, a person may also experience mental blocking, which involves:

- Blanking out on test questions
- Only remembering the correct answers to the questions when the test has already finished.

Fortunately for test anxiety sufferers, beating these feelings, to a large degree, has to do with proper preparation. When a test taker has a feeling of preparedness, then anxiety will be dramatically lessened.

The first step to resolving anxiety issues is to distinguish which of the two types of anxiety are being suffered. If the anxiety is a direct result of a lack of preparation, this should be considered a normal reaction, and the anxiety level (as opposed to the test results) shouldn't be anything to worry about. However, if, when adequately prepared, the test-taker still panics, blanks out, or seems to overreact, this is not a fully rational reaction. While this can be considered normal too, there are many ways to combat and overcome these effects.

Remember that anxiety cannot be entirely eliminated, however, there are ways to minimize it, to make the anxiety easier to manage. Preparation is one of the best ways to minimize test anxiety. Therefore the following techniques are wise in order to best fight off any anxiety that may want to build.

To begin with, try to avoid cramming before a test, whenever it is possible. By trying to memorize an entire term's worth of information in one day, you'll be shocking your system, and not giving yourself a very good chance to absorb the information. This is an easy path to anxiety, so for those who suffer from test anxiety, cramming should not even be considered an option.

Instead of cramming, work throughout the semester to combine all of the material which is presented throughout the semester, and work on it gradually as the course goes by, making sure to master the main concepts first, leaving minor details for a week or so before the test.

To study for the upcoming exam, be sure to pose questions that may be on the examination, to gauge the ability to answer them by integrating the ideas from your texts, notes and lectures, as well as any supplementary readings.

If it is truly impossible to cover all of the information that was covered in that particular term, concentrate on the most important portions, that can be covered very well. Learn these concepts as best as possible, so that when the test comes, a goal can be made to use these concepts as presentations of your knowledge.

In addition to study habits, changes in attitude are critical to beating a struggle with test anxiety. In fact, an improvement of the perspective over the entire test-taking experience can actually help a test taker to enjoy studying and therefore improve the overall experience. Be certain not to overemphasize the significance of the grade - know that the result of the test is neither a reflection of self worth, nor is it a measure of intelligence; one grade will not predict a person's future success.

To improve an overall testing outlook, the following steps should be tried:

- Keeping in mind that the most reasonable expectation for taking a test is to expect to try to demonstrate as much of what you know as you possibly can.
- Reminding ourselves that a test is only one test; this is not the only one, and there will be others.
- The thought of thinking of oneself in an irrational, all-or-nothing term should be avoided at all costs.
- A reward should be designated for after the test, so there's something to look forward to. Whether it be going to a movie, going out to eat, or simply visiting friends, schedule it in advance, and do it no matter what result is expected on the exam.

Test-takers should also keep in mind that the basics are some of the most important things, even beyond anti-anxiety techniques and studying. Never neglect the basic social, emotional and biological needs, in order to try to absorb information. In order to best achieve, these three factors must be held as just as important as the studying itself.

Study Steps

Remember the following important steps for studying:

- Maintain healthy nutrition and exercise habits. Continue both your recreational activities and social pass times. These both contribute to your physical and emotional well being.
- Be certain to get a good amount of sleep, especially the night before the test, because when you're overtired you are not able to perform to the best of your best ability.
- Keep the studying pace to a moderate level by taking breaks when they are needed, and varying the work whenever possible, to keep the mind fresh instead of getting bored.
- When enough studying has been done that all the material that can be learned has been learned, and the test taker is prepared for the test, stop studying and do something relaxing such as listening to music, watching a movie, or taking a warm bubble bath.

There are also many other techniques to minimize the uneasiness or apprehension that is experienced along with test anxiety before, during, or even after the examination. In fact, there are a great deal of things that can be done to stop anxiety from interfering with lifestyle and performance. Again, remember that anxiety will not be eliminated entirely, and it shouldn't be. Otherwise that "up" feeling for exams would not exist, and most of us depend on that sensation to perform better than usual. However, this anxiety has to be at a level that is manageable.

Of course, as we have just discussed, being prepared for the exam is half the battle right away. Attending all classes, finding out what knowledge will be expected on the exam, and knowing the exam schedules are easy steps to lowering anxiety. Keeping up with work will remove the need to cram, and efficient study habits will eliminate wasted time. Studying should be done in an ideal location for concentration, so that it is simple to become interested in the material and give it complete attention. A method such as SQ3R (Survey, Question, Read, Recite, Review) is a wonderful key to follow to make sure that the study habits are as effective as possible, especially in the case of learning from a textbook. Flashcards are great techniques for memorization. Learning to take good notes will mean that notes will be full of useful information, so that less sifting will need to be done to seek out what is pertinent for studying. Reviewing notes after class and then again on occasion will keep the information fresh in the mind. From notes that have been taken summary sheets and outlines can be made for simpler reviewing.

A study group can also be a very motivational and helpful place to study, as there will be a sharing of ideas, all of the minds can work together, to make sure that everyone understands, and the studying will be made more interesting because it will be a social occasion.

Basically, though, as long as the test-taker remains organized and self confident, with efficient study habits, less time will need to be spent studying, and higher grades will be achieved.

To become self confident, there are many useful steps. The first of these is "self talk." It has been shown through extensive research, that self-talk for students who suffer from test anxiety, should be well monitored, in order to make sure that it contributes to self confidence as opposed to sinking the student. Frequently the self talk of test-anxious students is negative or self-defeating, thinking that everyone else is smarter and faster, that they always mess up, and that if they don't do well, they'll fail the entire course. It is important to decreasing anxiety that awareness is made of self talk. Try writing any negative self thoughts and then disputing them with a positive statement instead. Begin self-encouragement as though it was a friend speaking. Repeat positive statements to help reprogram the mind to believing in successes instead of failures.

Helpful Techniques

Other extremely helpful techniques include:

- Self-visualization of doing well and reaching goals
- While aiming for an "A" level of understanding, don't try to "overprotect" by setting your expectations lower. This will only convince the mind to stop studying in order to meet the lower expectations.
- Don't make comparisons with the results or habits of other students. These are individual factors, and different things work for different people, causing different results.
- Strive to become an expert in learning what works well, and what can be done in order to improve. Consider collecting this data in a journal.
- Create rewards for after studying instead of doing things before studying that will only turn into avoidance behaviors.
- Make a practice of relaxing - by using methods such as progressive relaxation, self-hypnosis, guided imagery, etc - in order to make relaxation an automatic sensation.
- Work on creating a state of relaxed concentration so that concentrating will take on the focus of the mind, so that none will be wasted on worrying.
- Take good care of the physical self by eating well and getting enough sleep.
- Plan in time for exercise and stick to this plan.

Beyond these techniques, there are other methods to be used before, during and after the test that will help the test-taker perform well in addition to overcoming anxiety.

Before the exam comes the academic preparation. This involves establishing a study schedule and beginning at least one week before the actual date of the test. By doing this, the anxiety of not having enough time to study for the test will be automatically eliminated. Moreover, this will make

- 233 -

the studying a much more effective experience, ensuring that the learning will be an easier process. This relieves much undue pressure on the test-taker.

Summary sheets, note cards, and flash cards with the main concepts and examples of these main concepts should be prepared in advance of the actual studying time. A topic should never be eliminated from this process. By omitting a topic because it isn't expected to be on the test is only setting up the test-taker for anxiety should it actually appear on the exam. Utilize the course syllabus for laying out the topics that should be studied. Carefully go over the notes that were made in class, paying special attention to any of the issues that the professor took special care to emphasize while lecturing in class. In the textbooks, use the chapter review, or if possible, the chapter tests, to begin your review.

It may even be possible to ask the instructor what information will be covered on the exam, or what the format of the exam will be (for example, multiple choice, essay, free form, true-false). Additionally, see if it is possible to find out how many questions will be on the test. If a review sheet or sample test has been offered by the professor, make good use of it, above anything else, for the preparation for the test. Another great resource for getting to know the examination is reviewing tests from previous semesters. Use these tests to review, and aim to achieve a 100% score on each of the possible topics. With a few exceptions, the goal that you set for yourself is the highest one that you will reach.

Take all of the questions that were assigned as homework, and rework them to any other possible course material. The more problems reworked, the more skill and confidence will form as a result. When forming the solution to a problem, write out each of the steps. Don't simply do head work. By doing as many steps on paper as possible, much clarification and therefore confidence will be formed. Do this with as many homework problems as possible, before checking the answers. By checking the answer after each problem, a reinforcement will exist, that will not be on the exam. Study situations should be as exam-like as possible, to prime the test-taker's system for the experience. By waiting to check the answers at the end, a psychological advantage will be formed, to decrease the stress factor.

Another fantastic reason for not cramming is the avoidance of confusion in concepts, especially when it comes to mathematics. 8-10 hours of study will become one hundred percent more effective if it is spread out over a week or at least several days, instead of doing it all in one sitting. Recognize that the human brain requires time in order to assimilate new material, so frequent breaks and a span of study time over several days will be much more beneficial.

Additionally, don't study right up until the point of the exam. Studying should stop a minimum of one hour before the exam begins. This allows the brain to rest and put things in their proper order. This will also provide the time to become as relaxed as possible when going into the examination room. The test-taker will also have time to eat well and eat sensibly. Know that the brain needs food as much as the rest of the body. With enough food and enough sleep, as well as a relaxed attitude, the body and the mind are primed for success.

Avoid any anxious classmates who are talking about the exam. These students only spread anxiety, and are not worth sharing the anxious sentimentalities.

Before the test also involves creating a positive attitude, so mental preparation should also be a point of concentration. There are many keys to creating a positive attitude. Should fears become rushing in, make a visualization of taking the exam, doing well, and seeing an A written on the paper. Write out a list of affirmations that will bring a feeling of confidence, such as "I am doing well in my English class," "I studied well and know my material," "I enjoy this class." Even if the affirmations aren't believed at first, it sends a positive message to the subconscious which will result in an alteration of the overall belief system, which is the system that creates reality.

If a sensation of panic begins, work with the fear and imagine the very worst! Work through the entire scenario of not passing the test, failing the entire course, and dropping out of school, followed by not getting a job, and pushing a shopping cart through the dark alley where you'll live. This will place things into perspective! Then, practice deep breathing and create a visualization of the opposite situation - achieving an "A" on the exam, passing the entire course, receiving the degree at a graduation ceremony.

On the day of the test, there are many things to be done to ensure the best results, as well as the most calm outlook. The following stages are suggested in order to maximize test-taking potential:

Begin the examination day with a moderate breakfast, and avoid any coffee or beverages with caffeine if the test taker is prone to jitters. Even people who are used to managing caffeine can feel jittery or light-headed when it is taken on a test day.

Attempt to do something that is relaxing before the examination begins. As last minute cramming clouds the mastering of overall concepts, it is better to use this time to create a calming outlook.

Be certain to arrive at the test location well in advance, in order to provide time to select a location that is away from doors, windows and other distractions, as well as giving enough time to relax before the test begins.

Keep away from anxiety generating classmates who will upset the sensation of stability and relaxation that is being attempted before the exam.

Should the waiting period before the exam begins cause anxiety, create a self-distraction by reading a light magazine or something else that is relaxing and simple.

During the exam itself, read the entire exam from beginning to end, and find out how much time should be allotted to each individual problem. Once writing the exam, should more time be taken for a problem, it should be abandoned, in order to begin another problem. If there is time at the end, the unfinished problem can always be returned to and completed.

Read the instructions very carefully - twice - so that unpleasant surprises won't follow during or after the exam has ended.

When writing the exam, pretend that the situation is actually simply the completion of homework within a library, or at home. This will assist in forming a relaxed atmosphere, and will allow the brain extra focus for the complex thinking function.

Begin the exam with all of the questions with which the most confidence is felt. This will build the confidence level regarding the entire exam and will begin a quality momentum. This will also create encouragement for trying the problems where uncertainty resides.

Going with the "gut instinct" is always the way to go when solving a problem. Second guessing should be avoided at all costs. Have confidence in the ability to do well.

For essay questions, create an outline in advance that will keep the mind organized and make certain that all of the points are remembered. For multiple choice, read every answer, even if the correct one has been spotted - a better one may exist.

Continue at a pace that is reasonable and not rushed, in order to be able to work carefully. Provide enough time to go over the answers at the end, to check for small errors that can be corrected.

Should a feeling of panic begin, breathe deeply, and think of the feeling of the body releasing sand through its pores. Visualize a calm, peaceful place, and include all of the sights, sounds and sensations of this image. Continue the deep breathing, and take a few minutes to continue this with closed eyes. When all is well again, return to the test.

If a "blanking" occurs for a certain question, skip it and move on to the next question. There will be time to return to the other question later. Get everything done that can be done, first, to guarantee all the grades that can be compiled, and to build all of the confidence possible. Then return to the weaker questions to build the marks from there. Remember, one's own reality can be created, so as long as the belief is there, success will follow. And remember: anxiety can happen later, right now, there's an exam to be written!

After the examination is complete, whether there is a feeling for a good grade or a bad grade, don't dwell on the exam, and be certain to follow through on the reward that was promised...and enjoy it! Don't dwell on any mistakes that have been made, as there is nothing that can be done at this point anyway. Additionally, don't begin to study for the next test right away. Do something relaxing for a while, and let the mind relax and prepare itself to begin absorbing information again.

From the results of the exam - both the grade and the entire experience, be certain to learn from what has gone on. Perfect studying habits and work some more on confidence in order to make the next examination experience even better than the last one.

Learn to avoid places where openings occurred for laziness, procrastination and day dreaming.

Use the time between this exam and the next one to better learn to relax, even learning to relax on cue, so that any anxiety can be controlled during the next exam. Learn how to relax the body. Slouch in your chair if that helps. Tighten and then relax all of the different muscle groups, one group at a time, beginning with the feet and then working all the way up to the neck and face. This will ultimately relax the muscles more than they were to begin with. Learn how to breathe deeply and comfortably, and focus on this breathing going in and out as a relaxing thought. With every exhale, repeat the word "relax."

As common as test anxiety is, it is very possible to overcome it. Make yourself one of the test-takers who overcome this frustrating hindrance.

Additional Bonus Material

Due to our efforts to try to keep this book to a manageable length, we've created a link that will give you access to all of your additional bonus material.

Please visit http://www.mometrix.com/bonus948/fsot to access the information.